As expenditures on health in the United States will shortly exceed $1 trillion for the first time, public and private health care decision makers have called for more rigorous use of cost–effectiveness and cost–benefit analysis to guide spending. Concerns have arisen in the United States and in other countries, however, about the overall quality of such analyses. This book discusses and evaluates best-practice methods of conducting cost–effectiveness and cost–benefit studies of pharmaceuticals and other medical technologies. It encompasses a wide variety of topics, ranging from measuring cost and effectiveness to discounting to the use of dynamic modeling of cost–effectiveness. The book also includes conceptual and practical aspects of cost–effectiveness analysis by researchers who have conducted applied research in these areas. Rarely does the book provide a singular solution to a measurement problem; rather, the reader is directed to choices among alternative approaches and an analysis of the advantages and disadvantages of each.

D1506331

Valuing health care

Valuing health care

Costs, benefits, and effectiveness of
pharmaceuticals and other medical technologies

Edited by
FRANK A. SLOAN
Duke University

CAMBRIDGE
UNIVERSITY PRESS

PUBLISHED BY THE PRESS SYNDICATE OF THE UNIVERSITY OF CAMBRIDGE
The Pitt Building, Trumpington Street, Cambridge CB2 1RP, United Kingdom

CAMBRIDGE UNIVERSITY PRESS
The Edinburgh Building, Cambridge CB2 2RU, UK http: //www.cup.cam.ac.uk
40 West 20th Street, New York, NY 10011-4211, USA http: //www.cup.org
10 Stamford Road, Oakleigh, Melbourne 3166, Australia

First published 1995
First paperback edition 1996
Reprinted 1998

Typeset in Times

A catalogue record for this book is available from the British Library

Library of Congress Cataloguing-in-Publication Data is available

ISBN 0-521-47020-X hardback
ISBN 0-521-57646-6 paperback

Transferred to digital printing 2002

Contents

Tables

Figures

Boxes

Acknowledgments

This study was supported in part by a grant from Eli Lilly and Company. Although Eli Lilly originally suggested the idea of a book on best-practice techniques of cost–effectiveness analysis, the ideas in the book are totally the authors'. Douglas Cocks of Eli Lilly provided helpful advice and support throughout the study.

Early drafts of the chapters were presented at the Conference on Cost–Effectiveness of Pharmaceuticals held at Vanderbilt University on 22–23 September 1992. Partial support for this conference came from Eli Lilly and Company and G. D. Searle.

The project benefited from an excellent support staff. Sharon Stanley, secretary at Vanderbilt's Health Policy Center, organized the details of the conference and was responsible for the manuscripts in the early stages of the project. She was succeeded at Vanderbilt by Dorothy Adams, who helped shepherd the chapters through their intermediate stages. After I moved to Duke, Billie Maciunas of the Center for Health Policy Research and Education (CHPRE) was responsible for editing and helped to bring the book to completion. Kate Whetten-Goldstein, an Associate in Research at CHPRE, worked with the authors and provided oversight during the project's final months.

Last but not least, I wish to thank the authors. At a planning meeting held at Vanderbilt at the beginning of the project, participants helped me identify the key issues in cost–effectiveness analysis and the best persons to write on each issue. Fortunately, my first choices agreed to participate.

Frank A. Sloan

CHAPTER 1

Introduction

Frank A. Sloan

In a world with unlimited resources, it would be unnecessary to have methods to determine the best way to allocate those resources among alternative uses. But resources are limited: in 1994, U.S. health spending will exceed $1 trillion for the first time and spending is projected to grow 50 percent faster than gross domestic product for the remainder of the decade (Burner, McKusick, and Waldo 1992). Similar trends are evident in other countries (Schieber, Poullier, and Greenwald 1993). Throughout the world, there are pressures on public budgets. Policymakers and the public have begun to recognize that every dollar spent on health care is no longer available for spending on education, crime control, or infrastructure improvement. Further, much of what we now spend is wasted on care that does not improve our health or yields small improvements in health at exorbitant cost (Siu et al. 1986; Winslow et al. 1988; Enthoven and Kronick 1989; CBO 1992a).

In the public sector, even in the face of mounting cost pressures, the balancing of benefits and costs has typically not been a criterion in deciding whether medical services should be made available or should be covered under public insurance. At one extreme, policymakers have focused exclusively on costs, rejecting higher cost alternatives without any consideration of their potential benefits (e.g., some state Medicaid programs in the United States). Others have focused exclusively on benefits while ignoring the costs of achieving these benefits. Even today the U.S. Food and Drug Administration and Medicare do not use cost–effectiveness as a criterion for making what are, in essence, decisions about resource allocation. In the private sector, hospitals, health maintenance organizations (HMOs), insurers, and other decision makers may be more willing to use such criteria, but formal analysis of costs and benefits does not appear to be widespread. In the face of tighter budget constraints, public and private decision makers have made forays in the direction of adopting formal analysis of benefits versus costs. Examples in the public sector include the Oregon priority-setting method (Hadorn 1991; OTA 1992b; Fox and Leichter 1993; Chaps. 3 and 10, this volume) and Australia's guidelines for subsidized pharmaceuticals (Drummond 1992; Johannesson 1992a; Chap. 10, this volume). The news media report private health decision makers' greater use of studies that evaluate both costs and benefits of pharmaceuticals and other medical technologies (Winslow 1992; Tanouye 1993). Although there is greater demand for information about returns to investment in health care by numerous parties, including employers and public and private insurers, questions have been raised about the quality of many of the studies conducted to date (Lee and Sanchez 1991; Udvarhelyi et al. 1992).

Cost–benefit analysis has been used in public finance and therefore has had a social perspective in that calculations have weighed social costs and benefits. Such studies were used when individual decisions alone did not lead to an optimal allocation of resources (market failure). In other words, these studies were used by public decision makers to supplant the market. In most situations, however, individual consumers could be relied upon to weigh costs and benefits prior to making a purchase, with the consequence that the sum of individual wants produced the correct allocation of resources.

Formal methods were also applied to health care, but with several important differences. First, there was an overwhelming reluctance to attach money values to benefits. Second, costs largely were limited to those that appear in public or private budgets and that are more narrowly defined than social costs. Third, because of the pervasiveness of consumer ignorance and, more recently, uncertainty among health care providers about the effectiveness of many preventive, diagnostic and therapeutic interventions, there has been demand, even among private decision makers, for information about outcomes that may be obtained from such interventions. Thus, many of the clients for such analyses are in the private sector. Added to such private demand is the increasing public demand as additional medical services are collectivized either through an explicit tax-and-subsidize mechanism or through mandates on private parties.

Major objectives of this book

As in any field for which there is a substantial growth in demand, two concerns about quality may well be raised. One is that parties will skew the results of formal analyses without users of such information being able to detect it. The second is that even well-intentioned authors of such analyses may go astray because they are unaware of alternative methodological approaches. Fearing this, public policymakers may tend to specify details of methodology in a regulatory format or to perform such analyses themselves. As a reading of this book will indicate, at each step along the way there are so many plausible alternatives, each with its own strengths and weaknesses, that standardization or regulation of methods is likely be counterproductive.

A major objective of this book is to summarize the current state of the art in cost–effectiveness/cost–benefit analyses as they are applied to medical problems and to discuss aspects of these methods that have received comparatively little attention in these applications, such as measuring quality of life, costs, discounting, downstream treatment effects, and the sensitivity of findings to underlying assumptions. Several different audiences will find this book useful. First, the book serves as a reference for those who are or aspire to be users of cost–effectiveness/cost–benefit analysis. It is not a "how-to" manual in these methods; such exist elsewhere (e.g., Weinstein and Stason 1976; Warner and Luce 1982; DHHS 1992b). Our goal is to systematically review the methods now in use, assess their underlying conceptual foundations, and summarize their relative strengths and weaknesses. For example, the reader who wants to know how to structure time trade-off questions or use Markov chains for analyses of long-term effects of health care interventions will have to look elsewhere but can use this book to find out where to look. Second, the book provides some guidance for methodologists who have an interest in extending the analytical frontiers on which cost–effectiveness/cost–benefit analyses are based. Experts are likely to be well versed in some aspects of such analyses but fairly uninformed about aspects outside their own discipline. We have not attempted to push the current methodological frontiers but to clearly identify current boundaries that may suggest questions for further research. Third, the book can assist policymakers in showing the strengths and limitations of current methods. Chapter 10 in particular focuses on the problems and pitfalls of using these methods in policymaking.

Though not limited to pharmaceuticals, many of the examples included in this book come from pharmaceutical studies. The superior evidence on efficacy makes it easier to conduct cost–effectiveness or cost–benefit analysis. At the same time, the relative ease of conducting such studies increases the expectation that such information will be provided as part of the coverage decision-making process. Aside from the relatively greater availability of data on efficacy of pharmaceuticals, the evaluation of pharmaceuticals is not inherently different from the evaluation of medical devices and other medical procedures.

What is cost–effectiveness/cost–benefit analysis?

Cost–effectiveness/cost–benefit analyses are formal methods for comparing the benefits and costs of a medical intervention in order to determine whether it is worth doing. The only difference between the two is that cost–effectiveness analysis measures benefits in terms of some standard of clinical outcome or effectiveness, such as mortality rates, years of added life, or quality-adjusted life years, whereas cost–benefit analysis converts these benefits into a monetary value. A growing trend in cost–effectiveness studies has been to measure effectiveness in terms of patient preferences, often expressed as utilities (e.g., quality-adjusted life years), and the term "cost–utility analysis" has been used to describe this subset of cost–effectiveness studies (DHHS 1992b). The underlying goal of cost–effectiveness/cost–benefit analyses is to find which alternative provides maximum aggregate health benefits for a given level of resources or, equivalently, which alternative provides a given level of health benefits at the lowest cost.

The basic approach is to measure all relevant costs and benefits and determine the ratio between the two. All other things being equal, an alternative with a lower cost–benefit ratio (whether benefits are measured in terms of dollars or some other metric) is preferable to an alternative with a higher cost–benefit ratio. However, in the case of mutually exclusive interventions (e.g., surgery or drugs but never both), the issue is whether the additional improvement in benefits is worth the additional cost. In such cases, incremental cost–effectiveness or cost–benefit analysis is required. Similarly, as the scale of a particular intervention increases (e.g., more visits per patient or expansion of a service to greater numbers of patients), diminishing marginal returns are likely, such as a decline in the net benefit per patient. In such cases, marginal cost–effectiveness analysis is needed.

Several formal methods use certain elements of cost–effectiveness/cost–benefit analyses. For example, cost-of-illness analysis attempts to measure the social costs associated with a particular disease, including direct costs like medical services and indirect costs like loss of productivity due either to illness or to premature death. Decision analysis is used to guide individuals faced with complex choices that typically entail substantial uncertainty or complicated value judgments. Because so many medical decisions contain both of these elements, many cost–effectiveness/cost–benefit analyses use a decision-analytic framework. However, the purpose of decision analysis is to find which choice maximizes individual utility (well-being) regardless of whether costs enter the picture. Thus, not all decision analyses are cost–effectiveness analyses, nor do all cost–effectiveness analyses make use of decision analysis.

The six basic steps in cost–effectiveness/cost–benefit analysis (derived from DHHS 1992b) are as follows:

1. Define the intervention. This includes specifying the nature of the intervention, the types of patient to be treated, and what alternative the intervention is replacing. In some cases, a medical intervention is compared to the natural history of a disease without any treatment; but more commonly, an intervention is compared to an alternative intervention that could be used.

2. Identify relevant costs. These usually include direct (medical) costs but may also include indirect costs, such as patient time, lost earnings, or other social costs associated with an intervention.
3. Identify relevant benefits. These include the net health benefits to the patient (after deducting any adverse side effects) but may also include indirect benefits such as greater productivity.
4. Measure costs. This requires attaching a monetary value to all components of costs, which entails placing a value on medical inputs and an individual's time. In the case of costs that occur in the future, a discount rate is typically used to convert all costs into present-value terms.
5. Measure benefits. In the case of cost–effectiveness analysis, measuring benefits entails converting all benefits into a single metric (e.g., quality-adjusted life years). In the case of cost–benefit analysis, all benefits must be converted into dollars. In the case of benefits that occur in the future, a discount rate is sometimes used to convert all benefits into present-value terms.
6. Account for uncertainties. This entails using sensitivity analysis, Monte Carlo simulation, or other methods to test the robustness of conclusions to uncertainties in the measurement of costs and benefits.

Although the basic steps in a cost–effectiveness or a cost–benefit analysis are the same, it should be strongly emphasized that there is no consensus method for conducting cost–effectiveness/cost–benefit studies, even at the conceptual level. That is, at every step shown, different analysts will use different methods to complete the task. In part, this reflects an imperfection in the method itself. No method of measurement is perfect, and each has strengths and weaknesses depending upon the problem. For example, however conceptually desirable it may be to elicit patient preferences, this approach cannot work for certain patients, such as those who are comatose. But another element of disagreement concerns differences among analysts themselves. Based partly on background and experience, each analyst attaches different weights to the strengths and weaknesses of alternative methods and draws different conclusions about what is best to do in a certain situation. Sometimes a judgment about what is "best" may unfortunately be consciously or unconsciously guided by what approach best serves a client's interest (i.e., makes Company A's product look better than Company B's). Finally, differences may reflect a core conceptual disagreement: some analysts argue vehemently that discounting of health benefits is essential to avoid a biased conclusion, whereas others argue with equal fervor that such discounting is totally inappropriate.

This book should clarify many of the important differences in methods that exist today. Despite the imperfections of the methods themselves and the lack of consensus regarding which to use, one should avoid the fallacy of analytical nihilism. However imperfect these methods may be, they are superior to the alternative, which is global subjective human judgment unaided by formal analysis (Eddy 1984). The kinds of problems for which cost–effectiveness/cost–benefit analyses are needed are far too complicated to be solved in someone's head. And adopting a method, even if not perfect, is preferable to doing nothing when choices must be made. However, an alternative danger is the assumption that anything goes. Even if analysts cannot agree on a standardized approach, there can be a consensus about well conducted studies versus poorly conducted studies. Studies that ignore whole categories of costs or benefits that ought to be measured or those that select methods or parameters designed to bias results are clearly flawed. A discount rate of 50 percent is outside any plausible range of reasonableness. We hope that readers of this book will better appreciate the difference between high-quality studies and those of lower caliber. Caveat emptor!

Chapter plan

This book is organized into four parts. First, Chapters 2, 3, and 4 deal with the building blocks of cost–effectiveness/cost–benefit analyses: measurement of outcomes and cost. Second, Chapters 5 and 6 combine cost and outcomes/benefit measurement to discuss rules that decision makers might use to decide which among alternative programs to adopt. The analysis is sufficiently general to include private sector as well as public sector decision makers. In examining these funding decisions, the authors of these two chapters also consider some measurement issues. Such discussion is important, since the decision rule adopted hinges in part on the ability of analysts to measure the underlying concepts accurately. Third, Chapters 7, 8, and 9 are about special topics in cost–effectiveness/cost–benefit analyses: discounting future costs and benefits, statistical issues, and modeling long-term effects of programs. Fourth, Chapter 10 summarizes major points of the book and describes both the potential and the limitations of such analyses as a practical tool for making choices about resource allocation in the health field, in both the public and the private sectors.

Although most readers will undoubtedly learn something new from each chapter, they do differ in their degree of technical difficulty and in their assumptions about the reader's background. The first seven chapters assume relatively less prior technical knowledge, although issues of interest to specialists as well as generalists are often discussed. Like the authors, who have varying educational backgrounds – economics, medicine, psychology, and mathematics – readers come from a variety of disciplines. For example, a reader might be well versed in the conduct of randomized controlled trials (RCTs) but know virtually nothing about measuring quality of life or cost. Another reader might find the discussion of cost to be a useful review, perhaps because of the studies described, but learn the rudiments of quality of life measurement for the first time. Still other readers may be expert in mathematical statistics but know relatively little about the health field.

Sufficient material is presented to introduce the reader to a topic. To become an adept practitioner of cost–effectiveness and cost–benefit analysis, readers will typically need to read more, including some of the studies contained in the book's reference section. Again, this is not a how-to book. Rather, we present the state of the art, pointing readers in the right direction for avoiding many of the pitfalls and directing them to where they can learn more.

Chapters 8 and 9 assume a certain amount of technical knowledge on the reader's part. Readers with little knowledge of statistics may want to concentrate on the statistical discussion in Chapter 2, which is far less technical and provides an introduction to many of the key statistical issues developed in greater detail in Chapter 8. The reader who has great faith in the value of RCTs as a source of information for cost–effectiveness analysis is likely to become more skeptical after reading Chapters 2 and 8. Although Chapter 9 briefly describes all of the fundamental concepts used there, some prior knowledge of mathematical statistics in general, and of such concepts as Markov processes and simulation in particular, is helpful for gaining more from the material.

A reader who just wants a quick discussion of some of the major issues, advantages, and disadvantages of cost–effectiveness/cost–benefit analyses for making decisions about resource allocation might read the rest of this chapter and then turn to Chapter 10, with this one important caveat: even though there is some agreement about the fundamentals of cost–effectiveness/cost–benefit analyses, there is much disagreement about specific details. No consensus exists about many aspects of such analyses, even among the authors of this book. Thus, any summary of major points represents one interpretation of where the field stands. A strength of this book is that it presents subject matter from different disciplinary perspectives and practical experiences.

Description of specific chapters

In Chapter 2, "Evidence of Effectiveness: Evaluating Its Quality," Allan Detsky, who is both a physician and an economist, discusses measurement of effectiveness of a clinical strategy or program. Often the choice is between an older, lower-cost technology and a higher-cost alternative that perhaps offers a higher benefit. Then the analyst is concerned with the incremental cost–effectiveness of the program, that is, the ratio of the change (extra) in cost to change in effect. In other cases the choice is not among mutually exclusive alternatives. In either situation, measurement of effectiveness is a fundamental component of the analysis.

As Detsky explains, there is a difference between *efficacy*, whether or not a clinical strategy achieves its goal if applied under optimal circumstances, and *effectiveness*, which refers to the impact of a strategy as it is likely to be applied in practice. The "gold standard" of clinical studies, the RCT, demonstrates efficacy rather than effectiveness. Thus, there is some question whether the evidence on efficacy generalizes to situations of interest to private and public decision makers.

Detsky presents an approach for grading the evidence on effectiveness. Compared to evidence from observational or nonexperimental data, RCT-based evidence is relatively sound. However, RCTs also have limitations as sources of information in cost–effectiveness studies. Limitations as discussed by Detsky are (*a*) exclusion of pertinent patient types from the sample, (*b*) low statistical power for measuring relatively rare outcomes, and (*c*) a short time span encompassed by the study. The first limitation is particularly important when effects of a treatment differ among patients and the treatment is likely to be applied to patients who are different in terms of demography, comorbidities, severity of illness, allergic reactions, etc. Often a long lag time occurs between intervention and outcome, particularly for screening and primary prevention programs. Short and even modestly long trials may be too short to capture these longer-term effects. Also, technological change may alter a program's effect. Most cost–effectiveness studies use some form of simulation. Often it is necessary to use a best guess about the value of a parameter representing program effectiveness until evidence from an RCT becomes available.

A first step in measuring effect is to define the outcome or unit of outcome. Detsky refers to these as the *end points*. The most common end points in studies conducted to date are measures of mortality and clinical indicators such as blood pressure. The simplest outcome measure is mortality or life expectancy. The problem with this type of outcome measure is that everyone who remains alive receives the same score. Many health care interventions, especially in developed countries, aim to improve quality of life rather than merely to extend life. Alternative measures incorporate the concept of utility of various health states, which is the subject of Chapter 3.

In Chapter 3, "Utility Assessment for Estimating Quality-Adjusted Life Years," Robert Kaplan, a psychologist, discusses quality-adjusted life years (QALYs) and the related concept of utility assessment. Although one can always express the many health status changes attributed to a clinical strategy in terms of a number of outcome measures, the approach rapidly becomes cumbersome, especially when there are many outcomes and programs to compare. Thus, having a single number to represent many dimensions of quality of life has great potential appeal, especially to users. With QALYs, one no longer speaks about saving x years of life. Rather, if the quality of life during the period of life extension is low, the corresponding QALY is likely to be much less than x. The proof of the pudding is not so much in the desirability of having a number like a QALY but rather in the validity and reliability of QALYs. Thus, most of the chapter deals with measurement issues.

Several approaches assess the utilities of health states. Some rely on posing explicit trade-offs to individuals and inferring utilities about various health states from the responses. Other approaches do not rely on such trade-offs. The approaches Kaplan describes are rating scales, magnitude estimation, standard gamble, time trade-off, and person trade-off. The standard gamble is appealing, especially to many economists, but psychological studies have provided empirical evidence of preference reversals (inconsistent responses about preferences by individuals surveyed) and unexpected preferences that stem from respondents misunderstanding of the choices posed by the survey.

In studies using rating scales, respondents are given a range, say from 0 (death) to 10 (optimum function) and are asked to assign a numerical value within the interval to represent the utility of the health state described by the scenario. Economists have criticized rating scales on grounds that aggregating individual preferences for health, as revealed by the responses to surveys, violates principles of microeconomic theory. Psychological research, on the other hand, provides more favorable evidence on this behavioral approach. Kaplan concludes that considerably more theoretical and empirical research on the alternative methods of utility assessment is needed.

Given that the utility of individuals is being measured, the question arises of whose preferences count. The usual answer is that preferences should represent the general public rather than administrators. But one might also expect to find heterogeneity in preferences among members of the general public. Kaplan presents evidence that preferences for various health states are quite homogeneous, even between patients and the general population.

The Oregon Medicaid program provides a case study in which QALYs have been used as measures of program outcome. As Kaplan explains, the U.S. government during the Bush administration rejected Oregon's approach, which was based on principles of cost–effectiveness. In rejecting the waiver application as proposed, the U.S. government maintained that Oregon's method did not adequately account for health state preferences of disabled persons, and hence the allocations proposed discriminated against such persons. Kaplan is critical of this decision because it ignored important empirical evidence on preferences. Subsequently, the Clinton administration approved the waiver, based on a slightly revised priority list.

The other half of a cost–effectiveness ratio refers to cost. In the past, issues of cost measurement have typically taken the backseat to effectiveness. Many studies have been very casual about measuring costs. Important components of cost have been excluded, and cost estimates have been drawn from very small and unrepresentative samples. Learning about the cost of a clinical strategy is only very rarely a part of an RCT.

In Chapter 4, "Measuring Costs," David Dranove, an economist, addresses two issues: (1) which costs to measure and (2) how to measure them. The concept of opportunity cost is basic to the economist's view of cost. Opportunity cost represents the value of the resources used as inputs in a clinical strategy or program if such resources were previously employed elsewhere. In this sense, a charge that incorporates a monopoly profit overstates cost. In practice, not all parties may view opportunity costs as the relevant cost. Plausibly, patients care about the charges they pay net of payments by insurers. Hospitals paid a fixed price per case should be concerned about the inputs devoted to the diagnosis and treatment of a case. Insurers view charges they pay as costs. In principle, at least, social planners should be concerned about opportunity costs. In practice, they may be more concerned about certain costs than others. The costs that count depend in large part on the client's perspective. Eliminating certain costs from the analysis can lead to very different recommendations about the optimal resource allocation.

Several problems arise in measuring costs. Dranove discusses treatment of sunk versus incremental costs, joint costs, and how to incorporate cost change resulting from learning by doing. As users of a new technology such as a surgical procedure become more familiar with it, cost per unit of output may fall. Such decreases should be considered when computing cost.

Dranove provides practical advice about measuring specific types of cost. It is necessary not only to quantify input units, such as time involved in administering a drug, but to value units of such time, such as the appropriate wage rate to use for the person administering the drug. Many elements of cost, such as patient travel time to health care providers, work loss time, and costs incurred by family members other than the patient, are likely to not be part of providers' clinical or financial databases.

Chapter 5, "From Cost–Effectiveness Ratios to Resource Allocation: Where to Draw the Line?" by Milton Weinstein, an economist, is the first of two chapters to address the choice of programs given evidence on cost and effectiveness. Probably because it avoids translating health consequences into monetary units, cost–effectiveness analysis is much more commonly used than is cost–benefit analysis. Even so, with cost–effectiveness analysis one cannot avoid the question, Is the program worth funding?

The chapter addresses three issues. First, Weinstein explains that in order to compare the desirability of programs, the cost–effectiveness ratios must be based on comparable definitions of cost and outcome. He asks what types of lack of comparability are likely to arise. Second, he explains the concept of incremental cost–effectiveness and how to avoid common pitfalls in applying this concept. Third, he explains how one decides where to draw the line between those programs that merit funding or adoption and those that do not. The dollar value of the highest (least desirable) cost–effectiveness ratio that merits funding or adoption is sometimes referred to as the *cut point*.

A problem in comparing program costs is that studies may differ in the types of cost they include in the numerator of the cost–effectiveness ratio. For example, the value of time that patients spend in obtaining care or the value of the reduction in work loss due to health improvement is often excluded from cost–effectiveness analysis. Inclusion/exclusion may have a substantial effect on the cost–effectiveness ratio.

Weinstein discusses six approaches for arriving at cut points: (1) shadow price of explicit budget constraint, (2) opportunity cost in the absence of explicit budget constraint, (3) comparison with other (funded) health programs, (4) cost–effectiveness criteria inferred from prior funding decisions, (5) cost–benefit methods, and (6) rules of thumb. Some approaches are much more elegant than others, but in certain situations, such as when there is no explicit budget constraint, it is necessary to use more informal and ad hoc approaches.

In cost–benefit analysis, all end points are in monetary units. In Chapter 6, "Valuing Health Care Benefits in Money Terms," Mark Pauly, an economist, takes the position that cost–benefit analysis is preferable on balance to cost–effectiveness analysis for purposes of making decisions about resource allocation in health care programs. His chapter addresses two major issues. First, what are the differences between cost–effectiveness and cost–benefit analysis? Second, to the extent that there are differences, which approach should the decision maker use?

Pauly starts with the premise that the objective of the public decision maker should be to select the portfolio of programs that maximizes the well-being of persons served. The goal is achieved when benefits are gauged in terms of the maximum amounts individuals are willing to pay for various programs. The relevant benefit measure reflects the sum of willingness to pay on the part of individuals. Other measures of benefit such as wage gains or addition to gross national product are relevant only to the extent that they are proxies for maximum willingness to pay.

Private decision makers naturally have a more limited perspective of benefit. For example, an administrator of an HMO should gauge the benefit of adding a program to its coverage if the anticipated increase in premium income is greater than or equal to the program's cost. The added premium income reflects policyholder willingness to pay for the program.

Underlying the sum of individuals' maximum willingness to pay may be differences in individual preferences. Suppose rich people attach a higher marginal value to a program than poor people. Then by simply summing willingness to pay and using this as a criterion for program funding, decisions may favor the rich. If this is seen as socially or ethically objectionable, the social planner can adjust the weights to give greater weight to the preferences of low-income persons.

A concern that measuring outcomes or benefits in monetary units will lead to inequitable funding decisions has led many policymakers and analysts to reject cost–benefit in favor of cost–effectiveness analysis. Another concern is the accuracy of measures of willingness to pay. As Pauly explains, willingness to pay may be measured directly from surveys or inferred indirectly from decisions that individuals make. Direct measurement does raise some concerns, such as that respondents may give strategic answers to willingness-to-pay questions. Unfortunately, not much empirical evidence exists on the accuracy of direct measures (some references are given in the chapter). An alternative is to measure willingness to pay from market data. For example, one can infer the value of reductions in risk of dying from amounts needed to compensate workers for taking risky jobs. An alternative to measuring benefits in monetary units is to use QALYs as measures of benefit. But to make funding decisions, as Pauly explains, sooner or later one must attach a monetary value to a QALY.

In most cost–effectiveness studies, analysts simply state that they used a discount rate without justifying that rate or they do not discount at all. As explained in Chapter 7, "Discounting Health Effects for Medical Decisions," by Kip Viscusi, an economist, it is important to discount and to think about the discount rate to be used. Choice of rate can have an important impact on the relative ranking of programs, especially when there are substantial differences in the timing of program costs and benefits.

A unique feature of health care as opposed to commodities is that it is not possible to trade health either across time or across individuals. The fact that one makes decisions about health does not affect the necessity of discounting, but there is some question about the discount rate that should be used to discount health benefits. Is it the same as or different from the one used to discount financial returns or other benefits?

Unfortunately, there is no clear answer to the last question. Implicit rates of discount for health inferred from behavioral studies differ widely, from 1.0 to 14.2 percent, but so do rates applicable to other contexts, such as for the decision to purchase a refrigerator. Given the appreciable ranges of discount rates that have been obtained, it is not possible to state that discount rates applicable to health are different.

In Chapter 8, "Statistical Issues in Cost–Effectiveness Analyses," John Mullahy and Willard Manning, both economists who include econometrics among their fields of specialization, concentrate on a number of statistical issues in comparing alternative health programs. Much of the chapter involves problems that arise in the use of observational data and with data generated from RCTs.

Statistical problems arise when the variable representing the treatment or program, or some other important covariate, is correlated with the equations error term. Such correlations are likely to occur in observational data because the treatment the patient received did not occur at random but likely reflects some factor, probably an unmeasured one, specific to the patient. Even though evidence from RCTs tends to be better, RCTs also have their limitations. Some adverse effects of treatment and the costs associated with such effects may be too rare to be detected with the sample sizes commonly used in RCTs. As Detsky also noted, the time frame covered by an RCT may be too limited to provide a full accounting of either benefits or costs. Nonrandom selection may be a problem for RCTs as well as for observational studies because patient entry into the study and attrition from the study may be systematically related to the treatment. Patients may fail to comply with the prescribed treatment regimen, and failure to fully comply may not be recorded, leading to an error in measuring the treatment.

Mullahy and Manning describe several estimation approaches that are suitable when there is a nonzero correlation between treatments or other covariates and the error term, including use of longitudinal data from a program that allows the individual to act as his or her own control, and instrumental variables estimation. Toward the end of the chapter, Mullahy and Manning discuss problems of inference in cost–effectiveness analysis. They caution against gauging the effects of varying assumptions only singly in sensitivity analysis of cost–effectiveness ratios, since there may be important interaction effects among the changes. Also, since the change in outcome appears in the denominator of the cost–effectiveness ratio and the true change in outcome may be small, even small changes in effect could have a major influence on the ratio. The other chapters suggest a way to handle this problem.

Many health programs have very delayed effects. For example, an antihypertensive or an anticholesterol agent may affect health outcomes in the distant future. Nevertheless, such outcomes are relevant and should be reflected in cost–effectiveness and cost–benefit calculations. To incorporate information on long-term effects it is usually necessary to piece together information from several sources.

In Chapter 9, "Decision Trees and Markov Models in Cost–Effectiveness Research," Emmett Keeler, a mathematician, shows how decision trees can be used to study long-term effects. The chapter begins by showing how decision trees display choices and uncertainties involved in diagnosis and treatment decisions. The second half of the chapter discusses models used to predict long-run outcomes of treatment in order of increasing complexity: formulas for life expectancy, Markov chains, Markov processes, and simulations. For each, the reader is provided with a brief explanation of the approach and is told where to go to learn more. Keeler advises the analyst to use the simplest model that fits.

Chapter 10, "The Use of Cost–Effectiveness/Cost–Benefit Analysis in Actual Decision Making: Current Status and Prospects," by Frank Sloan and Christopher Conover, has three objectives: (1) to summarize key points of agreement and disagreement among the authors; (2) to describe and evaluate how cost–effectiveness analysis is being used by public decision makers in Oregon, Australia, and Canada to decide which prescription drugs and other technologies should be covered by health insurance; and (3) to discuss the usefulness of these tools for making choices, given the current state of the art.

CHAPTER 2

Evidence of effectiveness: evaluating its quality

Allan S. Detsky

The basic components of a cost–effectiveness analysis are demonstration of the relative effectiveness of the new technology compared to the old, conversion of the effectiveness of the new technology into a common unit of measurement of benefit in order to make this measurement comparable to that of other, competing technologies, and the measurement of the incremental costs. This chapter focuses on the quality of the evidence supporting the effectiveness of the new technology compared to older technologies; that is, the measurement of incremental effectiveness (Effect). Later chapters will review the principles of measuring costs and converting estimates of effectiveness into common units of measurement such as utility and benefit.

Nature of the evidence

Assessing relative effectiveness of a new technology

To understand the nature of the evidence supporting the effectiveness of new health care technologies, it is useful to review the types of health care technologies under consideration. A health care technology includes all interventions that require the use of both labor (e.g., clinicians) and nonlabor (e.g., pharmaceutical products or diagnostic equipment) resources. A wide variety of health care technologies is aimed at reducing the burden of disease, including pharmaceutical products, surgical techniques, diagnostic equipment, diagnosis and development and delivery of treatment plans, counseling services, and interdisciplinary programs involving combinations of all of the above. Measurements of effectiveness require demonstration that the new technology does more good than harm compared with the older technology when applied to a target group of patients and provided by a particular group of providers. The very essence of effectiveness requires comparison with alternative methods of caring for patients with particular health states. Consequently, demonstrations of effectiveness universally must be comparative, measuring the clinical course for a group of subjects treated with and without the new health care technology.

High-quality evidence will result in a quantitative estimate of the relative effectiveness of the new health care technology that is both valid (i.e., estimates the true, unbiased effectiveness) and reliable (i.e., is reproducible if subsequent estimates of relative effectiveness are undertaken). Issues of validity are related to the design of the study estimating effectiveness, whereas issues of reliability and precision are usually related to the sample size of the study. There are two types of validity that are important to consider: internal validity and external validity. Internal validity asks whether the conclusions drawn from the evidence (i.e., that treatments either differ or result in the same outcomes) are true for the subjects who are enrolled in the study (i.e., internal to the trial). External validity, also known as generalizability, refers to the extent to which the results of this study can be applied to other subjects (i.e., external to the trial) who may have different characteristics.

Alternative study designs

Study design is based on the following principles (Fletcher, Fletcher, and Wagner 1982; Feinstein 1985; Sackett, Hayes, and Tugwell 1985). Estimation of the relative effectiveness of new versus old health care technologies requires following two groups of patients for the development of good and bad (or adverse) outcomes, one treated with the new technology and the other treated with the old. To conclude that the treatments are either different or equivalent relies on the assumption that the only difference between the two groups is the application of the new or the old health care technology. For this to be true, the two groups of subjects first must be similar with respect to their prognosis or risk of developing good and bad outcomes over time prior to receiving the therapy. If so, the distribution of prognostic factors in the two groups of subjects allocated to the two different therapies must be similar. There must be no differences in the distribution of either known or unknown prognostic factors for the two groups. Second, one must assume that the only difference in the way the two groups of subjects were treated during the course of the study was the actual application of the new versus the old technology; that patients receiving the new technology did not also receive some additional health care services such as more intensive monitoring of their overall health, called *co-interventions*. If patients did receive such co-interventions, then that must be considered as part of the new technology for purposes of evaluating effectiveness. Last, one must assume that the development of good and bad outcomes was assessed in exactly the same way for the two groups of subjects. Those who assessed whether good or bad outcomes occurred should have used the same criteria and should have been blinded as to whether the patient received the new or the old technology. Similarly the subjects themselves may be unduly influenced by knowledge of which treatment they were receiving when reporting symptoms, and the study design should try to protect against such bias.

The *randomized double-blind controlled trial* is a study design aimed at fulfilling the above assumptions and is the "gold standard" methodology in terms of internal validity. The word "randomized" implies that the subjects were not allocated by any individual who might knowingly or unknowingly allocate patients with a better risk profile into one of the two treatment groups. The word "controlled" implies that there is a comparison group. The words "double-blind" imply that neither the patient nor the individual assessing the development of good or bad outcomes has knowledge of which treatment group the patient was assigned to, thereby minimizing the threat of biased interpretation. The phrase "the randomized double-blind controlled trial" is sometimes shortened to "randomized controlled trial" (RCT). Since the word "randomized" implies the existence of more than one treatment group, one may even further shorten the phrase to the "randomized trial."

Over the last fifteen years there has been tremendous growth in the use of the RCT as a study design for the evaluation of health care technologies. The vast majority of RCTs involve the assessment of new medications such as antibiotics, antihypertensive agents, lipid-lowering agents (Goldman et al. 1991), chemotherapeutic agents for cancer, and medications for psychiatric illnesses such as depression (Stark and Hardison 1985), to name a few. In recent years new classes of pharmaceutical agents have been developed, such as Sumatriptan for migraine (Subcutaneous Sumatriptan International Study Group 1991), the genetically engineered "biological response modifiers" to stimulate production of white blood cells (Crawford et al. 1991), and combat endotoxin from gram negative bacteria (Ziegler et al. 1991). A smaller number of very important trials have compared surgical techniques such as extra-cranial–intracranial bypass (EC/IC Bypass Study Group 1985), carotid endarterectomy (North American Symptomatic Carotid Endarterectomy Trial Collaborators 1991; European Carotid Surgery Trialists' Collaborative Group 1991), and coronary artery bypass (Killip and Ryan 1985). Trials of invasive techniques such as coronary angioplasty and coronary atherectomy are presently being undertaken to compare these procedures with medical therapy or more invasive surgical therapy such as coronary bypass surgery. Still other RCTs have been undertaken to evaluate the effectiveness of screening patients for asymptomatic stages of a variety of cancers, including breast cancer (Miller et al. 1992). A much smaller number of trials have been undertaken to evaluate technologies such as counseling and multidisciplinary programs such as risk factor intervention for coronary disease as a health promotion intervention.

Unlike many economic studies aimed at measuring the difference in outcomes attributable to the use of resources, evaluating the effectiveness of health care interventions has the luxury of using this powerful experimental design. However, nonexperimental approaches must sometimes be employed or are often used as precursors to RCTs to determine whether an RCT would be feasible or likely to add knowledge (Abrams et al. 1988). These nonexperimental designs include *cohort analytical studies*, where two groups of patients, one treated with the new technology and the other treated with the old technology, are identified but not randomly allocated to receive those interventions and are prospectively followed for the development of outcomes. This design is much less powerful in terms of the validity of the conclusion that can be drawn from its results because it violates the assumption that the two groups have not been systematically selected on the basis of prognosis or the clinician's belief in the patient's likely response to a particular therapy.

Perhaps the best known cohort studies supporting a health care intervention are those demonstrating that smoking was related to the subsequent development of lung cancer (Doll and Hill 1950; Doll and Peto 1976). Although RCTs (Rose et al. 1982), following the cohort studies, demonstrated the risk of smoking (thereby supporting interventions aimed at helping patients stop smoking or preventing them from starting at all), they did not demonstrate a statistically significant positive relationship. In fact, the cohort studies form the largest body of evidence supporting smoking cessation as a mechanism for reducing the burden of disease among smokers.

In some circumstances prospective studies are deemed to be either too expensive or premature. Retrospective studies assessing the frequency of exposure to new and old health care technologies among patients who have good or bad outcomes can be undertaken to support the evidence of effectiveness of health care technologies. These studies are called *case-control studies*, and they inherently contain several biases because of their retrospective nature and the difficulty in assembling a meaningful group of control subjects. Case-control studies are rarely convincing enough to support the adoption of clinical interventions.

Occasionally clinical investigators will use a single group of patients, all of whom are treated with a new health care technology in order to support the evidence of the effectiveness of that technology. Such studies are called *case series*. This type of evidence is generally unacceptable because one cannot compare the clinical course among a similar group of untreated patients. Also, the clinical courses of most diseases are variable, with long lag times between the potential beginning of treatment and the development of outcomes. The only possible scenario where a case series might be considered acceptable evidence supporting the effectiveness of an intervention is one where the group of subjects being studied has a uniformly fatal outlook within a very short period of time. Patients with diseases such as acute myelogenous leukemia (AML) could constitute such a group. However, some investigators have demonstrated that even for a disease such as AML one can drastically alter the prognosis as measured by five year survival rates depending on the inclusion/exclusion criteria for the case series (Toronto Leukemia Study Group 1986). Therefore it is difficult to imagine a case series being acceptable as a standard of evidence supporting effectiveness.

Quality of the evidence

Demonstrating effectiveness: efficacy versus effectiveness

Clinicians must make numerous decisions about patient care management in the course of treating individual patients. The kinds of decisions they must make include whether or not to screen patients for potentially treatable diseases when they are asymptomatic, pursue a set of signs and symptoms with further diagnostic tests, treat patients with medical or surgical therapies, or pursue further information in order to predict the future clinical course for patients. Each of these decisions is based on the clinician's subjective impression of the relative benefits and risks of pursuing each of the strategies. When the use of resources is not a consideration (the usual circumstance for patient–clinician interactions), these decisions are based solely on the grounds of effectiveness.

Demonstration of *effectiveness* requires evidence that the clinical strategy does more good than harm when used in the specific clinical circumstance applicable to a particular patient. *Efficacy* implies that clinical strategies can achieve their stated goal of improving clinical outcomes when used in optimal circumstances. The major difference, therefore, between effectiveness and efficacy is the difference in both the type of patient to which the clinical strategy would be applied and the nature of the system delivering the care. Most clinical studies, particularly RCTs, demonstrate efficacy rather than effectiveness because they apply the therapy to a narrow spectrum of homogeneous patients and deliver care in a very controlled fashion, both of which optimize the chances of demonstrating benefit. As noted earlier, they are the "gold standard" for achieving internal validity. Whether the results of the clinical study supporting the efficacy of a particular health care technology are applicable to other patients in other care settings is a matter that often requires judgment concerning generalizability or external validity. In some circumstances, evidence from RCTs must be supplemented by evidence comparing the effectiveness of the technology for other patients who receive care in usual settings. This supplementary evidence is usually derived from studies using nonexperimental designs and occasionally involves large administrative databases that can be used for outcomes research. At the present time there is no standard approach to integrating information aimed at maximizing internal validity (e.g., efficacy of RCTs) with that aimed at establishing external validity.

There are two good examples of the use of administrative databases (Medicaid) to document the impact of medications in a general population (as opposed to a sample contained in an RCT). Carson and his colleagues used Medicaid data to provide estimates of severe and relatively rare adverse events such as gastrointestinal bleeding from nonsteroidal anti-inflammatory drugs (Carson et al. 1987a, 1987b; Strom et al. 1987; Strom and Carson 1989). Because the rates of these events are relatively low, estimates derived in this way are more precise (narrower confidence limits) as well as more generalizable than those derived from RCTs. Weisbrod (1983) used Medicaid data to document the economic impact of the introduction of a new drug class in the 1970s, H_2-blockers (e.g., cimetidine). He was able to use these data and econometric techniques to document the reduction in the costs of treating ulcer disease after H_2-blockers were adopted.

Grading levels of evidence

It is well known that the majority of clinical strategies undertaken in modern medicine are not supported by high-quality evidence, yet clinicians must make decisions about strategies even in its absence. Clinical policymakers have recently begun to develop guidelines for clinicians, establishing in some cases sets of rules of evidence to support clinical recommendations. For example, Cook, Guyatt, Laupacis, and Sackett (1992) established a set of guidelines that related a "grade of recommendation" to the level of evidence supporting the use of antithrombotic agents. Such a system is outlined in Table 2.1.

The levels of evidence displayed in this system are based on two criteria: whether the effectiveness has been demonstrated in a randomized trial, and whether the randomized trial was large enough to provide a precise estimate of the potential benefit. Examples of Grade A recommendations are aspirin for patients with transient ischemic attacks or unstable angina (Antiplatelet Trialists' Collaboration Group 1988), carotid endarterectomy for patients with a greater than 70 percent stenosis of the carotid artery (North American Symptomatic Carotid Endarterectomy Trial Collaborators 1991; European Carotid Surgery Trialists' Collaborative Group 1991), and AZT for patients with HIV infection (Fischl et al. 1987). A clinical strategy that carries a Grade B recommendation is heparin (an anticoagulant) for patients with unstable angina (Theroux et al. 1988; RISC Group 1990), and an example of a Grade C recommendation is antibiotic prophylaxis for the prevention of bacterial endocarditis (Dajani et al. 1990).

Table 2.1. *The relation between levels of evidence and grades of recommendation*

Level of evidence		Grade of recommendation
Level I:	Large randomized trials with clear-cut results (and low risk of error)	Grade A
Level II:	Small randomized trials with uncertain results (and moderate to high risk of error)	Grade B
Level III:	Nonrandomized, contemporaneous controls	Grade B
Level IV:	Nonrandomized, historical controls	Grade C
Level V:	No controls, case series only	Grade C

Source: Cook et al. (1992).

It is interesting to note that many of the recommendations for using antithrombotic agents in specific clinical conditions are supported by Grade C evidence (Dalen and Hirsh 1992). On the other hand, it is gratifying to note that many practices that previously were supported by Grade C evidence, such as the use of anticoagulant in nonrheumatic atrial fibrillation (Laupacis et al. 1992a) and carotid endarterectomy for patients with carotid stenosis greater than 70 percent (North American Symptomatic Carotid Endarterectomy Trial Collaborators 1991), are now supported by Grade A evidence.

The Department of Clinical Epidemiology and Biostatistics (1981) developed a detailed list of questions to help assess the quality of clinical studies supporting the therapeutic effectiveness of clinical interventions and technologies (see Table 2.2). These questions encompass the measurement and design issues in order to assess the validity and reliability of the evidence. Questions 1, 2, the first two parts of 5, and 6 relate to internal validity. Question 3 and the last part of 5 relate to the external validity, or generalizability, of the trial. Could patients with a different spectrum of clinical characteristics be expected to receive the same kinds of benefits? Question 4 raises two important issues. The determination of "clinical significance" or "clinical importance" in the absence of consideration of resources is clearly subjective. However, question 4b relates to the precision (reliability) of the estimate of effectiveness and, most importantly, to the issue of whether the trial was large enough to demonstrate a clinically important difference if in truth such a difference existed (Detsky et al. 1987). This last issue relates to the power of the trial, the sensitivity of the trial for detecting a true difference, or its complement, and the risk of making a Type 2 error (declaring a therapy ineffective when in truth it

Table 2.2. *Methodologic criteria for the critical assessment of a therapy article*

1. Was the assignment of patients to treatments really randomized?
   a. Was similarity between groups documented?
   b. Was prognostic stratification used in allocation?
2. Were all clinically relevant outcomes reported?
   a. Was mortality as well as morbidity reported?
   b. Were deaths from all causes reported?
   c. Were quality of life assessments conducted?
   d. Was outcome assessment blind?
3. Were the study patients recognizably similar to your own?
   a. Are reproducibly defined exclusion criteria stated?
   b. Was the setting primary or tertiary care?
4. Were both statistical and clinical significance considered?
   a. If statistically significant, was the difference clinically important?
   b. If not statistically significant, was the study large enough to show a clinically important difference if it should occur?
5. Is the therapeutic maneuver feasible in your practice?
   a. Is it available; affordable; sensible?
   b. Were contamination and co-intervention avoided?
   c. Was the maneuver administered blind?
   d. Was compliance measured?
6. Were all patients who entered the study accounted for at its conclusion?
   a. Were dropouts, withdrawals, noncompliers, and those who crossed over handled appropriately in the analysis?

Source: Department of Clinical Epidemiology and Biostatistics 1981.

is effective). Consumers of clinical trials throughout North America have used the checklist of questions (Table 2.2) when critically appraising evidence supporting therapeutic strategies. A similar checklist of questions can be used for evaluating the evidence of diagnostic technologies.

Chalmers et al. (1981) developed an even more complex system of assessing the quality of evidence derived from randomized trials. His system encompasses a much longer list of questions, including details about issues such as the method of randomization (to assess the risk of clinicians' somehow having put patients with a better prognosis in either of the two treatment groups), details about blinding patients and clinicians as to the therapeutic strategy (e.g., whether the investigator tested for equivalent appearance and taste of medications), and a more detailed analysis of the statistical procedures utilized in the studies.

Table 2.3. *Examples of cost–effectiveness studies that use different kinds of effectiveness evidence*

Intervention	References	Nature of evidence supporting effectiveness
Beta blockers after fatal/morbid myocardial infarction	Goldman et al. 1988	RCTs measuring end points
Streptokinase in acute myocardial infarctions	Krumholz et al. 1992	RCTs measuring fatal/morbid end points
Cholesterol lowering to prevent cardiac disease	Oster and Epstein 1987	RCTs measuring fatal/morbid end points
	Goldman et al. 1991	RCTs measuring cholesterol reduction only
	Schulman et al. 1990	Epidemiological data
Hormone replacement to prevent bone fractures	Tosteson et al. 1990	RCTs for intermediate outcome cohort and case-control studies for morbid outcomes
Angioplasty, coronary bypass surgery	Wong et al. 1990	RCTs for surgery and medication and case series for angioplasty medication
Neonatal intensive care	Boyle et al. 1983	Population cohort study (before-and-after design)
Low osmolar contrast agents	Goel, Deber, and Detsky 1989	Guess by experts
	Barrett et al. 1992	RCT

Meta analysis

In some circumstances, investigators estimating the incremental cost–effectiveness of technologies will use a *meta analysis* of the evidence supporting the effectiveness of the intervention in order to form a quantitative estimate of the effectiveness. Meta analysis is a technique of combining information from a variety of individual studies to draw an overall conclusion. The principles of meta analysis require the development of a research protocol that has the following components: description of the literature search techniques, inclusion/exclusion criteria for individual studies, choice of end points, records of individual study characteristics (e.g., patient characteristics), details about the therapy (e.g., dose), tests of statistical homogeneity, statistical pooling procedures, and sensitivity analyses (Detsky et al. 1987). Meta analyses can be very powerful sources of information concerning the effectiveness of technologies because they take advantage of a much larger sample size, giving greater precision to the estimate, and often allow an assessment of the generalizability of results from individual studies. In addition, differences in study designs, such as inclusion of patients with different characteristics or different doses of medication, can be used to answer questions that cannot be answered from individual studies. Meta analyses have been used to estimate the effectiveness of antiplatelet agents for patients with cardiovascular disease (Antiplatelet Trialists' Collaboration Group 1988), aminophylline for patients with asthma (Littenberg 1988), and parenteral nutritional support for patients undergoing surgery (Detsky et al. 1987) or intensive chemotherapy (McGeer, Detsky, and O'Rourke 1990). Recently, some investigators have shown that a cumulative meta analysis, that is, one that adds each successive trial in chronological order over time, is a powerful technique for determining when the weight of accumulating evidence clearly supports the conclusion that a therapy is effective (Lau et al. 1992). They note that the time when such evidence accumulates to support effectiveness often precedes by as much as ten years the time when clinical experts recommend the adoption of those therapies in textbooks and traditional review articles. This supports the use of meta analysis to provide precise estimates of treatment effect.

Although the RCT or meta analysis of RCTs is the method of choice for establishing the efficacy of an intervention, it may fall short of providing the information required to estimate cost–effectiveness for a variety of interventions under consideration for resource allocation. Reasons for this failure include the limited target population used in the trial, unanticipated additional findings that raise more questions, low power, choice of the wrong therapy, and the "moving target" nature of technologies over time. Additionally, certain interventions such as screening and primary prevention are much more difficult to evaluate using RCTs because of the long lag time between the intervention and the outcomes. Policymakers measuring the cost–effectiveness of these interventions may have to proceed with incomplete evidence. However, when considering new pharmaceutical products, it is unlikely that evidence from RCTs will be lacking, because of the requirements of pharmaceutical licensing bodies such as the U.S. Food and Drug Administration. Even so, the systems of grading evidence of effectiveness described previously may be more useful to clinicians and policymakers in determining which therapies are likely to result in more good than harm for some specific patients than in determining whether the quantitative estimate of relative effectiveness is valid for estimating cost–effectiveness.

As a result, the majority of cost–effectiveness analyses use simulation models (see the next section of this chapter and Chap. 9) combining data from multiple sources. Even the estimates of effectiveness must rely on combining data from RCTs with other data. For example, in estimating the cost–effectiveness of cholesterol reducing drugs, Oster and Epstein (1987) used an RCT of cholestyramine (the Lipid Research Clinics Trial), which measured fatal and morbid outcomes, and combined it with epidemiological data from the Framingham Study (Table 2.3). Sometimes, RCTs only estimate the impact of the intervention on an intermediate variable, and extrapolation to fatal and morbid events must be derived by adding epidemiological data. Goldman et al. (1991) and Schulman et al. (1990) used this strategy by combining RCTs of HMG-CoA reductase inhibitors, which only measured the impact on cholesterol, with epidemiological data. In some cases, investigators have used a best guess of the relative effectiveness of agents and then advocated RCTs to obtain better evidence. Goel, Deber, and Detsky (1989) did so in estimating the cost–effectiveness of low osmolar contrast agents, and subsequently, better evidence came from RCTs (Steinberg et al. 1992; Barrett et al. 1992).

Extensions of effectiveness evidence required for estimation of cost–effectiveness

Evidence supporting the adoption of new technologies often stops with a conclusion that they are effective; that is, they do more good than harm when used for appropriate patients. However, to perform a cost–effectiveness analysis, the data derived from effectiveness studies must be extended in several important ways.

Choice of alternative therapies

Because all cost–effectiveness analyses are comparative, the cost and clinical outcomes of the health care technology must be compared to those associated with an alternative strategy for treating the same group of patients. Most clinical trials on which evidence of effectiveness is based would also have control therapies. However, the control therapy used in a clinical trial may not be an alternative therapy that is appropriate for cost–effectiveness analysis. For example, a pharmaceutical company may establish the effectiveness of a new medication in a series of RCTs that compare that medication to placebo. However, an organization making allocative decisions such as whether or not to utilize the new medication will not be only interested in its effectiveness relative to placebo but rather its effectiveness, and particularly its cost–effectiveness, relative to other medications that could treat those patients. For example, Sumatriptan is a new medication for treating patients with migraine. All but two of the trials demonstrating the effectiveness of Sumatriptan compared it to placebo for patients with episodes of migraine (Subcutaneous

Sumatriptan International Study Group 1991). However, in considering whether or not to add it to a hospital or third-party payer formulary, the relevant comparison would be to other medications currently used to treat patients with migraine, such as Tylenol with codeine, Cafergot, or Fiorinal.

In some cases the choice of the alternative therapy is quite clear. For example, in estimating the relative effectiveness of a thrombolytic agent for treating patients with acute myocardial infarction such as tissue plasminogen activator, the appropriate comparison would be to the standard thrombolytic therapy streptokinase (Third International Study of Infarct Survival Collaborative Group 1992). In estimating the relative effectiveness of an antiplatelet agent such as Ticlopidine in preventing strokes, the appropriate comparison should be aspirin, which is the standard therapy (Hass et al. 1989). In other cases there will be several possible choices for other therapies. For example, a new cephalosporin for treating bronchitis or otitis media could be compared to a wide variety of antibiotics used to treat these conditions. For breakthrough pharmaceutical products, the appropriate comparison might be placebo (if there is no currently known effective therapy) or nonpharmacological interventions such as surgery or psychotherapy.

The choice of alternative therapeutic strategy is further complicated if the alternative therapeutic strategy can be purchased at a variety of prices.[1] For example, a new antibiotic or nonsteroidal anti-inflammatory might be compared to one of the older products in its class that now has a generic equivalent. In performing the cost–effectiveness analysis the difference in price between the new product and the old product will obviously be very sensitive to the choice of whether or not one wishes to use a brand name price or a generic price. Several different perspectives can be taken. For a purchasing party such as an insurer or hospital that can control the brand of the alternative therapy used and that is solely interested in maximizing the net benefits derived from a fixed budget, the appropriate approach would be to find the lowest priced product and perform the incremental cost–effectiveness analysis relative to that product. For an agency that is estimating incremental cost–effectiveness but does not have control over the brand or price of the alternative therapeutic strategy, the appropriate approach would be to model the alternative therapeutic strategy according to current patterns of care. For example, if 80 percent of the current market uses a brand name nonsteroidal anti-inflammatory while 20 percent uses a generic product, then the appropriate price for the alternative strategy would be a weighted average of the prices of the two products using the proportion of use in the market as the weights. The incremental effectiveness should also be modeled comparing the effectiveness of the new product to a weighted average of the effectiveness of the other products currently used in the market. In performing a cost–effectiveness analysis, it is important that the analyst understood the expectation of the consumer of the report. The safest approach would be to perform an analysis in several ways, each relevant to a different perspective.

Time horizon and modeling issues

Many effects of interventions are delayed, but the information at hand only applies to a relatively short time interval. The analyst must use some method for extending the evidence on effectiveness to cover the time interval over which effectiveness could logically apply. Most randomized trials report outcomes in terms of proportions, such as the proportion of patients who survive or die over a fixed period of time, usually no more than five to seven years. Let P_t be the observed proportion of adverse events such as death in the patients treated with the new technology and P_c be the same proportion for patients treated with the old technology. The difference in the two proportions (or the effect size) can be summarized in a number of ways, such as the proportionate risk reduction, $(P_c - P_t)/P_c$, or the absolute risk reduction, $P_c - P_t$. Extension of this information about effectiveness to cost–effectiveness requires caution, especially if the adverse event of interest is death over a fixed time period.

For example, suppose an RCT is carried out over five years. In patients receiving a new therapy the proportion who die over the five-year time frame is 0.1 and the proportion who die in the control group is 0.2. In this case, the proportion of risk reduction would be 50 percent, or $(0.2 - 0.1)/0.2$, and the absolute risk reduction would be 0.1, or $0.2 - 0.1$. It would be correct to conclude that this therapy is associated with a reduction in mortality but only over the five-year period, because obviously if one were to observe the treatment and control cohorts over a long enough period, the mortality rate in both groups would be exactly the same, 100 percent.

The therapy in this example is effective in increasing life expectancy by delaying "premature" deaths from the specific disease. To extrapolate from the evidence that establishes the effectiveness in reducing premature mortality, the cost–effectiveness analysis must use quantitative estimates of those gains in health over a period that usually extends well beyond the time frame of the trial. Complex decision analytic models (discussed in Chap. 9) can be used to make such extrapolations. However, it is important to note that analysts must make a considerable number of assumptions about what will happen in the period beyond time frame of the trial. For example, the excess mortality associated with a specific disease, such as cardiac disease, may well increase subsequently above the rate estimated from the trial. Lacking hard evidence, the analyst must make an assumption about how fast this increase takes place. Further, the effectiveness of the intervention may well be expected to decline in the time period after the trial's time frame. The analyst also is forced to assume how quickly the effectiveness will decline.

End points

Randomized trials usually estimate discrete end points such as death, nonfatal events such as myocardial infarctions or strokes, or periods of "disease-free survival," a term used in examining the outcomes for patients with cancer. To calculate cost–effectiveness ratios for individual new technologies, the outcomes must be expressed in common units to allow incremental cost–effectiveness ratios to be compared. This is not a requirement for studies that establish only the effectiveness of individual technologies, and therefore it is likely that the evidence of effectiveness of different technologies will use different units of measurement. The conversion of these units of measurement into a common unit of measurement can be difficult. Decision analytic models can convert various outcome measures to a single metric: life expectancy. Then the gains would be measured in extensions in life expectancy. However, a measure of change in life expectancy fails to recognize improvements in quality of life attributable to many modern health care technologies such as pharmaceutical products.

Conceptually there are two approaches to moving beyond effectiveness measures that are limited to discrete end points such as fatal and nonfatal adverse events such as strokes. Utility is a nonmonetary concept for estimating the value to society of improvements in health status. There are several methods for converting end points into utilities. The use of quality-adjusted life years (QALYs) has been popular as a proxy for utilities (see Chap. 3). QALYs are a weighted average of the periods of time that an individual lives in each health state over the remainder of his or her lifetime weighted by the quality of life estimate (sometimes measured using a utility instrument). However, QALYs are only a proxy for utility and are the same as a utility only under severe restrictive assumptions (Torrance and Feeny 1989). Another method for converting clinical end points into a common metric for economic analyses would be to use monetary units based on approaches such as willingness to pay.[2]

Heterogeneity of population using a drug or other technology

Most health care technologies are delivered to a variety of patients whose different clinical characteristics will almost certainly affect the relative effectiveness and cost. Examples of such clinical characteristics are age, sex, presence of comorbid conditions (other illnesses), and type of primary illness for which the technology is known to improve outcomes. Examples of the last characteristic are coronary artery disease, cerebrovascular disease, prosthetic valves, or atrial fibrillation, for which the same thrombotic agent could be used. Therefore, incremental cost–effectiveness will vary for different groups of patients, in some cases quite considerably. Most cost–effectiveness analyses deal with this problem by using sensitivity analyses, that is, by varying estimates of the variables in the model to reflect these differenct populations (Goel, Deber, and Detsky 1989). Some ignore this issue altogether. In some cases, investigators model different groups of patients separately. For example, researchers have assessed the cost–effectiveness of strategies involving lipid lowering drugs aimed at lowering the risk in patient populations without current cardiac disease (primary prevention) separately from those aimed at improving health outcomes in those with already established cardiac disease (secondary prevention) (Goldman et al. 1991). These studies are improved by having available results from separate RCTs in primary and secondary prevention. Most cost–effectiveness analyses do not have the benefit of such information.

As mentioned earlier, the use of technologies in actual practice may vary considerably from the use in patients included in the studies from which effectiveness estimates are derived. In practice, patients who are inappropriate candidates may receive a particular diagnostic or therapeutic procedure. To the extent this occurs, the effectiveness of particular technologies from trials may overstate actual effectiveness. Although not easily dealt with in the absence of data, this issue is rarely considered in economic analyses.

Summary

This chapter has reviewed the study designs used to support the evidence of effectiveness, one of the basic building blocks in estimating the incremental cost–effectiveness of new health care technologies. The majority of pharmaceutical products will have their effectiveness studied in the form of randomized controlled clinical trials, the study design that maximizes the internal validity of the result. However, as outlined in this chapter, this evidence must be expanded in several important ways to be useful for estimating the incremental cost–effectiveness of these technologies. In addition, several important questions concerning the internal and external validity of the trials themselves help the reviewer assess the quality of the evidence.

CHAPTER 3

Utility assessment for estimating quality-adjusted life years

Robert M. Kaplan

Programs in health care have varying objectives. The objective of prenatal care might be a reduction in infant mortality. Rheumatologists strive to make their patients more functional, whereas primary care providers often focus on shortening the cycle of acute illness. All of these providers are attempting to improve the health of their patients. However, they each measure health in a different way. Comparing the productivity of a rheumatologist with that of a neonatologist may be like comparing apples to oranges.

The diversity of outcomes to health care has led many analysts to focus on the simplest common ground, typically, mortality or life expectancy. Those who are alive are statistically coded as 1, and those who are dead are statistically coded as 0. Mortality allows the comparison between different diseases. For example, we can state the life expectancy of those who will eventually die of heart disease and compare it to the life expectancy of those who eventually die of cancer. The difficulty is that everyone who remains alive is given the same score. A person confined to bed with an irreversible coma is alive and is counted the same as someone who is actively playing volleyball at a picnic. Utility assessment, on the other hand, allows the quantification of levels of wellness on the continuum anchored by death and optimum function.

This chapter reviews the concept of utility in relation to the evaluation of cost–effectiveness of pharmaceutical products. The concept of quality-adjusted life years and the related concept of utility are first reviewed. Then, methods of utility assessment are considered. Differences in economic and psychological approaches to utility assessment are reviewed and evaluated, as well as practical issues relevant to whose preferences should be used in the model. Finally, applications of cost–effectiveness models in resource allocation are reviewed.

Conceptual framework

To evaluate health-related quality of life, one must consider all of the different ways that illness and its treatment affect outcomes. Health concerns can be reduced to two categories: life duration and quality of life. Individuals are concerned about illness, disability, and effects of treatment because they can affect life expectancy and quality of life. Assessment of a pharmaceutical treatment should consider a few basic questions:

1. Does the illness or its treatment make life last a shorter duration of time?
2. Does the condition or its treatment make life less desirable and, if so, how much less desirable?
3. What are the duration effects: how much life is lost or how long is the period of undesirable health effects?

This chapter focuses on the second issue. Determining how illness or treatment affects desirability of life is a matter of preference or utility. Such evaluations require that health states be compared to one another.

Within the last few years interest has been growing in using quality of life data to help evaluate the benefits of health care programs. In cost–effectiveness analysis, the benefits of medical care, behavioral interventions, or preventive programs can be expressed in terms of well years. Others have chosen to describe outcomes in quality-adjusted life years (QALYs; Weinstein and Stason 1976) or health years of life (Russell 1986). The term "QALY" has become most popular and is therefore used here. QALYs integrate mortality and morbidity to express health status in terms of equivalents of well years of life. If a woman dies of lupus at age fifty and one would have expected her to live to age seventy-five, the disease was associated with twenty-five lost life years. If 100 women died at age fifty (and also had a life expectancy of seventy-five years), 2,500 (100 × 25 years) life years would be lost. Yet, death is not the only outcome of concern in lupus. The disease leaves many adults somewhat disabled over long periods of time. Although still alive, the quality of their lives has diminished. QALYs take into consideration the quality-of-life consequences of these illnesses. For example, a disease that reduces quality of life by one-half will take away 0.5 QALYs over the course of one year. If it affects two people, it will take away 1 QALY (2 × 0.5) over a one-year period. A medical treatment that improves quality of life by 0.2 for each of five individuals will result in the equivalent of 1 QALY if the benefit is maintained over a one-year period. This system has the advantage of considering both benefits and side effects of programs in terms of the common QALY units. Although QALYs are typically assessed for patients, they can be measured for others, including caregivers who are placed at risk because they experience stressful life events.

The concept of relative importance

Dimensions of quality of life

Nearly all health-related quality-of-life measures have multiple dimensions, such as pain and lack of mobility. The exact dimensions vary from measure to measure. There is considerable debate in the field about which dimensions should be included (Wiklund et al. 1992). For example, the most commonly included dimensions are physical functioning, role functioning, and mental health. The Medical Outcomes Study (MOS) includes eight health concepts (Stewart and Ware 1993). Although many questionnaires include different dimensions, they still may be tapping the same constructs. For example, a measure without a mental health component does not necessarily neglect mental health. Mental health symptoms may be included and the impact of mental health, cognitive functioning, or mental retardation may be represented in questions about role functioning. Some measures have multiple dimensions for mental health symptoms, whereas others include fewer items and ask about problems in general. Although a common strategy is to report outcomes along multiple dimensions, it is not clear that multiple dimensions are more capable of detecting clinical differences. This remains an empirical question for systematic analysis.

Relative importance of dimensions

Most treatments have side effects as well as benefits. Generally, the frequencies of various side effects are tabulated. Thus, a medication to control high blood pressure might be associated with low probabilities of dizziness, tiredness, impotence, and shortness of breath. The major challenge is in determining what it means when someone experiences a side effect. Should the patient who feels sleepy discontinue the medication? How do we determine whether or not observable side effects are important? Should a patient with insulin dependent diabetes mellitus (IDDM) discontinue therapy because he or she develops skin problems at the injection sites? Clearly, local irritation is a side effect of treatment. But without treatment the patient would die. Often the issue is not whether treatment causes side effects, but how we should place these side effects within the perspective of total health. Ultimately, we must decide whether treatment produces a net benefit or a net deficit in health status.

Many measures of health-related quality of life simply tabulate frequencies for different symptoms or represent health status using profiles of outcomes. A representation of three hypothetical treatment profiles is shown in Figure 3.1. It is common in the presentation of these profiles to connect the points, even though increments on the category axis (*x*-axis) are not meaningful. *T*-scores

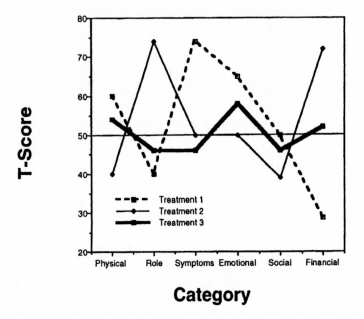

Figure 3.1. Comparison of profiles for three hypothetical treatments. (*Source*: Kaplan and Coons 1992, 31.)

(*y*-axis) are standardized scores with a mean of 50 and a standard deviation of 10. Treatment 1 may produce benefits for physical functioning but decrements for role functioning. Treatment 2 may produce decrements for physical functioning but increments for role functioning. This information may be valuable for diagnostic purposes. However, ultimately, clinicians make some general interpretations of the profile by applying a weighting system. They might decide that they are more concerned about physical, rather than role, functioning or vice versa. Judging the relative importance of various dimensions is common and typically is done implicitly, arbitrarily, and in an idiosyncratic way. Physicians may ignore a particular test result or a particular symptom because another one is more important to them. The process by which relative importance is evaluated can be studied explicitly and be part of the overall model.

If one accepts that preference, or utility, assessment is central to valuing a service relative to its cost, several conceptual issues must be considered (Froberg and Kane 1989a, 1989b, 1989c, 1989d). For example, a variety of approaches to the measurement of preference can yield different results (see the Froberg and Kane studies for a review). However, these differences are to be expected: the various approaches to preference assessment are based on different underlying conceptual models, which then require that different questions be asked.

The concept of utility

The concept of QALYs has been in the literature for nearly twenty-five years. Perhaps the first application was suggested by Fanshel and Bush (1970), and later Torrance (1976) introduced a conceptually similar model. Since then, a variety of applications have appeared.

Despite the differences in approach, some important assumptions are similar. All approaches set one completely healthy year of life at 1. Years of life at less than optimal health are scored as less than 1. The basic assumption is that two years scored as 0.5 add up to the equivalent of one year of complete wellness. Similarly, four years scored as 0.25 are equivalent to one completely well year of life. A treatment that boosts a patient's health from 0.5 to 0.75 produces the equivalent of 0.25 QALYs. If applied to four individuals, and the duration of the treatment effect is one year, the effect of the treatment would be equivalent to one completely well year of life. The disagreement is not over the QALY concept but rather over how the weights for cases between 0 and 1 are obtained.

Health utility assessment has its roots in the classic work of von Neumann and Morgenstern (1944). Their mathematical decision theory characterized how a rational individual should make decisions when faced with uncertain outcomes. Von Neumann and Morgenstern outlined axioms of choice that have become basic foundations of decision analysis in business, government, and health care. This work was expanded upon by Raiffa (1968) and several others (see reviews by Bell and Farquhar 1986; Howard 1988). Torrance and Feeney (1989), who reviewed the history of utility theory and its applications to health outcome assessment, argued that the use of the term "utility theory" by von Neumann and Morgenstern was unfortunate. Their reference to utility differs from the more common uses by economists that emphasize consumer satisfaction with commodities that are received with certainty. Nineteenth century philosophers and economists assumed the existence of cardinal (or interval level) utilities for these functions. A characteristic of cardinal utilities is that they can be averaged across individuals and ultimately used in aggregates as the basis of utilitarian social policy.

By the turn of the century, Pareto challenged the value of cardinal utilities and demonstrated that ordinal utilities could represent consumer choice (Bator 1957). Arrow (1951) further argued that there are inconsistencies in individual preferences under certainty and that meaningful cardinal preferences cannot be measured and may not even exist. As a result, many economists have come to doubt the value of preference ratings (Nord 1991).

Perhaps the most important statement against the aggregation of individual preferences was Arrow's impossibility theorem (Arrow 1951). In this classic work, Arrow considered the expected group decision based on the individual preferences of the group members. After laying out a set of very reasonable assumptions about how an aggregate decision should not contradict the apparent preferences of group members, Arrow demonstrated how aggregate decisions can violate the apparent will of the individual decision makers.

Arrow's impossibility theorem may not be applicable to the aggregation of utilities in the assessment of QALYs for several reasons. First, utility expressions for QALYs are expressions of probabilistic outcomes, not goods received with certainty. Von Neumann and Morgenstern emphasized decisions under uncertainty, an approach theoretically distinct from Arrow's. The traditional criticisms of economists are directed toward decisions to obtain certain, rather than uncertain, outcomes (Torrance and Feeney 1989). Second, Arrow assumed that the metric underlying utility was not meaningful and not standardized across individuals. Substantial psychometric evidence now suggests that preferences can be measured using scales with meaningful interval or ratio properties. When cardinal (interval) utilities are used instead of rankings, many of the potential problems in the impossibility theorem are avoided (Keeney 1976).

Different approaches to the calculation of QALYs are based on very different underlying assumptions. One approach considers the duration of time someone is in a particular health state as conceptually independent from the utility for the state (Weinstein and Stason 1976; Kaplan and Anderson 1990). Another approach merges duration of stay and utility (Torrance and Feeney 1989). This distinction is central to understanding the difference in approaches and affects the evidence required to validate the utility assessment procedure.

In the approach advocated by Kaplan and Anderson (1990) and Weinstein and Stason (1976), utilities for health states are obtained at a single point in time. For example, suppose that the state of confinement to a wheelchair is assigned a weight of 0.5. The patients in this state are observed over the course of time to empirically determine their transitions to other states of wellness. If they remain in the state for one year, then they would lose the equivalent of 0.5 well years of life. The key to this approach is that the preference concerns only a single point in time and does not acknowledge duration and that the transition is determined through observation or expert judgment. The alternative approach emphasized by Torrance and Feeney (1989) and others (e.g., Nord 1992) obtains preference for both health state and duration. These approaches also consider the more complex problems of uncertainty. Thus, they are consistent with the von Neumann and Morgenstern notion of decision under uncertainty, in which probabilities and trade-offs are considered explicitly by the judge.

Methods for assessing utility

Different techniques have been used to assess these utilities for health states. These techniques will be summarized briefly, and then comparisons between the techniques will be considered. Some analysts do not measure utilities directly. Instead, they evaluate health outcome by simply assigning a reasonable utility (Weinstein and Stason 1983). However, most current approaches have respondents assign weights to different health states on a scale ranging from 0 (for dead) to 1 (for wellness). The most common techniques include category rating scales, magnitude estimations, the standard gamble, the time trade-off, and the equivalence person trade-off, each of which will be described briefly.

Rating scales

Rating scales provide simple techniques for assigning numerical values to objects. There are several methods for obtaining rating scale information. One approach, the category scale, is a simple partition method in which subjects are requested to assign a number to each case selected from a set of numbered categories representing equal intervals. This method, exemplified by the familiar ten-point rating scale, is efficient, easy to use, and applicable in a large number of settings. Typically, the subject reads the description of a case and rates it on a ten-point scale ranging from 0 for dead to 10 for asymptotic optimum function. End points of the scale are typically well defined; instructions, as the sample in Box 3.1 indicates, are straightforward. Another common rating method, the visual analogue method, shows subjects a line, typically 100 centimeters in length, with the end points well defined. The subject's task is to mark the line to indicate where their preference rests in relation to the two poles.

Appropriate applications of rating scale reflect contemporary developments in the cognitive sciences. Judgment/decision theory has been dominated by the belief that human decisions follow principles of optimality and rationality. Considerable research, however, has challenged the normative models that have attempted to demonstrate rational choice. Cognitive theories such as information integration theory (Anderson 1990) provide better explanations of the cognitive process of judgment. Information integration theory includes two constructs: integration and valuation. Integration describes the cognitive algebra of mentally combining multiple pieces of information during the judgment process. Valuation refers to the weight applied to a particular piece of information. Estimation of these weights requires a theory of measurement. Normative studies of decision making often use arbitrary weights, whereas the cognitive theory requires estimates of subjective value parameters. Although expected

Box 3.1 Instructions for category scaling

Each page in this booklet [OPEN BOOKLET TO SAMPLE ITEM] tells how an imaginary person is affected by a health problem on one day of his or her life. I want you to look at each health situation and rate it on a ladder with steps numbered from zero (0) to ten (10). The information on each page tells (1) the person's age group, (2) whether the person could drive or use public transportation, (3) how well the person could walk, (4) how well the person could perform the activities usual for his or her age, and (5) what symptom or problem was bothering the person.

This sheet [HAND DEFINITION SHEET] tells what the lines mean. Please notice, for example, that the word "hospital" includes nursing homes, mental institutions, and similar places, that "special unit" means a restricted area of a hospital such as an operating room or intensive care unit, and that "self-care" means specifically bathing, dressing, eating, and using the bathroom.

Think about the day described on each page and rate it by choosing a step on the ladder from 0 to 10. All health situations can be placed on one of the steps. If the page describes someone who is completely well, then choose the top step, 10. If you think the situation described is about as bad as dying, then choose the bottom step, 0. If you think the person's situation is about halfway between being dead and being completely well, then choose step 5. Step 6 is one step better than 5, 5 is one step better than 4, and so on. You can choose any of the steps from 0 to 10 depending on how bad or good you think that day was.

The problem on the bottom line of each page could be caused by many different diseases or injuries. The line does not tell how severe the problem is. You must judge that from how the problem affected the person's activities. Also, there is no way to tell for sure whether the problem will get much better or much worse on the next day. So just assume that the person is getting the best medical treatment possible on that day, and that he feels and performs as well as his condition or treatment would permit.

Read the situation, and when I call off the number of the page, tell me the step on the ladder that you choose. Give your opinion about the *situation on that day only*. Don't worry about what tomorrow will be like. There are no right or wrong answers; this is simply your opinion. Are there any questions? [ANSWER ANY QUESTIONS.] O.K. then, let's begin.

utility theory, which has its origin in the work of von Neumann and Morgenstern (1944), uses subjective values, the estimates are not guided by substantive theory. In information integration theory, properties of measurement can be confirmed by empirical evidence when the rule of integration is known. For example, when it is known that information is integrated by an averaging rule, subjective values should obey specified patterns, but only if the underlying measurement metric is a linear response scale. A large body of evidence indicates that rating scales provide meaningful metrics for the expression of these subjective preferences (Anderson 1990). Although there have been some challenges to the use of rating scales, most biases can be overcome with the use of just a few simple precautions, such as clear definitions of the end points and preliminary practice with cases that make the end points salient (Anderson 1990).

Magnitude estimation

Magnitude estimation is a common psychometric method that is believed by psychophysicists to yield ratio scale scores (Stevens 1966). In magnitude estimation, a specific case is selected as a standard and assigned a particular number. Then, other cases are rated in relation to the standard. Suppose, for example, the standard is assigned the number 10. If a case is regarded as half as desirable as the standard, it is given the number 5. If it is regarded as twice as desirable, it is given the number 20. Ratings across subjects are standardized to a common metric and aggregated using the geometric mean. Advocates for magnitude estimation argue that the method is meaningful because it provides a direct estimate of the subjective ratio (Stevens 1966). Thus, they believe, the magnitude estimate has the properties of a ratio scale.

However, magnitude estimation has been challenged on several grounds. The method is not based on any specific theory of measurement and gains credibility only through face validity (Anderson 1990). Further, the meaning of the score has been challenged. For example, the values are not linked directly to any decision process. What does it mean if one case is rated as half as desirable as another? Does it mean that the respondent would be indifferent between a 50-50 chance of the higher valued outcome and a certainty of the alternative valued as half as desirable? These issues have not been systematically addressed in the health status literatures.

Standard gamble

Category rating and magnitude estimation are methods commonly used by psychometricians. Typically, the tasks emphasize wellness at a particular point in time and do not ask subjects to make trades or to consider aspects of uncertainty. By contrast, several methods more explicitly consider decision under uncertainty. The standard gamble offers a choice between two alternatives: living in health state A with certainty or taking a gamble on treatment, for which the outcome is uncertain (Fig. 3.2). The respondent is told that treatment will lead to perfect health with a probability of p or immediate death with a probability of $1 - p$ (choice B). The health state described in A is intermediate between wellness and death. The probability (p) is varied until the subject is indifferent between choices A and B.

An attractive feature of the standard gamble is that it is based on the axioms of utility theory. The choice between a certain outcome and a gamble conforms to the exercises originally proposed by von Neumann and Morgenstern. Although the interval properties of the data obtained using the gamble have been assumed, they have not been empirically demonstrated (Froberg and Kane 1989b). A variety of other problems with the gamble have also become apparent. For example, it has often been stated that the standard gamble has face validity because it approximates choices made by patients (Mulley 1989). However, treatment of most chronic diseases does not approximate the gamble. There is no product that will make a patient with arthritis better; nor is there one that is likely to result in immediate death. In other words, the decision-making experience of the patient is not likely to include an option that has a realistic gamble. Further, the cognitive demands of the task are high.

Time trade-off

The concept of probability is difficult for most respondents and requires the use of visual aids or props to assist in the interview. Thus, an alternative to the

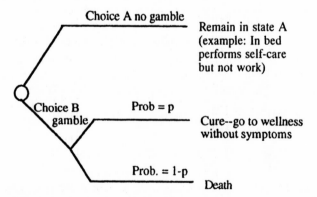

Figure 3.2. Illustration of the standard gamble. (Adapted from Torrance and Feeny 1989.)

standard gamble, also consistent with the von Neumann and Morgenstern axioms of choice, uses a trade-off in time. Here, the subject is offered a choice of living for a defined amount of time in perfect health or a variable amount of time in an alternative state that is less desirable. Presumably, all subjects would choose a year of wellness versus a year with some health problem. However, by reducing the time of wellness and leaving the time in the sub-optimal health state fixed (such as one year), an indifference point can be determined. For example, a subject may rate being in a wheelchair for two years as equivalent to perfect wellness for one year. The time trade-off is theoretically appealing because it asks subjects to explicitly state their preferences in terms of life year equivalents.

Person trade-off

Finally, a person trade-off technique allows comparisons of the numbers of people helped in different states. For example, respondents might be asked to evaluate the equivalencies between the number of persons helped by different programs. They might be asked how many persons in state B must be helped to provide a benefit equivalent to helping one person in state A. From a policy perspective, the person trade-off directly seeks information similar to that required as the basis for policy decision.

Comparisons of the methods

Several articles, reviewed by Nord (1992), have compared utilities for health states as captured by different methods. In general, standard gamble and time trade-off methods give higher values than rating scales in most, but not all, studies (Table 3.1). In about half of the studies reported, time trade-off yields lower utilities than standard gamble. In one of the earlier studies, Patrick, Bush, and Chen (1973) found that person trade-off methods gave the same results as rating scales. However, these findings were not confirmed in more recent studies (Nord 1991). Magnitude estimation has produced highly variable re-sults across studies (Nord 1992). Such variability of results across studies is hardly surprising. The methods differ substantially in the questions posed to respondents.

Psychological versus economic models

Psychometric models divide the decision process into component parts. Health states are observed and categorized. Utilities are observed and categorized. Preferences are obtained as weights for these health states and the ratings apply to a particular point in time and are analogous to consumer preferences under

Table 3.1. *Selected results from comparative valuation studies*

Study	N	Kind of subjects	Selected results SG	RS	ME	PTO	TTO	State
Torrance 1976	43	Students	.75	.61			.76	Not indicated
			.73	.58			.70	
			.60	.44			.63	
			.44	.26			.38	
Bombardier et al. 1982	52	Health care personnel, patients, family	.85	.65			.78	Needs walking stick
			.81	.47			.58	Needs walking frame
			.64	.29			.41	Needs supervision when walking
			.55	.18			.28	Needs one assistant for walking
			.38	.08			.11	Needs two assistants
Llewellyn-Thomas et al. 1984	64	Patients	.92	.74				Tired; sleepless
			.84	.68				Unable to work; some pain
			.75	.53				Limited walking; unable to work; tired
			.66	.47				In house; unable to work; vomiting
			.30	.30				In bed in hospital; needs help for self-care; trouble remembering
Read et al. 1984	60	Doctors	.90	.72			.83	Moderate angina
			.71	.35			.53	Severe angina
Richardson 1991	46	Health care personnel	.86	.75			.80	Breast cancer: Removed breast; unconcerned
			.44	.48			.41	Removed breast; stiff arm; tired; anxious; difficulties with sex
			.19	.24			16	Cancer spread; constant pain; tired; expecting not to live long
Patrick et al. 1973	30	Students		.78	.85	.71		Skin defect
				.60	.66	.58		Pain in abdomen; limited in social activities
				.50	.54	.42		Visual impairment; limited in traveling and social activities
				.37	.46	.36		Needs wheelchair; unable to work
				.28	.36	.32		In hospital; limited walking; back pain; needs help for self-care; loss of consciousness

Selected results

Study	N	Kind of subjects	SG	RS	ME	PTO	TTO	State
Kaplan et al. 1979	54	Psychology students		.93	.44			Polluted air
				.67	.13			Limited walking; pain in arms and/or legs
				.49	.06			Needs wheelchair; needs help for self care; large burn
				.25	.02			Small child; in bed; loss of consciousness
Sintonen 1981	60	Colleagues		.61	.72			Difficulties in moving outdoors
				.45	.51			Needs help outdoors
				.25	.34			Needs help indoors also
				.09	.15			Bedridden
				.04	.04			Unconscious
Buxton et al. 1987	121	Health care personnel, university staff			.997		.72	Breast cancer: Removed part of breast; occasionally concerned
					.994		.70	Removed breast; occasionally concerned
					.987		.68	Removed breast; occasionally concerned, also about appearance
					.917		.27	Removed part of breast; stiffness of arm; engulfed by fear; unable to meet people
				.910		.38		Removed whole breast; otherwise as previous case
Nord 1991, 1992[a]	22	General public		.71		.985		Moderate pain; depressed
				.65		.98		Unable to work; moderate pain
				.30		.97		Unable to work; limited leisure activity; moderate pain; depressed
				.20		.90		Problems with walking; unable to work; limited leisure activity; strong pain; depressed

Note: N = number; SG = standard gamble methods; RS = rating scale methods; ME = magnitude estimation methods; PTO = person trade-off methods; TTO = time trade-off methods.

Magnitude estimation values are obtained by applying the Rosser/Kind index (Rosser and Kind 1978).

[a] The person trade-off values are transformed from raw scores published in Nord 1991. This study did not include the state "dead." The transformations to a 1–0 scale are based on a subsequent separate valuation of "dead," still using person trade-off (Nord 1992).

Source: Nord 1992.

certainty. Probabilities are a separate dimension and are determined empirically. These models combine the empirically determined probabilities and the preferences. Psychologists and economists differ in their views about the most appropriate model. Economists have challenged the psychometric approaches (Richardson 1991; Nord 1992), emphasizing that data obtained using rating scales cannot be aggregated. They acknowledge that rating scales may provide ordinal data but contend that they do not provide interval level information necessary for aggregation. These judgments under certainty are subject to all of the difficulties outlined by Arrow (1951).

Psychologists have also challenged the use of rating scales. For example, Stevens (1966) questioned the assumption that subjective impressions can be discriminated equally at each level of a scale. He claimed that the rating scale method is biased because subjects will attempt to use categories equally often, thus spreading their responses when the cases are actually close together and compressing them when the true values are actually far apart. These biases would suggest that numbers obtained on rating scales cannot have meaning.

Armed with these arguments, economists have proposed standard gamble or time trade-off methods as validity criteria for rating scales. The basic assumption is that methods that conform to the von Neumann and Morgenstern axioms assess true utility. If rating scales produce results inconsistent with these utilities, they must be representing preferences incorrectly. As compelling as these arguments are, they disregard a substantial literature analyzing the process of human judgment.

Cognitive limitations

Evidence for the standard gamble and time trade-off techniques

Since the standard gamble technique meets the axiomatic requirements of the von Neumann and Morgenstern theory of decision under uncertainty, some experts believe that the gamble should serve as a gold standard for evaluating other methods. However, there are several concerns about the standard gamble and related techniques. One of the most important has been raised by Tversky, Slovic, and Kahneman (1990). In a series of laboratory experiments, these investigators demonstrated that subjects tend to reverse their previously revealed preferences. For example, in one experiment, subjects were presented with two lotteries. The lotteries had two outcomes: a cash prize or no win at all. In one lottery, the cash prize involved a high probability of winning a small amount of money, while the other lottery offered a cash prize with a low probability of winning a large amount of money. The participants were then asked to state the minimum price they would be willing to accept to sell each bet.

In the next phase of the experiment, the subjects were presented with pairs of bets. In each case, they were offered bets with a high probability of a low payoff versus a low probability of a high payoff. In some cases, the comparison was with the bet against a sure thing. In these cases, one of the options paid a specified sum of money with a probability of 1. This established the pricing. If subjects behave rationally, the alternatives should produce the same estimated value of the bets. However, they did not, and significant reversals occurred, such as a person choosing the high-probability/low-payoff bet over the low-probability/high-payoff bet but assigning the high-probability/low-payoff bet a lower selling price. In fact, 46 percent of subjects showed some reversal. The explanation for these results is that the subjects used inappropriate psychological representations and simplifying heuristics. How a question is framed can have a significant impact upon choice because it can evoke these inappropriate cognitive strategies. In general, humans are poor processors of probabilistic information. When confronted with complex decisions, they use simplifying rules that often misdirect decisions (Kahneman and Tversky 1984).

Several studies have documented unexpected preferences using standard gamble or time trade-off methodologies. For example, MacKeigan (1990) found that patients preferred immediate death to being in a state of mild to moderate dysfunction for three months. Apparently, some subjects misunderstand the nature of the trade-off or felt that any impaired quality of life is not worth enduring. McNeil, Weichselbaum, and Pauker (1981) obtained similar results. They found that if survival was less than five years, subjects were unwilling to trade any years of life to avoid losing their normal speech. These results suggest that either patients have unexpected preferences or that they have difficulty using the trade-off methodologies. Cognitive psychologists have suggested explanations for these problems. Some methods, such as the standard gamble, require only simple trade-offs. They may not require complex processing of probability information. However, other information processing biases may distort judgment. For instance, humans employ an anchoring and adjustment heuristic in decision making. Typically, information is processed in a serial fashion. Subjects begin with one piece of information and adjust their judgment as more information is added. However, experiments have suggested that the adjustments are often inadequate or biased (Kahneman and Tversky 1984). Use of the gamble and trade-off methods could evoke bias due to the anchoring and adjustment heuristic.

Other explanations for the inconsistent results in studies using trade-off methods have been proposed. Some studies have been poorly designed or conducted. For example, there have been problems in studies that request a choice between a mild disability and a very large disability. Often patients will not make this trade. However, a careful application of the methodology would identify a smaller trade-off that the patient would take. Some of the problems may be avoided with careful application of the methodology (Torrance and Feeny 1989).

Evidence for rating scales

Several lines of evidence argue against the use of rating scales. As noted above, rating scales are theoretically inconsistent with the utility under uncertainty provisions of the von Neumann and Morgenstern theory. From principles of microeconomic theory, rating scales should not produce data that can be aggregated. When compared against the theoretically more appealing standard gamble and time trade-off methods, rating scales produce different results. In addition, the use of rating scales has been challenged by psychophysicists who also argue that these methods produce, at best, ordinal level data (Stevens 1966).

Recent psychological research challenges these criticisms of rating scales (Anderson 1990). Although rating methods are subject to serious biases, most of these biases can be controlled. For example, it has been argued that subjects have a tendency to use each category in a ten-point rating scale equally often. Thus, for stimuli that are close together, subjects will use all categories from 0 through 10 on a ten-point rating scale. Similarly, for cases that represent broader variability in true wellness, subjects will also use the entire range. As a result, it has been argued that any numbers obtained from rating scales are meaningless (Parducci 1968). However, systematic studies of health case descriptions do not confirm this property. Kaplan and Ernst (1983), for example, were unable to document these context effects for health case descriptions. The real issue is whether or not rating scales can produce meaningful data. Most studies evaluating utilities have sought to demonstrate convergent validity (Revicki and Kaplan 1993). Convergent validity is achieved when different methods produce the same results. Many investigators have emphasized the standard gamble because they feel that it is theoretically more sound (Nord 1992).

Only recently have empirical tests evaluating the various approaches been conducted. An empirical test of scale property has been introduced within the last few years (Anderson 1990). The model takes into consideration the psychological process used in evaluating cases. Typically, utility assessment involves a global judgment of a case that is usually made up of multiple attributes. Common attributes of health status are shown in Table 3.2.

When the attributes of the case are systematically varied, parameters of the judgment process can be estimated. Substantial evidence suggests that human judges most often integrate multiattribute information using an averaging rule (Anderson 1990). The averaging rule yields an additive model of human judgment. This averaging process has been validated in specific experimental tests (see Anderson 1990 for a three-volume review of the evidence). Once the averaging process has been established, an analysis of variance model can be

Table 3.2. *Examples of quality-of-life health attributes and levels*

Attribute	Level
Physical function	No limitations
	Mild or moderate limitations
	Severe limitations
Social function	No limitations
	Mild or moderate limitations
	Severe limitations
Emotion well-being	No limitations
	Mild or moderate limitations
	Severe limitations
Pain	No pain
	Mild or moderate pain
	Severe pain
Cognitive ability	No limitations
	Mild or moderate limitations
	Severe limitations

Source: OTA 1992a.

used to evaluate the scale properties. Typically, this is done by systematically varying components of case descriptions as rows and columns in an experimental design. Global judgments are obtained for each cell within the resulting matrix. The analysis of variance model allows parameter estimation for scale values and weights.

According to the functional measurement model, the absence of a significant interaction effect in the analysis of variance establishes the interval property, assuming that the subjects are combining information using an averaging rule. The difference between utilities for two items that differ only by one attribute should be equal to the difference between two other items that differ only by that one attribute. Figure 3.3 shows several applications of the functional measurement test for health case descriptions. These data confirm a large number of other studies that have also shown the interval property for rating scales (Anderson 1990). However, studies have failed to confirm the interval property for magnitude estimation (Kaplan, Bush, and Berry 1979) or for trade-off methodologies (Zhu and Anderson 1991). The axioms underlying the functional measurement model have been published (Luce 1981).

It is of interest that the rating scale debate raged for nearly a century among psychophysicists. It was widely believed that rating scale methods could not

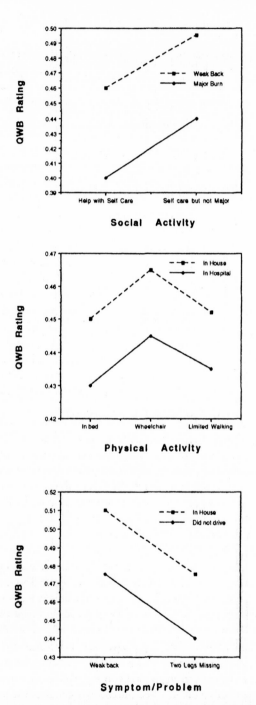

Figure 3.3. Functional measurement test showing lack of interaction among items that differ by the same levels on each two attributes (QWB = Quality of Well-Being Scale).

produce meaningful data, whereas methods requiring dichotomous choice or ratings of subjective intervals were regarded as true psychological metrics. Recent evidence, however, has challenged these beliefs and has confirmed that rating scales can produce data on an interval-level scale, and many psychophysicists have come to accept these methods (Anderson 1990).

In summary, there is substantial debate about which technique should be used to acquire utility information. Results obtained from different methods do not correspond although they typically have a high degree of similarity in the ranks they assign to outcomes. However, the differences in preferences yielded by different methods can result in different allocation of resources if the preferences are not obtained on a linear or interval response scale. For example, suppose that the difference between the effect of a drug and a placebo is 0.05 units of well-being as assessed by rating scales and 0.02 as measured by magnitude estimation. The benefit would have to last twenty years to produce 1 QALY if rating scale utilities were used and fifty years if magnitude estimation utilities were used. Aggregation of benefits necessarily requires an underlying linear response scale in which equal differences at different points along the response scale are equally meaningful. For example, the difference between 0.2 and 0.3 (0.1 QALY if the duration is one year) must have the same meaning as the difference between 0.7 and 0.8. A treatment that boosts patients from 0.2 to 0.3 must be considered of equal benefit to a treatment that brings patients from 0.7 to 0.8. Confirmation of this scale property has been presented for rating scales but not for the other methods.

Another difference between methods is the inclusion of information about uncertainty in the judgment process. Time trade-off, standard gambles, and person trade-off all theoretically include some judgment about duration of stay in a health state. Magnitude estimation and rating scales typically separate utility at a point in time from probability. Considerably more theoretical and empirical work will be necessary to evaluate these differences of approach.

Whose preferences should be used in the model?

Choices between alternatives in health care necessarily involve preference judgments. For example, deciding what services to include in a basic benefits package is an exercise in value, choice, or preference. Preference is expressed at many levels in the health care decision process. For example, an older man may decide to cope with the symptoms of urinary retention in order to avoid the ordeal and risk of prostate surgery. A physician may order expensive tests to ensure against the very low probability that a rare condition will be missed. Or an administrator may decide to allocate resources to prevention for large numbers of people instead of devoting the same resources to organ transplants for a smaller number.

In cost–utility analysis, preferences are used to express the relative impor-

tance of various health outcomes. There is a subjective or qualitative component to health outcome. Whether one prefers a headache or an upset stomach
caused by its remedy is a value judgment. Not all symptoms are of equal
importance. Most patients would prefer a mild itch to vomiting. Models of how
well treatments work and models that compare or rank treatments implicitly
include these judgments. Models require a precise numerical expression of this
preference. Cost–utility analysis explicitly includes a preference component to
represent these trade-offs.

The model advocated by our group incorporates preferences from random
samples of the general population (Kaplan 1993a). The rationale is that although administrators ultimately choose between alternative programs, preferences should represent the will of the general public, not administrators.

Some critics of cost–utility analysis begin with the assumption that preferences differ. For example, in most areas of preference assessment, it is easy to
identify differences between different groups or different individuals. It might
be argued that judgments about net health benefits for white Anglo men should
not be applied to Hispanic men, who may give different weight to some
symptoms. We all have different preferences for movies, clothing, and political
candidates. It is often assumed that differences must extend to health states and
that the entire analysis will be highly dependent upon the particular group that
provided the preference data. Allocation of resources to Medicaid recipients,
for example, should not depend on preferences from both Medicaid recipients
and nonrecipients (Daniels 1991). Other analysts have suggested that preference weights from the general population should not be applied to any particular patient group. Rather, patient preferences from every individual group
must be obtained.

The difference between instrumental and terminal preferences (Rokeach
1973) is important to understanding this debate. The difference between instrumental and terminal preference is analogous to the difference between
means and ends. Instrumental preferences describe the means by which various
assets are attained. For instance, socialists and capitalists hold different instrumental values with regard to the methods for achieving an optimally functioning society. Different individuals may have different preferences for how
they would like to achieve happiness, and evidence suggests that social and
demographic groups vary considerably on instrumental values.

Terminal values are the ends, or general states of being, that individuals seek
to achieve. The Rokeach (1973) classic study of values demonstrated that there
is very little variability among social groups for terminal preferences. There is
less reason to believe that different social or ethnic groups will have different
preferences for health outcomes. All groups agree that it is better to live free
of pain than to experience pain. Freedom from disability is universally preferred over disability states. It is often suggested that individuals with particular

disabilities have adapted to them. However, when asked, those with disabilities would prefer not to have them. If disability states were preferred to non-disability states, there would be no motivation to develop interventions to help those with problems causing disabilities.

Although critics commonly assume substantial variability in preferences, the evidence for differential preference is weak at best. An early study demonstrated some statistically significant, but very small, differences in preferences among social and ethnic groups (Kaplan, Bush, and Berry 1979). Other studies have found little evidence for preference difference between patients and the general population. For example, Balaban and colleagues (1986) compared preference weights obtained from arthritis patients with those obtained from the general population in San Diego. They found remarkable correspondence for ratings of cases involving arthritis patients (Fig. 3.4). The mean value for each of thirty scenarios rated by arthritis patients almost perfectly predicted the mean values for the same scenario provided by the general population in San Diego. A similar study of cancer patients by Nerenz and colleagues (1990) found that preference weights from Wisconsin cancer patients were very similar to those obtained from the San Diego general population.

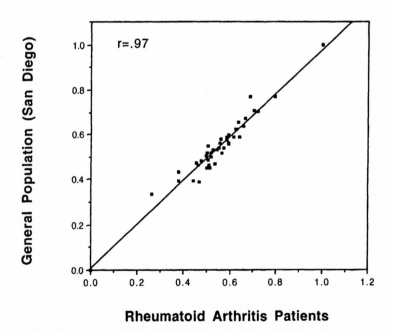

Figure 3.4. Comparison of rheumatoid arthritis patients versus general population. (*Source*: Balaban, Fagi, Goldfarb, and Nettler 1986.)

Also, preferences appear not to vary by location. Patrick and his colleagues (1985) found essentially no differences between preference for another health status measure among study subjects in the United Kingdom and in Seattle. Kaplan (1991) compared residents of the Navaho Nation living in rural Arizona with the general population in San Diego and found few differences. Differences between San Diego citizens evaluated in the 1970s and Oregon citizens evaluated in the 1990s were small even though the weights obtained by the Oregon Health Services Commission were based on a different scaling methodology and different wording of case descriptions (Kaplan, DeBon, and Anderson 1991).

A scaling methodology similar to that used by the Oregon Health Sevices Commission was used by the EuroQol Group in a series of European communities. The data from those studies suggest that differences in preference among the European communities are small and nonsignificant. In one analysis, ratings from European sites were similar to those obtained from respondents in San Diego and estimated approximate San Diego preferences for these cases (Fig. 3.5).

Clearly, overall preferences for health states appear to be quite similar.

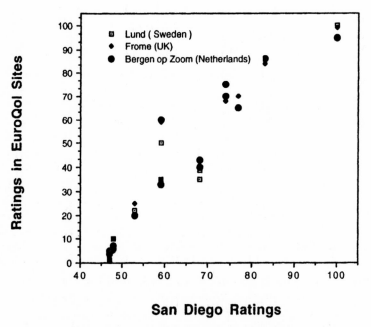

San Diego Ratings

Figure 3.5. Comparison of San Diego case ratings and ratings from sites in EuroQol utilities studies. (*Source*: Balaban, Fagi, Goldfarb, and Nettler 1986.)

There may be considerable variability in preferences for certain particular health states (Mulley 1989), but averaged across individuals, with some exceptions (Kaplan, Bush, and Berry 1978; Kaplan 1993b), the mean preference for different cases in different groups is remarkably similar. Further analysis is required to determine whether these small differences affect the conclusions of various analyses.

Fixed versus variable preference models

Most approaches to utility assessment use the mean preference for a particular case to represent all individuals so characterized. For example, suppose that the average utility for being in a wheelchair, being limited in major activities, and having missing limbs is 0.50. The models would assign the same number to all individuals who occupy that state. In individual decision models, however, decisions might be different if the patient's own utilities were used (O'Connor and Nease 1993).

As appealing as individual decision analysis can be, such analysis is time consuming. Also, Clancy, Cebul, and Williams (1988) demonstrated that the use of individual preferences rarely leads to different treatment courses than would be obtained from the use of aggregate preferences.

Application and criticism: the Oregon experiment

In 1987 a young boy in Oregon developed acute leukemia and his physicians decided that he needed a bone marrow transplant. In addition to his serious illness, the boy became the victim of a new change in the Oregon Medicaid program. With the state unable to afford many basic health services, there was some concern about whether the underfunded public program should be paying for very expensive organ transplantation procedures. A grassroots citizens group, known as Oregon Health Decisions, had created strong support for new approaches to resource allocation. The state legislature determined that thirty-four transplants to Medicaid patients during 1987–9 used the same financial resources as prenatal care and delivery for 1,500 pregnant women. The legislature recognized that they could use their limited resources to provide a small benefit to the large number of pregnant women instead of providing a larger benefit to a small number of people needing organ transplantation. The case attracted substantial media attention and forced the Oregon legislature to grapple with some very serious questions. During the debate, the family of the young leukemia sufferer attempted to raise money for the transplant, but the boy died before he could get the medical procedure.

The problems with financing Medicaid in Oregon are similar to those faced by essentially all other American states. The costs of health care are expanding much more rapidly than are the budgets for Medicaid. One alternative is to change eligibility criteria and remove some individuals from the Medicaid rolls. Oregon also recognized that American health care was not a two-tiered system but rather a three-tiered system. The three-tiered system included people who had regular insurance and could pay for their care; people enrolled in Medicaid, and a growing third tier of people who had no health insurance at all. In 1991, it was acknowledged that this third tier represented about one-fifth the population of the state. In Oregon, that accounts for about 450,000 citizens. And the number of uninsured is steadily increasing. Collectively, Oregon citizens spent approximately $6 billion on health care in 1989, three times what they spent in state income taxes (Kitzhaber 1993).

Stimulated by the community support from Oregon Health Decisions, Oregon concluded that they (and most other states) were rationing health care. Oregon passed three pieces of legislation to attack this issue. This chapter focuses most specifically on Senate Bill 27. This bill mandated that health services be prioritized in order to eliminate services that did not provide benefit.

A Health Services Commission was created to develop the prioritized list. This commission obtained several sources of information. First, they held public hearings to learn about preferences for medical care in the Oregon communities. These meetings helped clarify how citizens viewed medical services. Various approaches to care were rated and discussed. On the basis of forty-seven town meetings that were attended by more than a thousand people, thirteen community values emerged. These values included prevention, cost–effectiveness, quality of life, ability to function, and length of life. The major lesson from the community meetings was that citizens wanted primary care services. Further, the people consistently argued that the state should forgo expensive heroic treatments for individuals or small groups in order to offer basic services for everyone. To pay for preventive services, it was necessary to reduce spending elsewhere.

A major portion of the commissioners' activity was to evaluate services using the Quality of Well-Being (QWB) Scale from the General Health Policy Model (Kaplan and Anderson 1990). The commissioners could not possibly have conducted clinical trials for each of the many condition–treatment pairs (see Table 3.3). So the commission formed a medical committee that had expertise in essentially all specialty areas and had the participation of nearly all of the major provider groups in the state. Working together, the committee estimated the expected benefit from 709 condition–treatment pairs. The QWB Scale also requires preference weights. These weights are not medical expert judgments but should be obtained from community peers. Oregon citizens were particularly concerned about using weights from California to assign priorities in their state. Thus, 1,000 Oregon citizens participated in a telephone survey conducted by Oregon State University. This exercise became a central issue in the evaluation of the proposed program.

Table 3.3 *Examples of condition–treatment pairs*

Condition	Treatment
Rectal prolapse	Partial colectomy
Osteoporosis	Medical therapy
Ophthalmic injury	Closure
Obesity	Nutritional and lifestyle counseling

In 1990, the commission released its first prioritized list. Unfortunately, many of the rankings seemed counterintuitive, and the approach drew serious criticism in the popular press. As a result, the system was reorganized according to three basic categories of care: essential, very important, and valuable to certain individuals. Within these major groupings were seventeen subcategories. The commission decided to place greatest emphasis on problems that were acute and treatable yet potentially fatal if untreated. In these cases treatment prevents death and there is full recovery. Examples include appendectomy for appendicitis and nonsurgical treatment for whooping cough. Other categories classified as essential were maternity care, treatment for conditions that prevents death but does not allow full recovery, and preventive care for children. Nine categories were classified as essential. Listed as very important were treatments for nonfatal conditions that would return the individual to a previous state of health. Included in this category were acute nonfatal one-time treatments that might improve quality of life: hip replacements, cornea transplants, and so on. At the bottom of the list were treatments for fatal or nonfatal conditions that did not improve quality of life or extend life, including progressive treatments for the end stages of diseases such as cancer and AIDS or care for conditions in which the treatments were known to be ineffective. In the revised approach, the commission decided to ignore cost information and to allow their own subjective judgments to influence the rankings on the list. Conditions selected from the top, middle, and the bottom of the list are summarized in Table 3.4.

To implement the proposal, Oregon needed a waiver from the U.S. Department of Health and Human Services (DHHS). However, in August 1992, the DHHS rejected Oregon's application for a waiver on the grounds that the Oregon proposal violated the Americans with Disabilities Act of 1990 which became law in July 1992. The DHHS's position was that the Oregon preference survey on quality of life quantified stereotyped assumptions about persons with disability. According to the statement scholars have found that people without disability systematically undervalue the quality of life of those with disabilities. A paper by Hadorn (1991) and an analysis by the U.S. Office of Technology

Table 3.4. *Examples of condition–treatment pairs from top, middle and bottom of list*

Top 10
  1. Medical treatment for bacterial pneumonia
  2. Medical treatment of tuberculosis
  3. Medical or surgical treatment for peritonitis
  4. Removal of foreign body from pharynx, larynx, trachea bronchus, or esophagus
  5. Appendectomy
  6. Repair of ruptured intestine
  7. Repair of hernia with obstruction and/or gangrene
  8. Medical therapy for croup syndrome
  9. Medical therapy for acute orbital cellulitis
  10. Surgery for ectopic pregnancy

Middle 10
  350. Repair of open wounds
  351. Drainage and medical therapy for abscessed cysts of Bartholin's gland
  352. Medical therapy for polynodal cyst with abscess
  353. Medical therapy for acute thyroiditis
  354. Medical therapy for acute otitis media
  355. Pressure equalization tubes or tonsillectomy and adenoidectomy for chronic otitis media
  356. Surgical treatment for cholesteatoma
  357. Medical therapy for sinusitis
  358. Medical therapy for acute conjunctivitis
  359. Medical therapy for spina bifida without hydrocephalus

Bottom 10
  700. Mastopexy for gynecomastia
  701. Medical and surgical therapy for cyst of the kidney
  702. Medical therapy for end stage HIV disease (comfort care excluded – it is high on list)
  703. Surgery for chronic pancreatitis
  704. Medical therapy for superficial wounds without infection
  705. Medical therapy for constitutional aplastic anemia
  706. Surgical treatment for prolapsed urethral mucosa
  707. Paracentesis of aqueous humor for central retinal artery occlusion
  708. Life support for extremely low birth weight (<500 g) and under 23 week gestation
  709. Life support for anencephaly

Assessment (OTA 1992a) were cited to support this statement. However, the great bulk of the evidence summarized earlier in this chapter was ignored. Using Oregon data, utility differences across groups are small. For example, those who have ever been in a wheelchair versus those never in a wheelchair (Fig. 3.6), men and women (Fig. 3.7), and those insured and uninsured for health care (Fig. 3.8) have very similar utilities for thirty-one cases rated.

The DHHS's decision failed to acknowledge that resource allocation designs necessarily require human judgment. Ultimately, decisions are made by patients, physicians, administrators, or their surrogates. Oregon clearly recognized this and attempted to separate aspects of human judgment. For example, when decisions required medical knowledge, they depended upon a medical committee. When the decisions required in-depth understanding of human values, they depended on discussions held in open forums in Oregon towns. When the judgments involved an assessment of quality of life for those with either symptoms or disabilities, they depended on the preference of Oregon citizens. This exercise was unusual because all of these judgments were made publicly using methods that could be replicated by others.

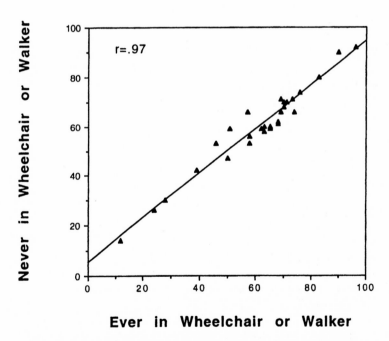

Figure 3.6. Ratings of thirty-one cases by those who have ever been confined to a wheelchair or walker and those who have not. (Data from Oregon Health Services Commission, Oregon State University.)

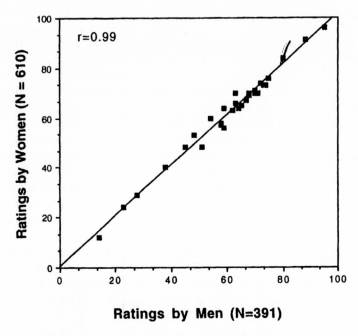

Figure 3.7. Ratings of thirty-one cases by men and women in Oregon.

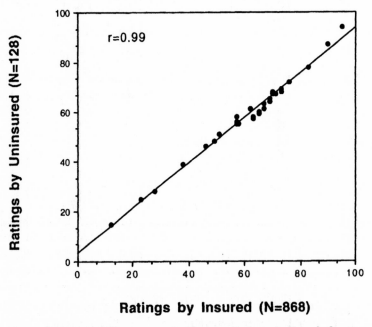

Figure 3.8. Ratings of thirty-one cases by insured and uninsured citizens in Oregon.

The analysis underlying the rejection of the Oregon application was not only misinformed, it was incorrect. It assumed that there would be discrimination against persons with disabilities because treatment could not improve their chronic problems. However, this analysis made a very serious conceptual error. Effectiveness of treatment is based on estimated course of the illness with and without treatment. A treatment that sustains life, even without improvements in quality of life, produces very substantial benefits. For example, suppose a person is in an accident that leaves him or her in a state rated 0.5 with treatment or in a state rated 0.0 (death) without treatment. According to the Oregon model, the treatment will produce 0.50 QALYs (calculated as 0.50 − 0.00) for each year the person remains in that state. That is a powerful treatment effect in comparison to most alternatives. The crucial element is that the treatment works. The system does attempt to exclude treatments that neither extend life nor make patients better. In other words, the targets for elimination are only treatments that use resources and make no difference.

The DHHS also misrepresented the meaning of quality-of-life scores. They assumed that having a low quality-of-life score was discriminatory because people with disabilities and those without disabilities would not be rated the same. However, the assumption contradicts the notion that people with disabilities need medical services. People who are at optimum health (1 on the QWB Scale) need fewer services than those who occupy lower levels. Quantifying these differences allows us to set priorities for future resource allocation. If, for the sake of argument, we decide to score people with disabilities 1, it would follow that we should not provide services for these individuals, because they have already achieved the optimum level of wellness. Scores lower than 1 suggest that resources should be used to improve these conditions.

Instead of debating these issues, Oregon chose to resubmit their application with the utility portion of the model excluded. Their revised waiver application considered probability of death and probability of moving from a symptomatic to an asymptomatic state. By giving up the utility component of the model, Oregon ignores the fact that health states are valued.

Summary

Cost–utility studies depend on measures of utility. In addition to the issue of whose preferences are obtained, we must also consider how preferences are measured. Economists and psychologists differ on their desired approach to preference measurement. Economists favor approaches based on expected utility theory. The axioms of choice (von Neumann and Morgenstern 1944) depend upon certain assumptions about gambling or trade-off. Thus, economists only acknowledge utility assessment methods that formally consider economic trades (Torrance 1986). The advantage of these methods is that they clearly are linked to economic theory. However, there are also some important disadvantages. For example, Kahneman and Tversky (1984) have shown empirically that many of the assumptions that underlie economic measurements of choice are open to challenge. Human information processors do poorly at integrating complex probability information when making decisions that involve risk. Further, economic analysis assumes that choices accurately correspond to the way rational humans assemble information.

A substantial literature from experimental psychology questions these assumptions. In particular, Anderson (1990) has presented evidence suggesting that methods commonly used for economic analysis do not represent the underlying true preference continuum. Newer research by economists employs integrated cognitive models (Viscusi 1989), and contemporary research by psychologists consider economic models of choice. However, significantly more exchange between economists and psychologists is needed to resolve the theoretical and practical difficulties of utility assessment.

In summary, a review of the literature on utility assessment suggests that preferences can be explicitly considered in a cost–utility analysis. A variety of studies have evaluated the generalizability (Kaplan, Bush, and Berry 1976), the validity, and the reliability of the preference measures (Kaplan, Bush and Berry 1976, 1979; Froberg and Kane 1989c). Methodological studies have tested some of the specific concerns about rating scale methods (Kaplan 1982; Kaplan and Ernst 1983). Preference differences across groups appear to be small and are not sufficiently large to justify their use in influencing policy decisions. This review of the evidence indicates that rating scales provide an appropriate method for utility assessment.

CHAPTER 4

Measuring costs

David Dranove

Ideals and realities in cost measurement

Medical treatment involving pharmaceuticals usually requires a substantial number and variety of additional medical resources. During a patient's hospital stay, for example, personnel, including nurses, technicians, therapists, and orderlies, will allocate some of their time to caring for and attending to the patient's many needs. In addition to these labor inputs, the attending physician may order the use of expensive equipment for diagnosis and treatment. Other medical supplies must be obtained and administered. Pharmaceutical treatment in other settings involves a similarly wide array of medical resources. The other principal resource used in the medical process is the time of the patient and his or her family.

When resources are used to provide medical care for one patient, they are unavailable for other patients and other societal uses. Thus, one cannot judge the merits of a medical intervention without understanding what one is giving up to provide that intervention. What providers and society give up to provide treatment for an individual is called the cost of the treatment.

This chapter presents a series of conceptual guidelines to help the researcher measure the costs of medical treatment. The fundamental economic concept of opportunity cost is introduced first. This concept is essential to understanding the importance of perspective, which is discussed in the next section. These points are then used to show how the analyst can determine which costs should be included in the analysis. Additional conceptual topics in cost measurement, including the distinction between fixed and sunk cost, learning effects, and the importance of duration of the study period are covered. Finally, practical guidance for estimating costs is provided.

Theoretical issues in cost measurement: opportunity costs

Medical treatments require resources that could have been employed elsewhere, which makes it important to measure costs. The *opportunity cost* of a treatment is the value of those resources if employed elsewhere. In order to measure cost with a common yardstick, economists usually express it in terms of dollars or some other currency.

Cost measurement requires two steps. First, the researcher must identify the resources used in an activity. The relevant resources to consider are those that could have been deployed elsewhere had the activity not been undertaken. Second, the researcher places a dollar value on those resources. Institutions may vary in the resources used in delivering care and in the dollar value of those resources. This implies that the specifics of cost analysis, such as which cost centers to consider and how to value particular resources, are likely to vary from one institution to the next. By paying attention to the concept of opportunity costs, the researcher can identify the relevant costs at each institution.

Whose costs are we measuring?

The answer to the question Is this service cost–effective? may depend on who is asking it. The decision maker may be a patient, a hospital, an insurer, or a social planner. Each has a set of concerns, as follows:

1. The patient cares about out-of-pocket medical costs and the time and inconvenience associated with treatment. Patients benefit from the improvement in health status resulting from the treatment.
2. Hospitals with fixed budgets or those providing treatment under a fixed reimbursement regime (e.g., Medicare prospective payment) care about the costs of providing care. Hospitals benefit from the expected revenues from increased demand because the hospital offers the treatment.
3. Insurers are concerned with their payments to providers and the costs of processing claims. Note that in the case of insurers, the benefits are largely the expected revenues from increased demand for their services, because the insurer pays for the treatment. When the insurer is a government agency, the benefits are associated with political support.
4. The social planner is concerned with all incremental resources associated with treatment, whether borne by patients, providers, or insurers. The social planner's benefits are largely identical to the consumer's, that is, improved health status.[1]

Obviously, each decision maker may reach different judgments about specific costs, such as the cost of research and development of new drugs. Most pharmaceutical cost–effectiveness research adopts the perspectives of providers and/or social planners, and this section concentrates on these perspectives.

The regulator and the social planner often make different valuations of costs. This difference is illustrated by considering the goal of minimizing total medical costs, which is often espoused in the cost–benefit literature (see Hollenberg et al. 1988; Podrid et al. 1991). Calvert and Urie (1991) discussed this goal within the context of a comparison of carboplatin and cisplatin treatment of ovarian cancer. Carboplatin and cisplatin are *imperfect substitutes* in the treatment of ovarian cancer. Carboplatin is more expensive but allows many patients to leave the hospital sooner than does cisplatin. From a societal perspective, the resources saved by the earlier discharge exceed the additional costs of carboplatin, thereby making it the more cost–effective treatment.

In spite of this evidence, the British National Health Service (NHS) does not pay for carboplatin. Calvin and Urie explain that the NHS does not attempt to maximize social welfare but rather, because of budget considerations, attempts to minimize total medical costs. The NHS reasons that if an ovarian cancer patient is able to go home, her bed will be filled by some other patient currently in queue for admission, thereby raising total NHS costs. Because the NHS is only concerned about medical costs, it ignores the time and medical costs borne by patients queuing up for admission, as well as any time and inconvenience costs borne by ovarian cancer patients forced to remain in the hospital. In Calvert and Urie's estimation, the policy to restrict use of carboplatin may lower medical costs but increase total societal costs.

I (Dranove 1989a) observed a similar divergence between medical costs and societal costs in my analysis of Medicaid formulary restrictions. Opening the formulary to cephalosporins raised the total medical costs of the Illinois Medicaid program. At the same time, however, it enabled Medicaid patients to receive faster cures. Using reasonable values of morbidity, I argued that, from a societal perspective, the benefits to Medicaid patients outweigh the added costs to Medicaid.

Similar issues arise when considering cost–effectiveness decisions on the part of private insurers. Private insurers must decide whether to cover services that produce medical benefits but do not necessarily lower medical costs. Although legal and ethical considerations guide most of these decisions, a substantial gray area exists, particularly regarding new drugs that represent marginal improvements over existing products. Unless the insurer believes that including a new drug in its formulary will boost the demand for its insurance product, it may undervalue (relative to society) the health benefits of new drugs relative to their added costs.

Which cost centers must be included?

The costs of treatment may be incurred in a number of *cost centers*. Such cost centers include the following:

1. Drug costs, including the costs of acquiring and administering the drug
2. Other hospital costs
3. Other institutional costs, such as nursing home costs
4. Labor costs not included in institutional costs, such as the costs of physician services and home health services
5. Costs borne by the patient and his or her family, including lost income from work, visitation costs, and less immediately identifiable costs, such as reduced career opportunities

A hospital perspective requires careful consideration of the first two cost centers. A societal perspective generally requires consideration of all five cost centers. This seemingly obvious distinction is sometimes overlooked. Freedberg, Tosteson, Cohen, and Cotton (1991), for example, claimed to take a societal perspective in measuring the costs of drug therapy for AIDS patients with pneumonia; yet they only considered drug and hospital costs.[2]

The researcher may safely eliminate a cost center from consideration if it is not affected by the medical intervention.[3] When comparing the costs of two drug therapies, for example, it may be possible to restrict one's attention to the costs of acquiring and administering the drugs, if the drugs are *perfect substitutes*. Drugs are perfect substitutes if they produce identical outcomes with identical side effects. Thus, the choice of drug will not affect resource use at other cost centers. Branded and generic formulations of aspirin are good examples of perfect substitutes, although some would argue that certain generics have variable dosage and digestibility, making them imperfect substitutes for branded drugs.

The perfect substitute assumption is implicit in several studies that compared alternative drug therapies: ceftazidime versus tobramycin/ticarcillin therapy for pneumonia and/or septicemia (Parr, Hansen, and Rapp 1988); the comparison of five ocular β-blockers (Ball and Schneider 1992); and cefonicid sodium therapy versus cefoxitin sodium therapy for prevention of postoperative infections after cesarean section (Briggs et al. 1987). Often it is clear that the perfect substitute assumption is not valid, and further cost analysis is warranted. In Briggs et al., for example, the authors compared costs of administering cefonicid sodium and cefoxitin sodium. They also identified differences in associated postoperative infection rates. They did not measure treatment costs associated with postoperative infections, however, thereby omitting a major element of cost.

These comparison studies can be contrasted with a study by Hay (1988), who compared the cost–effectiveness of different transdermal nitroglycerin patches. Hay calculated the initial cost of acquiring and applying patches, as well as the additional costs caused by patch failures and discontinuation of treatment. By analyzing these additional costs, Hay computed the full cost to society of alternative patches. Similarly, Rice, Duggan, and DeAngelis (1992) recognized that erythromycin and mupirocin are not perfect substitutes in the treatment of impetigo in children. They calculated costs associated with differences in time to resolution and differences in compliance.

The perfect substitute assumption also appears in a number of papers analyzing policies regarding drug formularies. Smith and MacClayton (1977) and Smith and McKercher (1984) restricted their analyses of Medicaid drug formularies to drug costs, implicitly assuming that drugs removed from a formulary are perfect substitutes for drugs retained. Himmelberg et al.'s (1991) analysis of a hospital's formulary restrictions on antimicrobial use made a similar assumption in its cost analysis. Himmelberg et al. actually documented changes in length of stay after restrictions were removed but did not measure any associated cost savings.

Adopting a societal perspective requires the researcher to consider the widest array of cost centers. Hay (1988) considered the cost of physician visits for patients who discontinue transdermal nitroglycerine patches. I (1989b) examined the costs borne by hospitals, physicians, home nurses, medical equipment lessors, and families in my assessment of the costs of home ventilation. Herve et al. (1990) included a similar array of costs in assessing thrombolysis for myocardial infarct patients.

Sunk versus incremental costs

Once relevant cost centers are identified, the next critical task is to identify the activities associated with the intervention. The relevant activities are those whose costs are borne or, alternatively, forgone because the intervention occurred. For example, if drug intervention facilitates an early hospital discharge, one must identify the hospital activities that would have been undertaken had the patient remained in the hospital. These might include "hotel services," lab tests, and certain administrative activities. The associated costs of these activities are *incremental*, or *marginal, costs*. Other activities must be undertaken whether the intervention occurs or not. Depreciation of property, plant, and equipment is included in this category. The associated costs are "*sunk*." Because sunk costs cannot be recovered by eliminating the activity, they should be ignored. A number of key issues arise when determining whether costs are incremental or sunk. The first is whether the activity involves a substantial fixed asset, such as major diagnostic equipment. The second is whether the activity is undertaken in tandem with some other activities, such as when a nurse administers a drug while also monitoring a patient's recovery. The third issue is the time horizon. From society's perspective, all costs are incremental in the long run.

Treatment of fixed costs: Perhaps as much as 20 percent of the typical provider's total costs include allocated expenses for property, plant, and durable medical equipment. These expenses would have been borne by the hospital regardless of whether the intervention occurred and should not be considered when computing incremental costs of specific treatments. A number of other labor-intensive activities, including administration, billing, and maintaining medical records, may appear to be fixed, since associated staffing does not appear to change with caseload. This is incorrect, however, because the associated inputs are *divisible*. Divisible costs are usually incremental.

To see why divisible inputs are usually incremental, consider the cost of maintaining medical records. An additional hospital admission will not likely cause the hospital to hire another medical records staffer. Even so, existing staff must work slightly harder, forgoing other valuable activities. Unless existing staff have genuine slack time that can be reduced as workloads expand, the incremental admission has created an incremental cost. The same argument applies to all other labor inputs, including management.

Joint products: Another area of confusion is the treatment of costs when a given task produces more than one output. This is frequently the case in a hospital – for example when a laboratory centrifuge spins several samples simultaneously or when a floor nurse visits a patient, administers a drug, and monitors the patient's condition. Given adequate data on total effort and the quantity of each specific output, the researcher can run a regression to determine the incremental cost of each output. Otherwise, the researcher must make educated guesses.

The decision maker's time horizon: A critical factor for social planners is the time horizon. Suppose a social planner is developing a rule regarding whether to permit a hospital to take magnetic resonance images (MRIs). For simplicity, suppose that price is set retrospectively to cover average total costs, so that the social planner is restricted to deciding whether to offer any reimbursement at all. Let the fixed cost of the MRI machine equal F and the constant marginal cost of an MRI equal C. The average cost of the image is therefore $F/N + C$, where N is the number of images taken by the hospital. These cost figures are captured by the cost curves AC (average cost) and MC (marginal cost) depicted in Figure 4.1.

Now suppose that the demand for the images is a true representation of their value to consumers and is represented by demand curve D in Figure 4.1. This

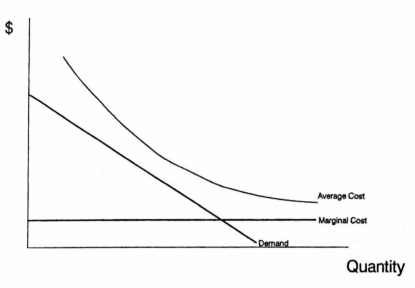

Figure 4.1. Short- versus long-run costs and benefits of new technology adoption.

demand curve is everywhere below the average-cost curve AC. If the hospital has not yet acquired the MRI machine, the social planner should not permit it to do so (i.e., it should deny reimbursements). Note, however, that the total area under the demand curve and above the MC curve is positive. Thus, if the hospital has already purchased the MRI, the correct short-run decision is to permit reimbursement for MRIs, since societal benefits exceed incremental societal costs.

Adoption of such a policy may create long-run inefficiencies, however. In particular, providers may perceive that once they have acquired equipment, the social planner will pay them enough to cover average total costs regardless of whether total value exceeds total cost. Unless the social planner sticks to the long-run optimal reimbursement rule, even when suboptimal in the short run, the best long-run allocation of resources will not be achieved.

Learning

Learning curves have been documented for many industrial production processes; a doubling of cumulative output generally leads to a 10–30 percent reduction in the costs of production. It is plausible that learning economies are also a factor in medical care. For example, the cost of treatment with new drugs should fall with cumulative experience as physicians learn the best dosages and identify early indications of side effects.

Learning curves have in fact received some attention in medical care. Luft,

Hunt, and Maerki (1987) documented learning effects for several surgical procedures.[4] Saywell et al. (1989) reported a nearly 50 percent reduction in the costs of heart transplants performed at a single hospital over a four-year period. Calvert and Urie (1991) observed that the incidence of acute renal failure is lower with cisplatin than with carboplatin. They attributed the decline in renal failure to practitioner experience, with consequent adjustments in dosage and regimen, in using the former drug. They forecasted that further experience with carboplatin should yield similar adjustments and reductions in renal failure. These studies indicate that failure to account for learning can impart serious bias to estimates of the cost of new technologies and procedures.

Box 4.1 illustrates how to adjust cost measurements to account for learning. In general, the higher the ratio of expected future use to current use, the greater the cost reductions from learning by doing. In fact, with very new technologies, such cost reductions can exceed nominal incremental costs, so that true marginal costs are negative! This is the philosophy underlying learning curve growth strategies in business, and the idea is equally valid for new medical technologies and procedures.

Box 4.1 Adjusting cost measurements to account for learning

Suppose that a new treatment has been provided 500 times and the current unit cost is $10,000 – call this the "naive" incremental cost. There is ongoing learning so that a doubling of cumulative experience is expected to lead to a 20 percent reduction in unit cost, to $8,000. This implies that one additional treatment (0.2 percent of the total done to date) will lead to a $4 reduction in the costs of each future treatment (0.04 percent of naive cost). It is estimated that 156 treatments will be performed each year for the next ten years, for a total of 1,560 treatments.

To calculate the correct incremental cost of the 501st treatment, we must consider its impact, via learning, on the costs of future treatments. Assume that the discount rate is 9 percent (see Chap. 7, this volume, for a discussion of discounting). In the absence of learning, the 1,560 treatments forecasted to be performed over the next ten years have a discounted present cost of $10,000,000. Because of the learning benefits of the 501st treatment, the actual cost of these 1,560 treatments will be $10,000,000 – (0.04 percent × 10,000,000) = $9,996,000. Thus, the 501st treatment produces a learning benefit of $4,000. This implies that the true incremental cost of the 501st treatment is only $6,000.

Duration of the study period and the calculation of cost

Restricting cost analysis to a fixed time period after the intervention may introduce bias into cost comparisons. Since a disproportionate amount of expenditures is made when a patient is near death, the treatment offering the shorter life expectancy will have higher costs, ceteris paribus. An example of this bias appears in a study of the costs of AZT treatment in the first twelve months after use began (Scitovsky, Cline, and Abrams 1990). Scitovsky et al. found that patients receiving AZT have total costs that are nearly 50 percent less than those not receiving AZT, mostly as a result of lower hospital inpatient costs. One reason for this difference was that those patients not on AZT were more likely to incur expenditures associated with the last stages of AIDS within the twelve-month window of analysis. Had the study been extended another year or two, the cost difference would have been much lower or could even have been reversed.

Practical advice for measuring costs

Drug costs

All cost analyses of pharmaceutical interventions must, at a minimum, measure the costs of the pharmaceuticals. This generally takes the form of measuring the *direct cost of obtaining and administering the drug required*. The cost of administering a drug is typically measured using *time and motion (TAM) methods*. For example, the researcher may measure the time it takes for a nurse to gather materials, prepare the medication, and administer the medication. TAM methods underlie "patient classification systems" used by many researchers to allocate nursing costs according to nursing intensity (see Sovie 1988 for a detailed discussion). Patient classification systems are usually too broad for studies that focus on drug costs. Such focused studies often require original TAM research.

TAM is a conceptually sound approach, as long as the true marginal time cost to the provider of preparing and administering a drug equals the sum of the time costs of the individual steps. This measurement requires careful consideration of the "production" process. As with any TAM study, the researcher should produce a process flowchart that includes all relevant steps in drug preparation and administration. The researcher should then determine if any of these occur simultaneously with other tasks, such as monitoring the patient's condition. If such "simultaneous production" does occur, then the time cost of the joint product should be allocated to each task rather than assigned exclusively to the cost of the drug.

An indication that TAM studies are susceptible to problems due to simultaneous production arises from an examination of the coefficients of variation of drug preparation and administration time reported in various studies.[5] The coefficients of variation in the TAM studies cited in the following pages range from 0.5 to 1.0. Since drug preparation and administration are usually standard tasks, the large variation in times suggests that providers may perform other tasks simultaneously. Researchers should be sensitive to this issue. Failure to account for multiple tasks leads to overstatement of the costs of labor-intensive treatments.

Most researchers determine the dollar cost of the time required to administer a drug by multiplying the time by an hourly wage. Many researchers base hourly wages on average nurse salaries; one used the salary of a first-year registered nurse (Hall et al. 1988). There are a host of issues associated with choosing the proper wage rate. For example, if hospitals generally overstaff to handle peak loads, and if drug administration can be scheduled during lulls, then the opportunity cost of a nurse's time is relatively low. In the absence of any simple method to determine the opportunity costs of time, one may use average hourly wages (see Goughnour and Arkinstall 1991). Some researchers have added fringe benefits to wages (Milkovich and Piazza 1991; Mamtani et al. 1990; Parr, Hansen, and Rapp 1988), and some include allocated vacation time (Lobo et al. 1991). These additions to the base salary are appropriate only if fringes are a proportion of wages (as may be the case for a pension but not generally for health insurance.)

The other major cost of drug therapy is the cost of the drug itself. Most researchers analyzing the costs of drugs used in the hospital try to obtain or approximate hospital acquisition costs (see Briggs et al. 1987; Hay 1988; Saxena, Endahl, and Shulman 1988; Goel, Deber, and Detsky 1989; Himmelberg et al. 1991; Milkovich and Piazza 1991). Researchers studying outpatient drugs have used prices charged by pharmacies (see Goldman et al. 1991; Ball and Schneider 1992; Rice, Duggan, and DeAngelis 1992). These are sensible approaches for measuring costs from the perspective of hospitals and patients, but probably not when measuring social cost.

The relevant cost of a drug from a societal perspective should approximate marginal economic cost. It is important to distinguish here between short-run and long-run marginal economic cost. The short-run marginal cost of acquiring a drug is the cost of production and distribution. Such cost is generally quite small, as evidenced by price reductions afforded by generic versus branded drugs. This suggests that most drugs with a positive health benefit would pass the test of societal benefits exceeding short-run societal costs. Long-run costs are those associated with research and development and initial marketing effort.

Hospital costs

Except in the specific case when the researcher is comparing two drugs that are perfect substitutes, other hospital costs should be examined. If hospitals reported costs for each type of service they performed, and such reports were perceived to approximate economic cost, then it would be simple for the researcher to identify the services provided to an individual patient and add up the appropriate costs. Hospitals do not report costs for individual services, however, and thus researchers must endeavor to estimate those costs themselves.

TAM studies are arguably the best way to determine the costs of most aspects of hospital care. They are also the most costly, for the researcher must either follow specific patients through all aspects of the hospital stay or conduct a comprehensive survey of hospital personnel to obtain estimates of the time involved in specific activities. To my knowledge, the only comprehensive TAM study directly pertinent to this discussion is a study of the costs of a wide range of hospital services used in the treatment of acute myeloblastic leukemia (Lobo et al. 1991). However, a serious limitation is that the estimates come from the experiences of a single patient.

Given the impracticality of hospital-wide TAM studies, how should the researcher proceed to measure marginal costs in the hospital? A number of approaches appear in the literature. These range from examining the bottom line on the hospital bill to sophisticated efforts to identify costs at individual cost centers.

In countries such as the United States and Germany, where hospitals bill insurers, the temptation is to estimate costs to equal the total charges reported on the hospital bill (Hollenberg et al. 1988; Chapekis, Burek, and Topol 1989; Scitovsky, Cline, and Abrams 1990). If the hospital is profit maximizing and is free to set prices, as in the private patient sector of the United States, charges represent the amount that the hospitals believe the least price-sensitive consumer or group of consumers is willing to bear. In regulated countries, charges are a result of a political process. In either case, as well as in cases when hospitals do not maximize profits, charges will not equal costs borne by providers, except by chance. It is possible that the use of charges is appropriate from the payer's perspective, but only if the payer pays full charges. This is increasingly rare in the United States, where Medicare and Medicaid obtain discounts as high as 50 percent or more, and many private insurers negotiate discounts nearly as large (Dranove, Shanley, and White 1991).

Fortunately, data on costs (rather than charges) as reported by hospitals are usually readily available. Hospitals need to know their own marginal costs to assess the performance of departments and the merits of specific programs. Hospitals typically obtain costs for given departments using traditional tools of cost accounting. The hospital may then report a cost-to-charge ratio (CCR). The researcher can use the charges and the CCR to calculate the underlying costs. If the researcher has a detailed medical bill, he or she can calculate costs for individual units of service and then aggregate to obtain total hospital costs.[6] If the researcher does not possess data down to the level of the cost center, he or she may then multiply charges by a hospital-wide CCR. My own work indicates that the costs obtained in this way are generally within 10 percent of costs obtained from cost center data.

The quality of these cost estimates is only as good as the quality of the hospitals' accounting. An important concern is that hospitals calculate costs for their own purposes, which may not coincide with those of the cost–effectiveness researcher. Thus, the hospitals determination of which costs are sunk and the resulting allocation of costs may differ from what the researcher would desire. For example, hospitals often allocate fixed costs such as property, plant, and equipment to individual departments, when these should generally be excluded from computations of marginal costs. Some data sets, such as the financial data reported by the California Office of Statewide Health Planning, distinguish between direct and indirect costs, but some costs included in indirect costs, such as for administrative personnel, are more properly included in marginal costs.

A second problem with applying the CCR within departments is that there may be tremendous intradepartment variation.[7] Consider my study of the costs of caring for ventilator-assisted children (1989b). The major hospital expense for these children was the "hotel charge" for intensive care. The hospitals that I studied billed the same per diem rate for all ICU patients. This was problematic because ventilator-assisted children, in comparison with the average ICU patient, systematically underutilized ICU nursing services. One solution, suggested by Ewald (1991), would be to divide the ICU service into various levels and estimate costs for patients at each level (in effect creating additional cost centers for accounting purposes). My solution was to use costs from "stepdown ICUs," which treat only ventilator-assisted children, to estimate the costs of caring for ventilator-assisted children in regular ICUs.[8]

Physician costs

Only a few of the cost–effectiveness studies that I examined include the cost of physician time. This appears to be the result of a failure to systematically identify the relevant perspective for analysis and the failure to make explicit assumptions about the relevant cost centers. For example, from a societal perspective, the omission of physician effort is acceptable only if the interventions involve exactly the same degree of physician involvement – an assumption that most studies do not appear to satisfy. Another possible explanation for the failure to consider physician time is that it is somewhat harder to estimate than hospital costs. The researcher may use the physician's fees for those services for which the physician bills separately but may have to impute labor costs (perhaps using TAM methods) when physicians are salaried. As always, the fees should reflect the opportunity cost of the physician's time. The underlying premise of the Resource-Based Relative Value Scale (Hsiao et al.

1988), however, is that no necessary correlation exists between fees and opportunity costs. There is much debate as to whether the fee schedule first estimated by Hsiao et al. (1988) and ultimately adopted by the U.S. Health Care Financing Administration is a better reflection of opportunity costs than are fees (Frech 1991).

Some possible guidance for estimating opportunity costs of time for physicians in the United States comes from the economic theory of price discrimination. The theory tells us that when a seller faces consumers paying different prices (such as a doctor treating privately insured patients and Medicare patients), he equates the marginal revenue from each group with his marginal costs. When price is fixed by fiat, as with public sector payers such as Medicare, then that fixed price equals marginal revenue, which by inference equals marginal cost. Although there are some questions about applying the theory exactly to physician pricing, the theory does suggest that when physicians treat both private and public patients, the fixed fees paid by public insurers may serve as a good lower bound on physician opportunity costs.

Other medical costs

Detailed cost center level data are usually not available for medical providers other than institutional providers. In the absence of cost data, the researcher has a number of options. If these sellers face fairly competitive conditions, then simple microeconomics tells us that their charges will correspond to their costs. Jacobson et al. (1987), for example, estimated the costs of a hepatitis B screening program by examining the market price for such services. I (1989b) estimated the cost of home nursing care by examining market prices. If sellers sell to the private and public sectors, then the theory of price discrimination suggests that the public sector price corresponds to costs. Even in seemingly competitive markets, however, charges and public sector prices rarely agree. The researcher might choose to use the public sector price and charges as lower and upper bounds on costs, respectively.

Most episodes of illness involve at least some care outside of institutional settings. Methods for calculating many of the associated costs, such as for follow-up visits to physicians or for prescription drugs, have already been discussed. A number of other costs, such as for home nursing care or home therapy, may be incurred. These costs can often be substantial.

Home care has become an increasingly important component of many treatments. Home care can include nursing care, therapy, drawing of samples for diagnosis, or homemaker services. The first three are clearly relevant to measuring treatment costs. As with the costs of nonhospital institutional care, home care costs can be bounded above by home care charges and below by public sector prices.

Treatment of chronic illnesses outside the hospital often requires costly medical equipment. Home respirators are common in the treatment of many diseases, such as amyotrophic lateral sclerosis. The patient's family often has a choice of purchasing or leasing the equipment. Leases are often accompanied by a maintenance agreement, although the family may elect to bear the financial risk of repairing equipment that breaks down. The proper cost of durable medical equipment, like the proper cost of any durable good, takes into account the amount that the equipment depreciates during use, plus maintenance. A lease price, properly calculated by the lessor, should approximate this cost. I therefore prefer using lease prices to estimate equipment costs.

Cost to patients and their families

The resources necessary to produce medical care include the patient's time. One study that itemizes patient travel and waiting times is that by Ashton (1991). Ashton examined the costs of three alternative ulcer medications: colloidal bismuth sulfate, cimetidine, and raniditine. The first is associated with fewer relapses (and fewer physician visits) within the first two years of treatment. Thus, it has lower associated travel costs. Another study that includes travel times is Rice et al.'s (1992) comparison of erythromycin and mupiricin treatment of impetigo in children.

Inclusion of time costs can often alter one's conclusions about a drug's cost–effectiveness. An example is in the study by Jönsson and Carlsson (1991) of medical costs in Sweden for treatment of peptic ulcers. Jönsson and Carlsson found that medical costs increased after the introduction of cimetidine but that overall costs, including costs of lost time from work, declined.

The researcher may also need to consider costs to other family members. Rice et al. (1992) considered family members' lost time from work when their child visits the physician. I (1989b) found family costs to be critical in my assessment of the costs of caring for ventilator-assisted children in the home. I found that many families elected to substitute family time for professional nursing time in the home. Family members learned such tasks as tube insertion, feeding, monitoring, and routine equipment maintenance. These tasks required at least as much time from family members as they would have from professional nurses. Many families reported that having their child at home led to disruptions that may have affected careers and the schooling of other children.

The costs of time can be considerable. If the patient or affected family member is working, then it follows from simple economic theory that the cost of an hour's time, on the margin, equals the wage rate.[9] Estimating the cost of time for a nonworking patient or spouse is more problematic. One possibility is to equate the value of time to a market wage for homeworker services. Costs associated with disrupted careers and schooling are even more difficult to assess.

Summary

Resources used to treat one patient cannot be used elsewhere. To determine if the treatment is worthwhile, it is necessary to measure the costs of those resources.

Measurement of the cost of a medical intervention begins with the identification of the perspective of the decision maker. From this perspective it is possible to determine which cost centers are affected by the intervention. Cost centers usually include medical providers (e.g., institutions and physicians) and may also include nonmedical costs incurred by the patient and his or her family. When calculating costs, the researcher must be sure to identify all resources affected by the intervention and exclude those resources not affected by the intervention. The researcher must also bear in mind the time horizon of the decision maker – costs that are sunk in the short run may be variable in the long run.

Once the researcher has identified the resources affected by an intervention, it is necessary to assign costs to those resources. Unfortunately, hospital cost accounting is not reliable, since it is generally not performed for the same purposes as accounting by the cost–effectiveness researcher. The costs of other inputs may be even harder to obtain, although in many cases one can rely on market prices to estimate input costs. Nonmedical costs, including lost time from work and the costs of family disruptions, may be critically important, but imputing dollar values to them can be especially difficult.

CHAPTER 5

From cost–effectiveness ratios to resource allocation: where to draw the line?

Milton C. Weinstein

In recent years, cost–effectiveness analysis has been the most prevalent type of economic evaluation of health care interventions, including pharmaceuticals (Torrance 1986; Eisenberg 1989; Detsky and Naglie 1990; Freund and Dittus 1992). Unlike cost–benefit analysis, which requires that health outcomes be valued in monetary units in order to calculate the net economic benefit of a program, cost–effectiveness analysis requires only that a quantitative measure of health effectiveness, or utility, be defined. Typically, effectiveness is measured by life years (LYs) or quality-adjusted life years (QALYs). The cost–effectiveness ratio (dollars per LY or dollars per QALY) serves as a yardstick for measuring the relative priority of health interventions that compete for limited resources.

Perhaps because it avoids translating health consequences into dollars, cost–effectiveness analysis has been more favorably received by the medical community than cost–benefit analysis and has been favored by government agencies that have proposed or adopted economic criteria for funding of health programs or paying for new drugs (Klevit et al. 1991; Henry 1992). Although economic valuation of health consequences is avoided in the analysis per se, the problem of deciding in absolute terms whether a program is worth funding or not rests on whether a particular value of the cost–effectiveness ratio (e.g., $100,000 per QALY) is acceptable.

Following a review of the theoretical framework that leads to the use of the cost–effectiveness ratio as a decision criterion, this chapter addresses three issues in interpreting cost–effectiveness ratios and in translating them into criteria for resource allocation.

The first issue concerns the problems of comparability between cost–effectiveness ratios based on different definitions of cost. As was explained in

Chapter 4, many perspectives on cost are possible in economic evaluation. Ideally, the cost concept should correspond to the constrained resource from the perspective of the decision-making entity. In this portion of the chapter, many of the principles developed more fully in Chapter 4 are applied to the interpretation of cost–effectiveness ratios derived from different perspectives.

The second issue concerns the often misunderstood concept of incremental cost–effectiveness to evaluate mutually exclusive programs, such as drug regimens, or different levels of a program, such as drug dosages. Examples reveal that incremental cost–effectiveness analysis may have surprising implications for the evaluation of new drugs.

The third issue is the choice of a critical, or cutoff, value of the cost–effectiveness ratio. The following methods of determining a critical value are discussed: explicit evaluation of the shadow price of a budget constraint; estimation of opportunity cost in the absence of an explicit budget constraint; comparison with other health programs; inference of criteria from prior decisions; explicit use of cost–benefit methods; and rules of thumb. The comparative merits of cost–effectiveness analysis and of cost–benefit analysis based on willingness to pay are briefly discussed. The chapter's conclusion reiterates some of the points raised in Chapter 4.

Examples of all of these issues and concepts are drawn both from published cost–effectiveness analyses of pharmaceuticals and from the experience of institutions that have used or are considering using cost–effectiveness analysis in the process of allocating medical resources or funding pharmaceuticals.

The basic cost–effectiveness model

Cost–effectiveness analysis is based on the solution to a simple optimization problem (Box 5.1). Given a budget constraint, an explicit objective such as QALYs, and a set of alternative programs, such as treatments, that use resources (cost C_i) and contribute to the objective (effectiveness E_i), the optimal resource allocation is to rank order the programs according to their cost–effectiveness ratios (C_i/E_i) and to select them from lowest to highest to the point where the resource budget is exhausted.[1] This allocation can be shown to yield the maximum total effectiveness, that is, QALYs gained, subject to the budget constraint (Weinstein and Zeckhauser 1972).

Programs may include different applications of the same medical intervention or drug. The same drug applied to persons with different demographic, clinical, or epidemiologic characteristics could have widely varying cost–effectiveness ratios in these uses. For example, cholesterol lowering in persons with different cholesterol levels, coronary heart disease risk factors, and coronary heart disease histories could be regarded as different programs that compete for resources, and cost–effectiveness would be different in each group.[2]

Box 5.1 Paradigm for cost–effectiveness analysis

A decision maker faces a menu of programs ($i = 1,2,\ldots,N$) from which to choose.

The decision maker has a cost budget (C).

The decision maker's objective is to maximize total benefits, or effectiveness (E).

Each program uses part of the budget, that is, has cost C_i.

Each program contributes to total benefits, that is, has effectiveness E_i.

Any combination of programs on the menu is feasible, provided that it satisfies the budget constraint.

The cost and effectiveness of any program are independent of which other programs are adopted.

Programs are not repeatable; their costs and benefits reflect full implementation.

All programs are divisible, with constant returns to scale.

An assumption of divisibility of programs with constant returns to scale is needed to strictly justify the optimality of the C/E allocation rule, but violations of this assumption are to be expected in practice. Deviations from optimality occur especially when programs are "lumpy," that is, when they consume relatively large proportions of the available budget. In such cases, more complex decision rules, such as solutions to integer programming problems, may be used (Weinstein and Zeckhauser 1972; Birch and Gafni 1992). In practice, departures from the divisibility assumption can be handled on a case-by-case basis.

A simple hypothetical example of the use of cost–effectiveness analysis to optimize the allocation of a budget is shown in Box 5.2. It may appear that the conditions under which this simple C/E rule (Box 5.1) is optimal are excessively restrictive. For example, if two of the programs are alternative drug regimens for the same condition (e.g., streptokinase versus recombinant tissue plasminogen activator for heart attack patients, or niacin versus lovastatin for lowering cholesterol), then the requirement that all combinations of programs are feasible would not be met. It is precisely under circumstances of competing, mutually exclusive alternatives for the same patients that *incremental* cost–effectiveness analysis must be used. That paradigm is described later in this chapter.

The cost–effectiveness ratio of the last program selected before the budget is exhausted is especially important: it serves as the standard against which

---

Box 5.2. Hypothetical example of the cost–effectiveness paradigm

The health department in a large metropolitan area has been given a budget of $10 million to spend on health programs. Its objective is to save the greatest aggregate number of QALYs. The department's analysts have developed a list of programs that could be implemented, together with estimates of their costs and benefits (in QALYs gained):

Program	Benefit (QALYs)	Cost ($)	C/E ratio ($)
A	500	1,000,000	2,000
B	500	2,000,000	4,000
C	200	1,200,000	6,000
D	250	2,000,000	8,000
E	100	1,200,000	12,000
F	50	800,000	16,000
G	100	1,800,000	18,000
H	100	2,200,000	22,000
I	150	4,500,000	30,000
J	100	5,000,000	50,000

For each program, the cost and benefit values listed reflect full implementation of the program; in other words, it is not possible to replicate programs.

The optimal allocation of the $10 million budget is to adopt programs A, B, C, D, E, F, and G, up to a cutoff of $18,000 per QALY. The total of 1,700 QALYs saved is the most possible.

With a budget of $3 million the optimal allocation would be to adopt programs A and B only, up to a cutoff of $4,000 per QALY.

---

programs that make claims against the budget can be judged.[3] In the example shown in Box 5.2, when the budget is $10 million, the last program selected is program G, with a C/E ratio of $18,000/QALY. This means that if a new program is added to the menu, it should be adopted only if its C/E ratio is less than $18,000/QALY. The reason is that unless each dollar applied to the new option can buy at least 1/18,000 of a QALY, it is better to leave the money where it is (i.e., in program G and in more cost–effective programs) than to divert it to the new program. Hence, the cost–effectiveness cutoff in this example is $18,000/QALY if the budget is $10 million. If the budget is only

$3 million, the marginal dollar is even more valuable, since it purchases 1/4,000 of a QALY in program B; hence the cutoff for new options would be lower, at $4,000/QALY.

Cost–effectiveness ratios from different perspectives

As can be seen from the paradigm (Box 5.1) and the example (Box 5.2), the decision rule for using the *C/E* ratio as a criterion for resource allocation depends on the existence of a decision-making entity with a well defined budget constraint and a well defined objective. Cost–effectiveness analysis in practice can be applied to resource allocation decisions of a variety of decision-making entities with explicit budgets, but it is also applied more broadly in economic evaluation from the societal perspective (Weinstein 1990).

Examples of decision-making entities with explicit budgets include local health departments and health maintenance organizations. Another example is the Oregon Medicaid program, which has attempted to prioritize health services according to their cost per QALY (Chap. 3, this volume; Klevit et al. 1991). More commonly, cost–effectiveness analysis is applied in circumstances in which the budget is not explicitly limited but where there is an implicit need to allocate resources to contain costs. When the decision-making entity is a governmental agency, it will often adopt the societal perspective, considering all costs regardless of their source of payment.

As a consequence of this multiplicity of decision-making entities, the meaning of a *C/E* ratio calculated from a particular budgetary perspective may be very different from a ratio calculated from another perspective or from the societal perspective. Theoretically, the "cost" that appears in the numerator of the *C/E* ratio of a program or intervention should be the net burden of the program on the constrained budget in question.

Different societal cost concepts

Even from the societal perspective, important differences in interpreting the cost concept can lead to different interpretations of the *C/E* ratio. These differences can lead to inclusion or exclusion of cost elements that can have a dramatic effect on the resulting *C/E* ratios and their interpretation. Examples of such items are induced medical costs in added years of life, direct nonmedical costs, and indirect costs such as those due to either the program itself or morbidity – prevented or induced – and mortality.

Medical costs in added years of life: The analysis of pneumococcal vaccine by Willems, Sanders, Riddiough, and Bell (1980) and the analysis of antihypertensive treatment by Weinstein and Stason (1976) both included among the induced costs of their respective interventions the medical care costs that patients would be expected to incur in the years their lives were extended. This practice reflects a variant of the societal perspective that might be more appropriately called the perspective of the health care sector (Weinstein 1990). The implicit budget in such analyses is the total expenditure on health care. In effect, the inclusion of these costs adds a "surcharge" on the cost per QALY equal to the age-specific medical cost of a year of life extension. For C/E ratios well above the average per capita expenditure on health care, this adjustment will not affect priorities significantly. For programs with smaller C/E ratios, this practice will tend to favor programs whose health effectiveness consists mainly of improvements in quality of life rather than life extension.

Even in analyses that do not explicitly include medical costs of life extension in the numerator of the C/E ratio, induced costs related to the disease in question are typically included, with similar effects. For example, several analyses of the cost–effectiveness of cholesterol-lowering drugs (Oster and Epstein 1987; Goldman et al. 1991) include lifetime costs of coronary heart disease but not other diseases. Implicitly, therefore, the costs of coronary heart disease in the years of life added by cholesterol reduction are considered induced costs of this intervention.

Direct nonmedical costs: From a societal perspective, costs not accounted for within health care expenditures are often associated with programs (Chap. 6). Examples are the cost of transportation to medical providers, child care while a parent is receiving medical care, and nonmedical supplies and equipment such as might be prescribed for exercise regimens. For most interventions, the costs of these items are small by comparison with medical costs. Care should be taken to ascertain whether or not these items have been included in an analysis before interpreting the C/E ratio.

Indirect costs and benefits: From the societal perspective, indirect costs and benefits, that is, the value of time spent or saved, can represent real resources forgone or recovered. These costs and benefits are not relevant if the constrained resource is health care cost and are therefore excluded if the health sector variant of the societal perspective is used. When they are included, the resulting C/E ratios can look very different, and they must be judged by a different set of standards.

Consider first indirect program costs. Examples include the value of time spent traveling to providers and receiving care and time spent undergoing treatment. An economic evaluation of exercise as a heart disease prevention program by Hatziandreu et al. (1988) considered the cost of time spent exercising as an indirect cost of the program, as well as nonmedical direct costs – such as the cost of exercise equipment and clothing – and the costs of medical care. Hatziandreu et al. calculated C/E ratios in two ways, by either including or excluding indirect costs. When direct costs only were included, the cost per QALY gained was $1,400; when direct and indirect costs were both included, the cost per QALY gained was $11,300 (amounts in 1985 U.S. dollars).

Next, consider indirect costs and benefits associated with morbidity. Patients whose treatments result in their ability to work productively generate an economic benefit to society.[4] Because this economic benefit does not directly offset budgetary costs, it is excluded from cost–effectiveness analyses from most perspectives. From the broad societal perspective, these economic gains may be included in the numerator of the C/E ratio, but this practice is controversial for economic and ethical reasons. The economic argument is that these gains and losses are already captured by quality-of-life adjustments in the denominator of the ratio. The ethical argument (Williams 1981) is that it tends to favor interventions that benefit persons in their "productive" years, not children and the elderly.

Current practices are inconsistent as to whether indirect morbidity benefits are included, and this may reflect adherence to the health sector perspective on costs, ethical concerns, or both. Some analyses report C/E ratios both with indirect morbidity benefits included and with them excluded, an example being the evaluation of neonatal intensive care by Boyle, Torrance, Sinclair, and Horwood (1983).

The interpretation of a C/E ratio depends significantly on whether indirect morbidity benefits have been included in the numerator. When indirect morbidity benefits are excluded, the ratio can be interpreted as if the indirect benefits were subsumed within the denominator. In other words, each QALY gained may carry with it some economic benefit as well as a utility benefit to the patient. Thus, $50,000 per QALY would mean that the direct medical cost of purchasing a QALY is $50,000, but that each QALY may carry with it certain economic benefits. The same $50,000 figure in an analysis that includes indirect morbidity benefits in the numerator would represent a less cost–effective intervention because the productivity gains associated with the QALYs have already been subtracted from the costs. In such evaluations, the interpretation of the cost per QALY is the net of any economic implications of the QALY gained.

Indirect benefits of life extension are also sometimes included in cost–effectiveness analyses by using forgone earnings. This practice is not consistent with any reasonable cost perspective in cost–effectiveness analysis and should be avoided. In effect, including these productivity benefits of life extension creates a human capital–based cost–benefit analysis in the numerator of the C/E ratio, which is then divided by the health benefits. This practice counts the health benefits both as human capital benefits in the numerator and as QALYs gained in the denominator. It also exacerbates the ethical objections to including indirect cost generally (Williams 1981). C/E ratios in which indirect mortality benefits have been included cannot be compared with ratios that exclude them. Moreover, comparisons among such ratios have no obvious justification based on the cost–effectiveness paradigm for resource allocation.

Implications for interpreting cost–effectiveness ratios

Since what is included in the budget varies across perspectives, the interpretation of the C/E ratio will likewise vary. Moreover, the judgment as to what is an acceptable level of the C/E ratio will undoubtedly vary from one perspective to another. It is dangerous, therefore, to compare C/E ratios calculated from different perspectives. When the perspective is societal, comparisons should be based on C/E ratios that include health sector costs and direct nonmedical costs but that exclude indirect costs. It is logical, therefore, that morbidity effects be incorporated in the measurement of program effects.

Incremental cost–effectiveness analysis

Many applications of cost–effectiveness analysis in health care involve comparisons among competing alternatives for the same condition. Examples include choices among drug regimens for hypertension or cholesterol reduction, alternative drug dosages for a given condition, and comparisons between drugs and nonpharmacologic treatment. Other examples include choices among various diagnostic strategies that involve different tests in different sequences and with different positivity criteria.

In such competing choice situations, the basic cost–effectiveness paradigm (Box 5.1) no longer applies without modification, because the alternatives (e.g., different drugs for the same condition) are no longer independent. As an obvious example, the benefits of giving two antihypertensive drugs to the same group of patients are not additive. The paradigm needs to be modified to incorporate the possibility of mutually exclusive competing choices for the same condition.

A hypothetical example

The following example illustrates the principle of incremental cost–effectiveness analysis in its simplest form. Actual problems introduce other complications not considered in this chapter. The interested reader should refer to articles and textbooks on the subject (Weinstein et al. 1980; Doubilet, Weinstein, and McNeil 1986; Eisenberg 1989).

Consider a modification of the hypothetical example in Box 5.2, as shown in Box 5.3. The first key to solving the resource allocation problem in Box 5.3

is to recognize that the funds to pay for this program must come out of the original budget. This means that the funds would come from program G, whose C/E ratio is $18,000 per QALY.

It is tempting to conclude that K_2 is the best choice, since program K_2 has a C/E ratio of $10,000, and $10,000 is less than $18,000. Clearly, diverting resources from program G to pay for K_2 would result in a net gain of QALYs. *But this analysis would be incorrect!* The reason the analysis would be incorrect is that it ignores the availability of option K_1, which can give two-thirds of the benefits of K_2 at one-third of the cost. The correct analysis examines the *incremental* cost of K_2 relative to K_1, as well as its *incremental* benefit.

We calculate the incremental C/E ratio for option K_1 in relation to doing nothing as $50,000/10 QALYs, or $5,000 per QALY. Clearly, this first $50,000 is worth taking out of program G (at $18,000/QALY).

Next, calculate the incremental ratio for K_2, relative to K_1. This ratio is ($150,000 − $50,000)/(15 − 10)QALYs, which equals ($100,000/5) QALYs. The result is $20,000/QALY, an amount that exceeds the critical value of $18,000. So the department loses, rather than gains, QALYs by spending the extra $100,000 to upgrade from K_1 to K_2, because the additional QALYs cost $20,000 each – more than they could be bought for in program G at

---

Box 5.3 Hypothetical example of the cost–effectiveness paradigm with competing choices

In addition to programs A–J (see Box 5.2), the health department may fund one of four options for screening for a particular type of cancer. The department may also elect to fund none of these options. The net costs and effects of these options are as follows:

Program	Benefit (QALYs)	Cost ($)
K_0 (no program)	0	0
K_1	10	50,000
K_2	15	150,000

Given the original $10 million budget, and the availability of the original programs as well, which if any of the screening programs should be funded? (Continue to assume that all programs are divisible with constant returns to scale.)

$18,000/QALY. The optimal allocation is, therefore, to fund K_1, reducing the original allocation to program G accordingly.

There is a pitfall in incremental cost–effectiveness analysis, as illustrated by the following example. Suppose that an advocate for K_2, noting the result of the analysis described above, points out that another option, $K_{1.5}$, has been left out. Suppose $K_{1.5}$ costs $120,000 and saves 12 QALYs. The advocate points out that the incremental C/E ratio for K_2 relative to $K_{1.5}$ is ($150,000 – $120,000)/(12 – 10)QALYs, which equals $15,000/QALY. So, the fallacious argument goes, K_2 really is cost–effective after all, because its C/E ratio is below the threshold of $18,000.

The argument is fallacious because $K_{1.5}$ is an inappropriate basis for comparison. This can be discovered by calculating its own incremental C/E ratio relative to the next less costly option, K_1, which is $35,000/QALY. Since $K_{1.5}$ has a higher incremental ratio than the more expensive K_2, it is never cost–effective and should be eliminated from consideration.[5]

This pitfall implies that the choice of a basis for comparison in calculating an incremental C/E ratio can be crucial. Any option can be made to look cost–effective if it is compared to a sufficiently cost–ineffective alternative! The optimal decision rule is consider only to options whose incremental C/E ratios are lower than every more expensive competing option.

Incremental cost–effectiveness ratios in practice

Often, it is the competing choice formulation of the cost–effectiveness paradigm that faces health care decision makers. This is because usually more than one treatment is available for a given condition. The pitfall in economic evaluation is failure to acknowledge the existence of less expensive, though somewhat less beneficial, options in evaluating the cost–effectiveness of a particular treatment. The correct measure of cost–effectiveness is the incremental C/E ratio of a treatment relative to less expensive options.

Three examples will be used to illustrate the principle of incremental cost–effectiveness analysis. The first concerns alternative doses of the drug lovastatin for cholesterol reduction in patients who have had a heart attack. The second concerns the relative cost–effectiveness of niacin and lovastatin for cholesterol reduction. The third example concerns the cost–effectiveness of alternative thrombolytic (clot-dissolving) drugs to improve survival after a heart attack.

Cholesterol reduction after heart attacks

The drug lovastatin has been shown to reduce serum cholesterol, and the amount of cholesterol reduction increases with increasing dose. Dosages of 20 mg, 40 mg, and 80 mg per day are typically prescribed. The benefits are reduced mortality and cost from heart disease. Goldman et al. (1991) evaluated the incremental cost–effectiveness of the three dosages (20 mg was compared with no treatment) among patients with cholesterol levels of at least 250 mg/dl who had suffered a previous heart attack (Box 5.4). For men aged sixty-five to seventy-four, the incremental costs per LY (dc/dLY) were \$10,400, \$26,650, and \$84,300, respectively, for the 20 mg, 40 mg, and 80 mg daily doses. If the critical value were \$50,000 per LY, for example, then 40 mg would be the cost–effective choice.

Note that one could easily be misled by using the average cost per LY for the 80 mg dose, which is \$25,800 (Box 5.4). This is *not* the correct cost–effectiveness ratio for the 80 mg treatment. Rather, the correct measure of its cost per LY is \$84,300, its incremental cost per LY compared to the lower dose.

For forty-five to fifty-four year old men, the error introduced by failing to use incremental cost–effectiveness ratios is even more striking (Box 5.4). Both

---

Box 5.4. Cost–effectiveness of alternative doses of lovastatin in secondary prevention of heart disease

Goldman et al. (1991) evaluated the aggregate net medical costs and life years resulting from three doses of the drug lovastatin for men with a history of coronary heart disease and a serum cholesterol level of at least 250 mg/dl. The model calculated present values of heart disease cost (C) and life years (LY) for the U.S. population over the period 1990–2015. A sample of their results follows:

Dose (daily)	Total cost (billions of \$)	Total LYs	C/LY (\$)	dC/dLY
Men, 65–74				
20 mg	3.615	348,272	10,400	10,400
40 mg	7.051	477,204	14,800	26,650
80 mg	14.657	567,468	25,800	84,300
Men, 45–54				
20 mg	−3.846	411,189	\$\$\$\$	\$\$\$\$
40 mg	−2.761	536,973	\$\$\$\$	8,630
80 mg	3.010	616,942	4,880	72,000

Note: \$\$\$\$ denotes cost saving.

The correct cost–effectiveness ratios for the 20 mg, 40 mg, and 80 mg daily doses, respectively, are the incremental costs per LY (*dC/dLY*) compared to the next lower dose, as shown in the column at the far right.

the 20 mg and the 40 mg daily doses are cost–saving compared to no treatment, and the 80 mg dose costs less than $5,000/LY compared to no treatment. However, the 40 mg and 80 mg daily doses actually have *incremental C/E* ratios of $8,630/LY and $72,000/LY, respectively. These are the correct *C/E* ratios to use in deciding whether it is worth diverting the resources to pay for the higher doses.

Choice of cholesterol-lowering drug

Schulman et al. (1990) evaluated the cost–effectiveness of alternative drugs for cholesterol reduction (Box 5.5). Their results are not directly comparable to those of Goldman et al. (1991), because they used an intermediate effectiveness measure: percentage reduction in cholesterol. However, their results can be used to evaluate the incremental cost–effectiveness of two drugs: niacin and lovastatin.

Box 5.5. Cost–effectiveness of alternative drugs for cholesterol reduction

Schulman et al. (1990) evaluated the five-year direct medical cost of drug regimens using niacin and lovastatin for cholesterol reduction and related these costs to the percentage reductions in total cholesterol and low-density lipoprotein cholesterol (LDL-C). A sample of their results is as follows:

Drug	Cost ($)	% change LDL-C	Incremental C/E ($)
Niacin	1,573	11	143
Lovastatin	3,713	20	238

Thus, the incremental cost per percentage point reduction in LDL-C is lower with niacin than with lovastatin. The decision as to which drug is cost–effective, however, depends on the relation between cholesterol reduction and LYs saved, which depends, in turn, on the coronary disease risk of the patient group considered. For high-risk patients, $238 might translate to an acceptably low cost/LY ratio or might even result in cost savings if the cost of preventing heart disease exceeds the treatment cost. For sufficiently low-risk patients, $143 might translate to an unacceptably high cost/LY ratio.

They found that the incremental cost per percentage point reduction in low-density lipoprotein cholesterol was $143 for niacin (3 g/day) and $238 for lovastatin (20 mg/day). Thus, the incremental *C/E* ratio for niacin is only about 60 percent as high as that for lovastatin. This does *not* necessarily imply, however, that niacin is more cost–effective than lovastatin.[6] That judgment would depend on whether the $238 per percentage point reduction was worth paying. According to the Goldman et al. (1991) study (Box 5.4), the incremental *C/E* ratio for 20 mg/day of lovastatin would be extremely favorable (possibly even resulting in a saving of direct medical costs) in patients with a history of heart disease. Niacin would be the treatment of choice for such patients only in exceedingly cost–constrained environments where the incremental *C/E* ratio of lovastatin would be judged too high but that of niacin acceptable.

In other, lower-risk patients, the incremental cost per percentage reduction in cholesterol would translate to higher incremental cost per LY saved than in the case shown in Box 5.4 (Goldman et al. 1991). In that case, the incremental *C/E* ratio for lovastatin might well be unacceptable, while that for niacin (approximately 60 percent as high as lovastatin) could be acceptable.

Thus, either drug could be cost–effective compared to alternative uses of resources, depending on the risk status of the patient population and on the cost–effectiveness criterion.

Choice of thrombolytic drug in acute myocardial infarction

Intravenous administration of the drug streptokinase during the hours immediately following a heart attack has been shown to reduce the risk of in-hospital mortality. Moreover, this treatment has been shown to be cost–effective, even in the elderly, for whom the relative mortality reduction is less than for younger patients (Krumholz et al. 1992). A newer drug, recombinant tissue plasminogen activator (rt-PA), is believed to be somewhat more effective than streptokinase. Concerns about the high cost of rt-PA (approximately $2,000, compared to $200 for streptokinase), as well as concerns about its adverse effects (possible increase in the risk of cerebral hemorrhage), have slowed its diffusion.

Assuming a hospital mortality rate of 7.7 percent, a 29 percent reduction with streptokinase for a sixty year-old, and a cost of $200, streptokinase costs $9,100 per life saved (about $1,300 per LY saved) (Box 5.6). If rt-PA were able to reduce mortality by another 20 percent, its incremental cost per LY saved, compared to streptokinase, would be $23,700. A 10 percent mortality advantage would result in an incremental *C/E* ratio of $47,400/LY. (Analogous figures for seventy-year-olds would be $13,000 and $26,000 per added LY saved, compared to streptokinase.) Hence, rt-PA could be reasonably cost–

Box 5.6. Streptokinase versus rt-PA as thrombolytic agents

Krumholz et al. (1992) performed a cost–effectiveness analysis of streptokinase, a commonly used drug which, if administered intravenously shortly after a heart attack, can reduce mortality. They estimated the cost per LY saved to be $21,200 in persons seventy to eighty years of age.

A newer drug based on recombinant technology, rt-PA (recombinant tissue plasminogen activator), costs about $2,000, compared with $200 for streptokinase, and its incremental effect on mortality is controversial. Nonetheless, considerable interest exists in the medical community for the use of rt-PA, despite its high cost.

Using data from Krumholz et al. (1992), this example estimates the incremental cost–effectiveness of rt-PA assuming either a 20 percent or a 10 percent mortality reduction compared to streptokinase. Krumholz et al. estimated in-hospital mortality to be 7.7 percent for sixty-year-olds and 17.6 percent for seventy-year-olds; they estimated a 29 percent mortality reduction with streptokinase for sixty-year-olds and 14 percent for seventy-year-olds. Assume further a remaining life expectancy (discounted) of 6.9 years for sixty-year-olds and 4.6 years for seventy-year-olds; and costs of $200 for streptokinase and $2,000 for rt-PA. For this example, ignore adverse effects and costs other than the initial administration of the drug. The results would be as follows, depending on whether rt-PA offers a 20 percent or a 10 percent advantage over streptokinase:

Treatment	Cost ($)	Mortality	dC/dLives ($)	dC/dLT ($)
60 year olds				
No treatment	0	0.077	—	—
Streptokinase	200	0.055	9,100	1,300
rt-PA				
20%	2,000	0.044	164,000	23,700
10%	2,000	0.0495	327,000	47,400
70 year olds				
No treatment	0	0.176	—	—
Streptokinase	200	0.150	7,700	1,700
rt-PA				
20%	2,000	0.120	60,000	13,000
10%	2,000	0.135	120,000	26,000

Thus, rt-PA may well be cost–effective if it confers a 10–20 percent benefit over streptokinase, if its adverse effects compared with streptokinase are modest, and if cost–effectiveness ratios of $13,000–$47,400 are judged acceptable.

effective despite a possible tenfold cost disadvantage. As in the previous example, whether rt-PA is judged cost–effective depends on whether its incremental cost per LY, compared to streptokinase, is judged acceptable.

Determining a critical ratio

All of the discussion and examples so far have avoided the question of what, after all, is an acceptable cost per LY or cost per QALY. No magic number will be cited here – not even an algorithm for calculating such a number. Regardless of the decision-making context, judgment and consideration of unquantified factors must come into play. The stringency of the resource constraint, whether explicit or implicit, must also play a role.

Six approaches to arriving at a reasonable cost–effectiveness criterion are discussed here. Some have actually been used or proposed for actual use in decision making. Some are alluded to in "discussion" sections of economic evaluations that seek to place their results in perspective. All have some theoretical merit, and a consensus on their relative roles in decision making continues to evolve.

Shadow price of an explicit budget constraint

The most direct and theoretically correct criterion for judging the acceptability of a C/E ratio is the *shadow price* of an explicit budget constraint. If a decision-making entity is truly operating under the assumptions of the cost–effectiveness paradigm (Box 5.1, modified to allow for competing choice options), then the C/E ratio of the marginal program (the shadow price) represents the opportunity cost of diverting resources to fund a new program.

In the hypothetical example (Box 5.2), assuming a $10 million budget, program G was the marginal program, and its C/E ratio was $18,000/QALY. Therefore, any new program that competes for resources must have a C/E ratio of $18,000/QALY or less to allow a reallocation of resources to the new program to result in a gain of QALYs.

Although decision-making entities rarely allocate resources according to such a strict cost–effectiveness paradigm, the original plan for the Oregon Medicaid program came very close (Chaps. 3 and 10, this volume; Klevit et al. 1991). According to the original Oregon system, health services would be ranked according to a cost/QALY ratio and funded in priority order as funds permitted. The C/E ratio for the lowest-ranked service receiving funds would serve, then, as the standard for new services.

The Oregon system was subsequently modified to exclude explicit cost considerations and to allow for more flexibility in judging health benefit. In concept, however, the shadow price criterion for evaluating new funding options remains relevant as long as the budget is constrained. The criterion would, of course, change as the budget expands (higher C/E ratios become acceptable) or contracts (lower C/E ratios become unacceptable) or as new health services displace old ones.

In principle, other organizations whose budgets are explicitly limited could use the shadow price criterion if they chose to define their objective explicitly and evaluate the cost–effectiveness of their options. Examples include prepaid health plans and public health departments. However, not all programs are explicitly evaluated by such organizations, and objectives are typically more complex than simple maximization of health-related utility. In such situations, the second approach to defining a cost–effectiveness criterion remains relevant.

Opportunity cost in the absence of an explicit budget constraint

Suppose a decision-making entity has a limited budget for health care but elects not to allocate resources strictly according to the cost–effectiveness paradigm. Even in that circumstance, decisions at the margin might well be based on an explicit assessment of health opportunity cost. What is required to apply this criterion is to specify the program(s) that would be displaced by the program being evaluated. The C/E ratio(s) of that (those) programs(s) would then serve as the criterion for assessing the cost–effectiveness of the proposed program.[7]

Consider our hypothetical example once again. Suppose that, for political reasons, program G is not likely to be cut. Instead, funds for new programs would come equally from programs D ($8,000/QALY) and E ($12,000/QALY). In that case, the relevant opportunity cost and standard for cost–effectiveness would be $9,600/QALY.[8]

This type of reasoning is highly applicable in decision making by public health agencies or by prepaid health plans considering changes to benefit packages. It is also applicable to hospitals' developing treatment guidelines for a particular condition within the budgetary confines of prospective payment. Very often, explicit options for budget trimming are considered by each of these decision-making entities when new programs are contemplated. Examples include a public health department's budget-neutral decision to screen for HIV but to reduce other services at sexually transmitted disease clinics, or a hospital's budget-neutral decision to use rt-PA rather than streptokinase but to admit fewer patients with chest pain to the coronary care unit.

Comparison with other health programs

Cost–effectiveness analysis is often applied in circumstances where the budget constraint is implicit rather than explicit. In that case, explicit consideration of health-related opportunity cost is not applicable. Such is typically the case in societal level decision making. Examples include decisions by government agencies to approve funding for new drugs or technologies, or development of treatment guidelines by medical professional societies. Such decisions have to be "cost–conscious," but there is no explicit budget constraint and no obvious way to predict what programs would be displaced by the new program.

The use of cost–effectiveness analysis in such circumstances is becoming more prevalent. Governments are beginning to require economic evaluations to support decisions to grant insurance coverage for new drugs. In Australia, the Commonwealth (national) government has required that economic evaluations be submitted to the Pharmaceutical Benefits Advisory Committee in support of applications to be listed in the schedule of benefits under national health insurance (Henry 1992; Chap. 10, this volume). In Ontario, Canada, similar initiatives are being developed, and other provinces may soon join (personal communication, Allan S. Detsky). Medical practice guidelines are being developed by medical specialty groups, often with the support of economic evaluations.

The Australian Guidelines for Pharmaceuticals require cost–effectiveness analyses and call for the development of "yardsticks" to measure the acceptability of C/E ratios (Henry 1992). The guidelines themselves are silent on what this yardstick might be but suggest that the source of the yardstick should be other health programs that currently use or could use resources. Henry cites the guidelines as follows: "It will be necessary to develop a yardstick that can be used to assess how the cost per life-year saved by a drug compares to the cost–effectiveness of other ways of using the resources" (1992, 65).

Torrance (1986), in his landmark article on cost–utility analysis, published an early example of what has become known as a *league table*, an ordered listing of C/E ratios (in 1983 U.S. dollars) for services such as coronary artery bypass surgery ($4,200 for left main coronary artery disease), treatment of high blood pressure ($9,400 for severe hypertension to $19,100 for mild hypertension), neonatal intensive care ($4,500 for 1,000–1,499 g infants to $31,800 for 500–999 g infants), and renal dialysis ($47,100 for peritoneal dialysis to $54,000 for hospital hemodialysis). The implication is that users of cost–effectiveness analysis can refer to this sort of table to decide whether the C/E ratio of the program under consideration is (*a*) lower than ratios for well-accepted programs (in which case it should be recommended), (*b*) higher than ratios for programs generally regarded as "expensive" or "unacceptable," or (*c*) somewhere in the middle.

This method works rather well when criterion *a* is met. Treatment of very high blood pressure, coronary bypass operations for left-main blockages, and neonatal intensive care for babies with a good prognosis truly are established and noncontroversial. When C/E ratios are higher, it becomes more difficult to assert that some target of comparison is "cost–ineffective," given current resource levels. When it was enacted, universal coverage for renal dialysis in the United States was controversial because of its cost, and it is still not covered in many countries. Heart and liver transplants are also sometimes used as "high-end" examples, but the cost–effectiveness of both procedures seems to be improving. A recent estimate for heart transplantation for fifty-year-olds with heart failure is $32,000/QALY (Institute of Medicine 1991b), and cardiac transplant is now covered routinely by many health insurers.

Sometimes, the C/E ratio of an intervention is so high that comparisons are almost unnecessary. Weeks, Tierney, and Weinstein (1991) reported a ratio of $6,000,000/QALY for administering immune globulin to chronic lymphocytic leukemia patients to prevent infections. The article compared this ratio to treatment of moderate hypertension and renal dialysis as examples of acceptable treatments but stopped short of identifying a higher ratio (but lower than $6,000,000) that is regarded as unacceptable.

Inference of cost–effectiveness criteria from prior decisions

Prior decisions to withhold ideal health care for economic reasons can be used as indirect evidence of a societal standard for cost–effectiveness. Although it is dangerous to assume rationality in institutional decision making, such decisions do provide some evidence regarding the opportunity cost of resources. As an example, Eddy (1980) developed cost–effectiveness analyses of cancer screening that were subsequently used by the American Cancer Society (ACS) to recommend screening guidelines. For cervical cancer screening, however, the ACS recommended screening every three years, not every one or two years. Although the incremental C/E ratios were not explicitly calculated, the implied value for annual screening was $24,000 in 1980 (Doubilet, Weinstein, and McNeil 1986), which is the equivalent of slightly more than $50,000 in 1992 dollars. The fact that the ACS did not recommend annual screening at that time suggests that $24,000 per LY was too high.

There are obvious caveats in inferring implicit cost–effectiveness criteria from actual decisions. Unquantified variables, professional preferences, bureaucratic inertia, and political compromising are among the factors that come into play. Nonetheless, when a reputable cost–effectiveness analysis of a program is in the public domain and a prominent decision-making entity makes a decision to allocate or not to allocate resources to such a program, a natural "yardstick" is provided.

Cost–benefit methods

Often cost–effectiveness analysis is performed in circumstances where budget constraints are not explicit and where it is not even clear that the opportunity cost takes the form of health outcomes. Funding a program may result in

reduced budgets for other government programs, or it may lead to higher
or higher insurance premiums. In either case, the opportunity cost of t
resources is in areas other than health, for example public roads, national
defense, or private consumption. The cost–effectiveness criterion then reduces
to a willingness to pay test: how much private consumption (or its equivalent
in public services) is society willing to give up for an additional (quality-
adjusted) year of life? What is the value of a QALY? In such a situation, the
assumptions of the cost–effectiveness paradigm have broken down to the point
that the constrained optimization model is no longer helpful. The tools of
cost–benefit analysis are needed.

Phelps and Mushlin (1991) have argued that the choice of a cutoff value for
a cost–effectiveness analysis is equivalent ("nearly") to the valuation of a
QALY in cost–benefit analysis. The "near" in the title of their paper refers to
the fact that a cost–benefit analysis need not value all QALYs equally. For
example, QALYs for different ages could be valued differently for reasons of
economic productivity. The value of a life year might also depend on the
probabilistic context in which the QALY gains or losses are realized (Weinstein, Shepard, and Pliskin 1980), with avoidance of imminent death receiving
more value than preventive programs that reduce already low probabilities still
further.

When cost–benefit analysis is based on human capital valuation of human
life, the per capita gross domestic product (GDP) emerges as an age-neutral
point of comparison.[9] When based on more appropriate willingness-to-pay
methods, the value of a QALY could be considerably higher. For example, an
age-neutral annualization (at 3 percent discounting) of a $2,000,000 willing-
ness to pay per *life* saved over a fifty-year life span would lead to a value of
$78,000 per *year* of life saved.

Rules of thumb

Finally, a number of arbitrary rules of thumb have been proposed for deciding
whether a *C/E* ratio is acceptable. Kaplan and Bush (1981, 74–75) suggested
that, based on inspection of programs that had been evaluated, $20,000/QALY
was "cost–effective by current standards," $20,000–$100,000/QALY was
"possibly controversial but justifiable by many current examples," and
$100,000/QALY or greater was "questionable in comparison with other health
care expenditures." Although these benchmarks are putatively based on comparisons with other programs, the source of the actual numbers is unclear. They
would seem to serve as round, easily remembered numerical thresholds. It is
worth noting that the lower threshold corresponds closely to the per capita
GDP, possibly another implicit justification for its use.

Laupacis, Feeny, Detsky, and Tugwell (1992) have suggested these same
thresholds for classifying the economic acceptability of new drugs. Ironically,

h thresholds referred to 1982 U.S. dollars, which had
value of 1992 Canadian dollars after correcting for
hange. Perhaps the real thresholds have changed, but
ınd numbers is lasting!

ѵ cost–effectiveness analysis?

ᴜᴄ next chapter introduces willingness to pay as a measure of health benefits
in cost–benefit analysis. There Mark Pauly argues that resource allocation
based on a single "value of a year of life" or "value of a QALY" will lead to
inefficiencies if preferences are heterogeneous in the affected population. The
claim is that health outcomes are valued differently by different individuals
and, therefore, that cost–benefit analysis using willingness to pay as a means
of valuing health outcomes differently for different members of the population
is needed to ensure that allocations are Pareto optimal. A similar point has been
raised by Birch and Gafni (1992) regarding heterogeneity of preferences in
longevity–quality trade-offs.

This position is theoretically correct in terms of allocative efficiency, but
society may want to value each year of life, or QALY, equally for reasons of
equity. Do we want to permit people who are willing, or able, to pay more
dollars for longevity in general to claim more resources for the health programs
that affect them?

Also, the willingness-to-pay approach raises questions of measurement
strategy. If we seek to assign individual values to health *programs,* the question
arises as to whether the objects of the willingness-to-pay questions are holistic
programs (hypertension treatment programs, e.g., as opposed to coronary bypass operations) or whether the objects of the willingness-to-pay questions are
the *consequences* of those programs (such as gains in survival or quality of life).
The validity of estimates of willingness to pay for holistic health programs,
whether revealed by market decisions or elicited by survey, is limited by
inadequate consumer information about the consequences of medical interventions. On the other hand, eliciting values for bundles of health consequences,
such as survival curves and quality-of-life profiles, raises methodological problems analogous to and possibly even more difficult than those that arise in
eliciting the types of nonmonetary utility and health status measures required
in cost–effectiveness analysis. Clearly, more research on willingness-to-pay
methods is needed, as pointed out in the next chapter.

Conclusion

In a decision-making entity where the budget is explicitly constrained, the
objective is well defined (i.e., QALYs saved), and the list of potential uses of

resources has been evaluated and is open to inspection, the cost–effectiveness threshold is endogenous to the constrained optimization problem. In other words, the cost–effectiveness ratio of the least cost–effective funded program provides the standard against which competing uses of resources must be measured. The original plan for Oregon's Medicaid program came very close to this situation.

In less structured resource allocation settings, implicit cost–effectiveness standards come into play. Among these are the cost–effectiveness ratios of programs that are likely to be cut back to accommodate a new program, cost–effectiveness ratios of programs that are regarded generally as "cost–effective" or not, implicit criteria from past decisions, cost–benefit criteria for valuing life years or QALYs, and rules of thumb. As public and private organizations gain experience in allocating resources under increasing economic pressure, and as the medical profession and the general public develop experience in this new marketplace, it is possible that a general consensus will emerge. Until then, the learning process will continue.

CHAPTER 6

Valuing health care benefits in money terms

Mark V. Pauly

This chapter discusses the measurement of benefits from health interventions in monetary terms and specifically why and how monetary values are attached to health benefits. This discussion explores in detail the relationship between two commonly used methods of measuring the desirability of new programs or new products, especially new drugs. One method, cost–benefit analysis, is the economic approach that measures both resource costs and health benefits in monetary terms. The other method is cost–effectiveness analysis, which measures health outcomes in nonmonetary terms either as physical or as utility measures, while maintaining monetary measures for explicit (budgetary) resource costs and, frequently, for implicit costs. The difference between the two methods consists entirely in the way good outcomes are measured. The processes, advantages, and disadvantages of measurement in monetary terms are thus illustrated in comparison with the alternative.

Two primary questions about cost–benefit and cost–effectiveness analysis are addressed in this chapter. The first question is what *differences* are there between these two methods? A method will be called different from some other method if it will, in at least some possible state of the world, lead to a different conclusion about which program is preferable. The second question is, if there are differences, which method *should* a decision maker use? Such a normative conclusion obviously depends on the decision maker's objectives, so this question will be addressed in an indirect way by showing which objectives are consistent with the choices made under each method. The choice of objective is obviously not one that conceptual analysis can make, but some objectives might be more likely to achieve a consensus than others. The decision between methods will also depend on practical feasibility. The final valuative criterion, however, is still the same: which method yields decisions that select preferred outcomes?

The reason for this investigation is that in decisions about health programs and pharmaceutical products, cost–effectiveness analysis is currently used much more frequently than is cost–benefit analysis. This is especially true in European countries that use cost–effectiveness analysis, formally or informally, in the drug approval process. In addition, many health specialists, noneconomist health policy analysts, and political experts assert that cost–effectiveness analysis is preferable to cost–benefit analysis on grounds both of practical feasibility, because willingness to pay is difficult to measure, and of consistency with alleged distributional objectives (Warner and Luce 1982).

However, the reasons for such preferences have never been explained in detail. It may be, for example, that cost–benefit and cost–effectiveness analysis are both useful, but for different types of policy questions. If so, what are the characteristics of those different policy questions for which one or the other method is best suited? It may also be the case that one method fits the preferences of some decision makers, such as managers of a socialized insurance system, better than the objectives of other decision makers, such as managers of a for-profit managed care plan. The question remains, which method is better for whom?

Standards and definitions

Gauging benefits: a monetary or a nonmonetary metric?

How can one make a judgment about alternative methods for performing analyses? It is obviously difficult to do so on a case-by-case basis because one method may be more persuasive or more plausible than another after the fact. But such a finding would not prove that a method is preferable overall, or even that it would have been the best choice for a particular study given the information available when the study began.

This chapter proposes an *expected utility* or *constitutional* standard. This standard asks: given a wide variety of decisions to be made and a wide variety of individual circumstances for any member of a given group, what method would maximize the average or expected well being of a person in that group? In effect, this standard assumes/argues that each person has the group-average probability of being in each of the circumstances that might occur.[1]

As already noted, a study is conventionally labeled a cost–benefit study when both benefits and costs are measured in monetary terms. In contrast, when at least some of the good outcomes are measured in some continuous, nonmonetary metric (Chaps. 3 and 5) and costs are measured in monetary terms, the study is labeled a cost–effectiveness study.

These definitions are somewhat restrictive and limited. One could undertake a study that measures benefits and costs in units that are the same and also nonmonetary. For instance, in principle one could evaluate an intervention by asking how an individual's sacrifice of consumption to make payments affects the quality of life. One might then compare the negative impact of that sacrifice on quality-adjusted life years (QALYs) (primarily through the impact on quality of life, although reduced levels of nonmedical consumption could also affect life years) with any QALYs gained. This would be a cost–benefit study with a different numeraire.

It is also possible to have a study that measures good outcomes in monetary terms and bad outcomes in physical terms. For instance, a program might involve a more painful method of treatment in order to save on medical costs. By "reversing the signs" by asking what would happen if the program already in place were canceled, one could convert a study to a cost–effectiveness framework, but at the cost of a realistic approach. The more conventional definition of cost–benefit analysis will generally be used in the remainder of this study.

The cost–benefit decision rule and the economic definition of benefits

The general cost–benefit decision rule, which holds regardless of how benefits are measured as long as they are measured in money, states: *That set of programs is to be preferred that maximizes the excess of benefits over costs, given the constraints in the problem* (Mishan 1976). Since costs can be considered as negative benefits, this rule is equivalent to preferring or choosing that set of programs that maximizes net benefits, measured in monetary terms.

The reason for preferring programs that maximize net benefits is simple: any such program can always be financed in such a way that everyone in society can be made better off. People who benefit from the program could pay something less than the gross benefit but more than a share of the cost of the program (with the shares adding up to 100 percent). Such payment would leave them better off, and the excess of their payment over cost could be used to make a small payment to everyone else. Conversely, if a program's costs exceed its benefits, there is no way to finance the program without harming someone. Thus, it is possible in principle to move to a Pareto optimal point in a Pareto optimal fashion. Conventional welfare economics then argues that for a program to be desirable it is not necessary that the transfers needed to make everyone better off actually occur. Although there are some unlikely circumstances in which this potential compensation test will be ambiguous, it is the one welfare economics generally uses (Stiglitz 1988). The constitutional perspective described earlier makes the potential compensation test more attractive. If society follows the cost–benefit rule, on average every person can expect to be better off; the chance that the person will win will more than offset, in expectational terms, the chance that the person will lose.

In welfare economic theory, there is only one accepted way to measure the benefits an individual gets from a program. Benefit is defined as *the individual's maximum willingness to pay for the program* when supplied with information as complete as it can be, given the scientific knowledge available at the time. Willingness to pay, in turn, represents the maximum amount of other goods, or a composite of other goods, measured in monetary terms, that an individual would be willing to sacrifice to obtain the benefits from the program. "Information as complete as it can be" means that the individual has as much information about the program as is available or feasible. Approximating such a full-information situation is often difficult in medical settings. Nevertheless, it is critical to note that the willingness to pay of persons who are uninformed is not the measure that is to be used in cost–benefit analysis.

The benefit from a program is then defined as *the sum of the willingnesses to pay of all persons whose welfare is affected by the program*. Note that this definition does not limit benefits to persons directly, or physically, affected by a program. If my welfare is affected by a program that affects my parents' health, my willingness to pay should be included (along with theirs) in defining the benefits from a program for elderly people. Altruistic concerns about one's fellow human beings can also generate a willingness to pay by others that should be added in.

The willingness-to-pay measure evaluates how much better off people are as a result of the program, as opposed to the effect on them of the program's absence. The idea is that if the individual got the benefit from the program and paid anything less than his or her maximum willingness to pay, he or she would be better off with the program than without it.

In this case, the gainers from the program are those who obtain the benefit from the program; if the gainers did pay, they would compensate those who supply inputs to the program enough to compensate them for those inputs, and all would be better off. Technically speaking, however, the desirability or efficiency of a program that passes the cost–benefit test does not require that the gainers actually pay the cost of the program (in proportion to their willingness to pay), only that they would be willing to do so. For example, a health program that benefits lower-income households need not be financed by taxes on or charges to such households in order for implementation of the program to be efficient; the taxes could be imposed on others, if that is the (separate) distributional decision society wishes to make. In this sense, cost–benefit analysis does not necessarily accept the *initial* income distribution, but it does accept the final distribution decision, made according to whatever rules society has chosen for making distributional decisions.

The rationale for this definition and the question of how to measure willingness to pay are discussed later. For the present, there is one point that needs strong emphasis: in economic theory, the willingness-to-pay definition of benefits is the *only* acceptable definition. All other methods of valuing benefits in monetary terms are to be judged in terms of the closeness with which they approximate this definition. In particular, such concepts as the addition to measured gross national product associated with a health program, the additional wages to beneficiaries or providers, or additional returns from investment now or in the future have validity only to the extent that they proxy willingness to pay.

The need and settings for analysis

Is this calculation necessary?

For ordinary products sold in ordinary markets, there is no need to perform either cost–benefit or cost–effectiveness analysis. The reason is not because the products are unimportant but rather because in these cases all the agents in the market are themselves performing such analysis without high-priced consultants. When I contemplate buying an ice cream cone on a hot summer day, I will perform a cost–benefit calculation. I will compare my own subjective estimate of the value or utility I would get from the ice cream cone with the cost I will have to pay for it, and the cost in turn represents the opportunities I forgo. If the cone costs $1.00, I have to decide whether the benefit to me – the maximum amount I would be willing to pay – is greater or less than what I would have received if I spent $1.00 in the next best way I could. That is, I calculate a money measure of the benefit to me and compare it with the opportunity cost (price) I would have to pay. If the benefit is greater than the cost, then I maximize net benefit by buying and eating the ice cream cone.

A firm's decision on an investment project is also a cost–benefit calculation: an investment incurs costs now in return for revenues later. A calculation is made by comparing the costs incurred now with the present discounted value of the stream of net revenues the investment will generate.

In both cases, there is no need for a formal cost–benefit analysis. Instead, in situations in which there are no externalities or public goods, no distorting taxes or monopolies, and where there are fully informed consumers, the competitive market itself acts as a giant (but decentralized) cost–benefit calculator. No second guessing by analysts or consultants is required.

Why, then, should we develop such methods for medical services, drugs, and health care programs? One simple answer is that, as a matter of empirical fact, many decisions on the allocation of resources to medical care and health are made by governments. Likewise, many government programs necessarily affect health outcomes. Whether or not specific government intervention is warranted, the fact is that government does provide or pay for some services and does not leave them to the market. In those cases, there are no reliable market signals to use to evaluate decisions.

The challenge in these cases, under the economic view of cost–benefit analysis, is quite precise: in estimating the money value of benefits, the analyst should try to guess the valuation that would have been placed on the service or project in a competitive market if one had existed. That is, cost–benefit analysis uses the same rationale for benefits as do competitive markets but is required to use a different technique for calculating them. A perfect cost–benefit analysis simulates the outcome of a perfectly competitive market.

There is, however, a special reason to use cost–benefit analysis for insured medical services or drugs that does not apply to other uses of this technique. Conventional insurance causes the prices insured people face at the point of use or purchase to deviate from the full market price for services. Market demand does not, in such circumstances, serve as a reliable guide for allocation, even when markets exist. If it is possible to specify in advance which services will be rendered when, it will be necessary to make an external determination of which services are worth their cost by the use of cost–benefit analysis. When managed care is possible, cost–benefit analysis has a special role to play in determining how care is to be managed.

It is not always possible, of course, to manage care so precisely. When user price must play a role in controlling the allocation of resources, a special type of cost–benefit analysis, discussed later in more detail, will be necessary. But in every case some determination must be made of the value of services, and that value must be compared with cost.

Constraints on analysis

It is conventional to note that how benefits and costs should be measured will depend on the perspective the analyst takes. Economic cost–benefit analysis defines a particular type of societal perspective and a rationale for taking that perspective. Analysis can be cut free from this mooring, but then its course becomes less clear. If, for instance, a Medicare or Medicaid program is not to take the economic (societal) perspective, what perspective should it take? It might, for instance, take a so-called budgetary perspective, calculating the cost on what it pays out, regardless of other payments or the relationship of its payment to true cost. The question of perspective can, of course, be settled by definition. There is, however, no particular logic that would indicate that costs should be measured from a societal perspective and benefits in some other way. If the cost of a project is $1,200, and the next best thing a citizen who pays for the project would have bought is a big screen TV, why should the decision maker accept that the TV is worth $1,200? One cannot pick and choose which tenets of welfare economics one wants to follow and still imagine that there is some coherent rationale for what one is doing. If one substitutes QALYs or some politically chosen measures of value for willingness-to-pay based benefits, one could also substitute some politically determined valuation of the alternative uses of productive resources for the cost figures. For instance, there is no particular rationale for using a pharmaceutical firm's price (wholesale or retail) as the "cost" of its product, especially if one is willing to make the political judgment that stockholders or research scientists are being excessively compensated. Even worse, one might use the average (fully allocated) cost figures that accountants generate. There is no sense in which decisions made according to such rules will lead to preferred outcomes, even though they can *appear* to be made in a scientific and rigorous way.

There are some constraints on the decision maker's ability to substitute alternative benefit measures for willingness to pay. The constraints depend on whether the results of that decision must be submitted to market approval or political approval.

Let us take the simple case of market approval first. A good example would be the choice of programs in a for-profit health maintenance organization (HMO) sold in a competitive insurance market. (I ignore the issue of the tax subsidy.) Which type of analysis, cost–benefit or cost–effectiveness, should the HMO manager use?

Cost–effectiveness analysis does not appear to be especially persuasive. In what way would choosing a more cost–effective program lead to higher profits for the HMO or advance other HMO objectives? If buyers of the HMOs insurance are all the same, they would be expected to prefer the HMO that offered them better health outcomes for the money. But this is the case in which both cost–benefit and cost–effectiveness analyses give the same answer, as will be shown. What about a case in which the methods give different answers, the case in which the program with smaller effects offers them to persons who attach higher willingness-to-pay values to them? Following cost–effectiveness measures rather than cost–benefit measures would lower HMO profits because the program with greater willingness to pay can add more to the maximum premium the HMO could charge than could the program that produces more health, but of lower value.

More directly, the HMO needs to analyze all programs as a part of its marketing. It needs to ask whether adding a costly program will add more to the premium it could charge than it will add to cost. The amount that people would pay as additional premium is approximately (with qualifications to be discussed later) what would be measured as benefit in a cost–benefit analysis.

For drugs added to an HMO's formulary, this "addition to premium" approach is the ideal one. That is, the HMO should want to know the maximum willingness to pay additional premiums caused by the addition of the drug, compared to the drug's acquisition cost. Of course, buyers of HMO coverage will hardly notice the presence or absence of one particular drug, but packaging information about the use of sets of effective medications, even when they add to cost and premiums, is a possible marketing strategy.

Public sector decision makers are not similarly constrained by the need to find what pleases consumers enough to persuade them to buy. But the public decision makers (one hopes) are also not really free to adopt whatever measure of outcome they like, since decision makers must ultimately please voters in a political process. This brings us back to questions of outcomes. Is there a rule that is more likely to result in a majority of persons being better off, so they will vote in favor of the decision maker who follows that rule? Neither the cost–benefit nor the cost–effectiveness rule are perfect in terms of political attractiveness, but the cost–effectiveness rule, because it treats all persons as attaching the same value to health, may come closer, even though it may lead to economically less efficient outcomes.

What difference does money make?

One way to get insight into the difference between the two methods of making decisions is to ask when the methods would lead to different decisions. Specifically, when does the decision about which is the preferred outcome depend on whether benefits are measured in monetary or physical terms?

Imagine a set of programs, with positive resource costs, that improves health outcomes. The programs are assumed to have independent effects on health. Assume that costs and outcomes both occur during the same time period.

Fixed budget, unidimensional effects, identical persons

Suppose first that there is a fixed budget to be devoted to medical services for a given population. There is a set of costly but beneficial health care programs whose total cost, if all were to be undertaken, would more than exhaust the budget. Individual programs are sufficiently small that indivisibilities are not an issue. The beneficial effects all relate to one aspect of health, for example, mortality at a given age. Finally, all persons have the same income, the same productivity, and the same preferences.

Which set of programs would be chosen if cost–benefit analysis were used? In this particular case, since costs are fixed by the budget, the general cost–benefit decision rule is to choose the set of actions with maximum monetary benefits. This choice could be made by arraying all programs in terms of the ratio of their benefits to their costs and then working down from the highest ratio until the budget is exhausted.[2] It is quite obvious, however, that a cost–

effectiveness approach would give exactly the same answer. It would array programs by the ratio of effects to costs and, likewise, work down from the highest ratio until the budget is exhausted. Indeed, this case is precisely the one in which the method of cost–effectiveness gives an answer about what actions to take without any additional (external or controversial) assumptions. The outcome does not need to be valued and physical outcomes can be summed across individuals without ethical qualms because all persons are identical. In short, in the case where the cost–effectiveness approach gives the most defensible answer, it gives the *same* answer as the cost–benefit approach.

Different preferences

Let us now modify the example by assuming that people have different preferences, tastes, or utility functions but continue to have the same income and productive capacity. The cost–effectiveness method would ignore these differences. In contrast, the cost–benefit approach, properly applied, would attach different monetary values to identical changes in health for different people; the differences would reflect various willingnesses to pay for health outcomes. Note that, in this case, there is no variation in income or wealth to affect monetary valuations; there is none of the alleged "bias" toward the well off that is sometimes said to characterize cost–benefit analysis (LaPuma and Lawlor 1990).[3]

Would the two methods lead to different selections from the list of eligible projects? If no correlation whatsoever existed between individual valuations and the size of health benefits, the answer would be negative. For instance, if all interventions truly resulted in public (good) health – adding equal numbers of pain-free days on average for all citizens – there would be no difference in the choices made.

In contrast, if some programs provided relatively more pain-free days per capita to persons who place high values on the outcome because, for example, their job requires performance of certain functions, then the cost–benefit approach would tend to select those programs, even if they provided fewer pain-free days, rather than programs that primarily benefited people with low valuations.

Which is the better decision rule? In the constitutional state, the person has a chance of having any of the possible utility functions or performances. He or she would then prefer the cost–benefit rule to the cost–effectiveness rule. The reason is that for the given fixed budget, he or she would be willing to sacrifice a few pain-free days with low values of pain avoidance that could have been gained from projects directed at those circumstances in order to have more pain-free days should he or she have a strong "taste" or need to avoid pain.

The implicit argument that different values for or tolerances of pain or morbidity ought to be taken into account might command general acceptance. The difference between cost–benefit and cost–effectiveness analysis starts to come into focus, however, if we consider instead an intervention that affects the probability of survival. It is likely that different people place different values on changes in their probability of survival.[4] Preferences vary both because attitudes toward risk per se vary and because attitudes toward death or the value of life vary, even among people of equal wealth. Cost–benefit analysis would allow these preferences to affect the final decision, whereas cost–effectiveness would not.

Even in the most innocuous of examples, one feels disquiet at forgoing a program that could save more lives just because the beneficiaries of that program place less value on life than do others. Should we allow people to value their lives differently, or is not one life necessarily of the same value as another life? There is no way to "settle" so profound a question as this. There are, however, some strong arguments for permitting such preference variations to affect outcomes. If the decision maker takes as a postulate that variations in individual valuations of life years or survival ought not to affect decisions about programs, then economic cost–benefit analysis is simply not an appropriate method.

Of course, decision makers do not necessarily feel that all lives are of *equal* value, even when they choose to disregard individual preferences as irrelevant, misinformed, or mistaken. The political decision maker can use different amounts of dollars to reflect his or her own valuations of different lives, despite the political difficulties of doing so explicitly. Such a method would not be *economic* cost–benefit analysis, although it would take the generic form of cost–benefit analysis. However, in this particular case, dividing the money value of one life by that of another would permit a return to cost–effectiveness analysis, that is, adjusted life years; the money valuation, if not based on willingness to pay, would be excess baggage.

Different incomes

Now we reverse the assumptions and assume that all persons have the same tastes or utility functions but that they have different incomes. Furthermore, we assume that the marginal willingness to pay for good health outcomes, at any level of outcome, rises with income. Good health is a normal economic good, as are most other goods.

A key issue is whether or not there is diminishing marginal utility of (real) income, that is, whether people are risk averse in the constitutional state. If they are risk neutral, it is clear that the cost–benefit rule will be preferred to the cost–effectiveness rule. In the state of the world in which people have high incomes, they gain more utility by spending more on health. In the state in which their income is low, they would prefer not to buy as much health as they would have chosen at middle- or high-income levels but instead would choose to divert spending that has positive but small effects on health to other goods of greater value.

Conclusions can be ambiguous, however, if people are risk averse. The intuitive reason is that the cost–effectiveness rule may result in providing more health in low-income states than would the cost–benefit rule. This process can offer a type of insurance-in-kind against the unlucky event of having low income (as well as being sick). If efficient insurance markets exist, or if the amount of redistribution of real welfare across states is already chosen to be at the socially optimal level (whatever that may mean), then there is no basis for making further transfers of health to the low-income state.

But if private and public insurance markets are imperfect, it is possible that the cost–effectiveness rule would lead to a constitutionally preferred outcome compared to a cost–benefit rule. However, in this situation, the best decision rule will generally be neither the cost–benefit rule nor the cost–effectiveness rule but something in between – a rule that weighs the net (after the person's cost share) willingness-to-pay benefits in every income state by the marginal utility of income.

The choice of a cost–benefit rule over a cost–effectiveness rule therefore becomes more ambiguous the smaller the variance in tastes, the larger the variance in income or wealth, the greater the degree of risk aversion, and the more imperfect other social instruments for insuring against the adverse event of low income, whether or not the low income is caused by poor health. As a practical matter, the ideal analytical technique is still a form of cost–benefit analysis, with some adjustment in the money value of benefits by income class (away from a willingness-to-pay measure) to reflect the insurance-like character of many public programs.

Variable budget, unidimensional effects, identical persons

We now return to the case of identical persons but permit the level of the budget to be a choice variable. The cost–benefit approach selects projects in this setting by initiating all projects for which benefits are greater than cost, that is, all projects for which the ratio of benefits to costs is greater than unity.

In contrast to this straightforward procedure, *the cost–effectiveness method in this case cannot on its own lead to a preference among programs.* Programs can be arrayed in terms of their effectiveness to cost ratios in the form of a league table, and programs that provide more effect per dollar of cost obviously ought to be undertaken before programs with less effect per dollar of cost are undertaken. The problem is that the cost–effectiveness method does not specify how low a project's ratio of effects to costs can fall and yet still be worth doing.

To solve the decision problem, one must introduce an external standard concerning the minimum acceptable ratio of effects to costs (Chap. 5). However, the external standard then represents a valuation of benefits in monetary terms, such that lives are to be treated as being worth that particular dollar amount. Consequently, the money valuation of health outcomes is not really avoided (Phelps and Mushlin 1988).

Conventionally, these cutoff ratios are chosen fairly arbitrarily by basing them on values implicit in other projects that were undertaken, picking "reasonable" values, or just giving the problem back to the decision maker. An alternative strategy is to pick some point on the array of projects, and then ask the decision maker whether the value of the cost per unit of outcome in the last project funded is above or below his or her subjective measure of benefit. Either way, such approaches seem to represent a misallocation of effort. Great care is put into the decision modeling and the data-quality aspects needed to develop the cost per QALY figures, and then decisions are made by multiplying the QALYs by an arbitrary number, chosen with much less attention to its validity. Viewed as a whole, the process is still arbitrary, since the product of a precise number and an arbitrary number is an arbitrary number. The informal way in which the money value of the effect is estimated in cost–effectiveness analysis is conceptually less attractive than the formal derivation in cost–benefit analysis. The key practical question, however, is how validly can these money values actually be measured?

Variable budget, unidimensional effects, different preferences, same outcome

One potentially attractive aspect of the cost–benefit approach is apparent when the budget and preferences are variable. In most cost–effectiveness applications, the nonmonetary measures of outcome are simply summed. Using a single and uniform "dollars per unit of outcome" cutoff, then, is equivalent to valuing all units of outcome the same. If people have different preferences, the cost–benefit approach is superior because it would take such preferences into account. It would, in effect, attach different cutoffs for different people and would produce preferred outcomes.

Multidimensional effects

Finally, we return to the simplified case of identical persons, but we imagine that programs may affect different dimensions of health. For instance, one program might primarily affect survival, while another might affect the quality of life. To solve this problem, cost–effectiveness analysis generally specifies a particular, and usually restrictive, form of a utility function that attaches relative utility values to different health attributes and then combines them. These values are based on empirically estimated and averaged trade-offs between alternative dimensions. The primary restriction is that some interactions are ruled out; for instance, the value of one attribute often is not permitted to change if the values of other attributes change. In practice, tractability requires that either the utility function impose severe restrictions on admissible preferences or a fairly complex series of questions be posed to elicit a measure of outcomes relative to "healthy years" as a numeraire.

In contrast, all aspects of an outcome are *automatically* included in the willingness-to-pay measure of cost–benefit analysis if the willingness to pay queried is that of the complete program. No restrictive assumptions are needed, and money serves as a natural numeraire, in contrast to "healthy years." Cost–benefit analysis need not necessarily ask for an evaluation of the complete program, but the fact that it *can* do so – and cost–utility analysis cannot – is an advantage.

Moreover, in the case of identical preferences, both methods would give the same ranking of alternatives. That is, given some income level, the trade-offs represented in willingness-to-pay-based benefits should be identical with those generated by a valid utility function representation.

Conclusion

This set of examples serves to illustrate both the concept of money measures of benefits in cost–benefit analysis and the differences between cost–benefit and cost–effectiveness analysis. When the budget is fixed and little or no variation in preferences exists, cost–effectiveness analysis makes sense but is no different from cost–benefit analysis. In the more general case – that is, with variable budgets and varying tastes – cost–effectiveness analysis is much less suitable, in theory, than cost–benefit analysis.

Measuring benefits

We now explore in more detail how a money measure of benefits might be constructed and the rationale for that construction. To do so, we turn to the question of the measurement of benefits in monetary terms. The most direct approach inquires directly about willingness to pay. Other approaches should be judged in terms of the closeness with which they approximate willingness to pay.

Direct measurement

The most direct method to determine willingness to pay is a questionnaire approach that asks people how willing they are to pay to avoid particular health risks (Acton 1973; Thompson 1986). In principle, such questions are quite similar to those used to determine quality adjustments in the QALYs approach of cost–effectiveness analysis. In either strategy, people are asked about their hypothetical willingness to make certain trade-offs. In the willingness-to-pay approach, the trade-off is between money and the health risk in question. In the standard gamble approach, which is frequently used to define QALYs, the trade-off is between gambles with payoffs in years of life at various quality levels (McNeil, Weichselbaum, and Pauker 1981; Chap. 3, this volume). In the time trade-off approach, the trade-off is between certain years at one level of health quality and various numbers of years at other levels (Chap. 3). Only the method of bisection does not share this explicit trade-off character, since individuals are only asked what difference in outcome is "halfway" between some initial differences, but an implicit trade-off may be embodied in the method (Chen, Glick, and Eisenberg 1989).

All of these methods are obviously subject to the criticism that hypothetical trade-offs are not validated. Presumably, in the willingness-to-pay case, that objection means that we cannot be sure that the subjects really will pay the amount they report and no more. In some cases it may be possible, with effort, to confront people with the explicit opportunity to pay for an improvement in health and see what they do. In both the standard gamble and time trade-off approaches, the same problem of validation occurs: we do not know if people really would take the gamble or make the trade-off in terms of time. In this sense, despite widespread use, these measures are not known to be valid.

Willingness to pay and time trade-off share the property that a potentially complex prospect is valued as a single entity and compared with some simpler numeraire – either money or years in good health. The standard gamble approach, in contrast, seeks to break such prospects down into more fundamental elements and is known to require a fairly restrictive set of assumptions about utility functions in order to be able to do so (Keeney and Raiffa 1976).

Two properties of direct measurement of willingness to pay will be discussed here. One concerns the relationship between willingness to pay and various measures of life years, and the other concerns the use or difficulty of measurement of each of these concepts.

Individuals face a wide variety of risks to health. These risks differ both in terms of their expected values and in terms of their character. For instance, all three of the following risks have an expected value of 0.5 lives lost: (1) facing a single individual with a 50-50 chance of death; (2) facing a population of 100 individuals with a 1 in 200 chance of death; (3) facing a population of 100,000 individuals with a 1 in 200,000 chance of death. Most QALY-type approaches would regard programs that avoid any of these risks as equivalent in terms of effectiveness.

However, the aggregate willingness to pay of a set of identical individuals to avoid each of the prospects would ordinarily not be identical (Weinstein, Shepard, and Pliskin 1980a). Probably, willingness to pay would be greatest against the first prospect and lowest against the last. Since a person cannot logically offer to pay more than his or her lifetime income, it is possible that the value for the first prospect is limited by the need to retain enough income to be able to survive once the specific risk is avoided (Conley 1976).

Is it possible to get reasonable answers to willingness-to-pay questions? Such questions have not been subject to nearly as much research as questions intended to elicit the trade-offs that define QALYS, although some investigation has taken place over a long period of time (Acton 1973; Thompson 1986; Berger et al. 1989; Appel et al. 1990). Acton's study measured willingness to pay for the availability of mobile coronary care units by investigating values attached to life saving. People were asked about their willingness to pay for risk reduction for themselves and for the community; values were largest for saving one's own life. Thompson, Read, and Liang (1984) and Thompson (1986) explored willingness to pay (as well as a standard gamble) for morbidity reduction in the care of rheumatoid arthritis symptoms. When people unused to paying for care were asked open-ended questions, the response rate was quite low. With an improved questionnaire design, the response rates to both the willingness to pay and standard gamble questions were above 80 percent. Appel et al. (1990) queried willingness to pay to reduce the risk of minor and major side effects of radiographic contrast media. Care was taken to present probability measures in easy-to-understand forms, and results indicated that a majority of persons would be willing to pay more than the cost of the superior media, with value increasing with income.

A more recent set of studies by Swedish researchers has estimated the willingness to pay for antihypertensive drugs and the overall costs and benefits of a nonpharmacologic treatment program for hypertension (Johannesson, Jönsson, and Borgquist 1991) and compared the two forms of the treatment (for older men) (Johannesson and Fagerberg 1992). The last study is of interest because it also included several forms of cost–effectiveness analyses, some of which showed a preference for the drug treatment – in contrast to the cost–benefit analysis, which showed no difference. The main reason for the difference was that the more costly form of treatment (diet modification), although producing relatively few or no health effects, did have a higher willingness to pay. In a direct comparison of three methods – willingness to pay, time trade-off, and maximum acceptable risk – the willingness to pay and time trade-off methods were found to be more plausible than the risk-based method (Johannesson 1992b). Likewise, high response rates were obtained in willingness to pay for alternative drug therapies for angina (Jönsson et al. 1988).

More work on measuring willingness to pay for health outcomes has been reported in the literature on environmental threats (Gerking and Stanley 1986) than in the literature on medical services. Neither the willingness-to-pay, standard gamble, nor time trade-off approach has been truly validated, as already noted. We do not know whether people would be willing to pay what they say and we also do not know whether people would take the gambles or make the time trade-offs they have reported.

As with questions designed to elicit utility valuations, getting reasonable answers to willingness-to-pay questions requires some care in phrasing and choice of subject. Most of the design is a matter of common sense. Not surprisingly, persons who are used to paying for medical services are more willing to answer questions about willingness to pay and to give reasonable answers than those with nearly complete public or private insurance coverage. It has also been claimed that in willingness-to-pay studies it is better to ask people what percentage of their income they are willing to pay rather than to ask them for an absolute dollar amount (Thompson 1986). This presumably avoids the strategic misrepresentation that might occur if low-income people suspected that they might be harmed if they reported low willingness to pay.

The question of willingness to pay does not seem to be intrinsically difficult for people to understand, despite occasional unsupported assertions that people are not able to understand and answer willingness-to-pay questions but are willing to talk about trade-offs among gambles or lengths of longevity to establish quality of life. Indeed, it is probably the case that in the American health care system, people make many more decisions about willingness to pay for medical services than they make about risk or time trade-offs. What is obviously undesirable, however, is to place willingness-to-pay questions in a context in which respondents, who tend not to behave like the passive "subjects" we analysts would like, find the line of questioning contradictory or upsetting. For instance, it may be desirable, though difficult, to avoid strategic responses by asking what the government should be willing to pay rather than what the individual is willing to pay (Donaldson 1990).

One clear mistake is to ask people about willingness to pay to avoid health threats that might be imposed on them. Toxic waste dumps, nuclear power plants, and the like are treated by people as imposed risks, and respondents probably answer strategically, refusing to give willingness-to-pay answers and quoting enormous numbers if they are asked what they would have to be paid to be subjected to such health risks.

A more subtle point is that the determination of willingness to pay for insured services is likely to be perceived as a nonsensical question: why say what you will pay for something you are going to get for free? This reinforces the desirability of asking willingness-to-pay questions of those who have had some experience with or some prospect of actually being able to pay for services (adjusting, of course, for other relevant characteristics).

Measuring willingness to pay from market data

An alternative to direct querying of willingness to pay is to estimate it from market data. Ordinarily, the market data are not generated by the project or product being valued. If the product could be sold in a competitive market, there would be no need for a cost–benefit analysis. Instead, some characteristics of the product are specified and then the implicit value of those characteristics is inferred from market data on products that are sold in markets and that have similar characteristics. For example, if a product that either cannot be or has not yet been marketed reduces mortality, one might infer the money value of life by observing different wages paid in jobs that differ in terms of their expected mortality. In principle, this approach looks at every product as a bundle of characteristics, and the "hedonic" value of those characteristics is what must be estimated.

The market based approach has been used to study product safety and public investment questions (Viscusi 1979; Olson 1981; Moore and Viscusi 1988; Atkinson and Halvorsen 1990) but has not been used in any formal way in connection with medical services.[5] This is a pity, since this approach exhibits some strong advantages. For one thing, it is self-validating; values are based on behavior, not on artificial answers to hypothetical questions. In addition, the market-based approach will raise fewer questions about the impact of wealth on values, as long as the populations that expose themselves to greater risk contain some people who are not poor.

However, there are also some reasons for caution in the use of results from market choice studies. The most obvious problem is that there may well be unique properties of the risk that cannot be approximated by a stock list of hedonic characteristics in a given situation, or that have a value in combination different from what would be implied by the sum of hedonic characteristics. If a job has an increased mortality risk and the risk of a nonfatal but uncomfortable injury, can that value be calculated by knowing separate estimates of the market value of mortality and injury risk?

A second obvious problem is that values in markets reflect the information available to people in markets. If people are not completely informed, a risk may not be assigned the value it would have under full disclosure. For instance, relating price differences across hospitals to severity-adjusted measures of mortality risk would probably not generate reliable measures of the value of risk, both because of consumer ignorance and because insurance coverage distorts the user prices buyers pay.

There is a third, less obvious, problem. If people differ in the values they place on risks, either across persons or as a function of the amount of risk they have already accepted, market values will not describe the risk of all such persons. Nor can they be interpreted as the average value, that is, as the value of the person with median tastes in some population. Instead, market prices describe the value for the *marginal* person and for the *marginal* unit. We know that the person who is indifferent between two jobs, one more risky than the other, places a value on risk that equals the wage differential. But most persons who take the riskier job probably are not indifferent; they are actually made better off by taking the risky job, since the value they attach to risk is less than the wage premium. Conversely, persons who choose the less risky job attach greater value to avoiding risk than is represented by the market wage differential. That is, the wage differential sets a lower bound on value for those who take the riskier job and an upper bound on value for those who do not. In a way, the number of persons choosing to accept or reject a risky opportunity is a more valuable piece of information than the wage or price differential itself.

This problem appears again when one tries to value a health risk by seeing what people are willing to pay to avoid it. For those who do pay, the risk is at least as costly as the expenditure, but it could be much more costly. For those who do not pay, all we know is that they value the risk at less than the cost of preventing it. The size of the expenditure depends partly on the technology of expenditure prevention and, in the limit in a competitive market, is equal to the marginal cost of production.

These problems can be dealt with to some extent by making assumptions about the inframarginal distribution of values (or the shape of the demand curve) and by measuring the number of buyers and nonbuyers. It also sometimes happens that the project being analyzed itself affects marginal buyers and marginal units, although this is not usually the case for prospective evaluation of a product that will eventually be sold in markets where users pay the full price.

There is an alternative market-based measure. The "human capital" approach to valuing survival or morbidity measures value by the value of the output (at market prices) that the persons would have produced if they had been healthy or survived (Weisbrod 1961). Sometimes the additional consumption of other goods (even medical services for unrelated health problems) is subtracted out, sometimes only the unrelated medical costs are subtracted out, and sometimes the (present value of) earnings figures are presented as gross estimates. Sometimes as well, time not used in market work is valued as if it were used in market work: leisure time is valued at the market work time wage rate, and housework time is valued either at the wage rate for domestics or at the wage the particular person could have earned in the market. This method has sometimes been used in studies of drugs, as described in Chapter 4.

The human capital approach has some difficulties, even given its own terms. How should mortality and morbidity for retirees be valued? For homemakers, one might use the domestic wage rate, even for someone who lives alone, but for other subjects, the appropriate procedure is less obvious.

More fundamentally, however, the human capital measure is conceptually invalid as an economic measure of benefit from medical services precisely because it does not measure an approximate willingness to pay very well. At best, lifetime earnings might be interpreted as a lower bound on willingness to pay, as long as leisure has value (Linnerooth 1979; Berger et al. 1989). The view that health only has value in adding to "national output" is inconsistent with welfare economics, which recognizes value in leisure time and in other activities that are not measured in gross national product. In short, the human capital measure should not ordinarily be used in cost–benefit studies.

Problems with willingness-to-pay measures

If it is feasible to get credible willingness-to-pay measures of benefits in money terms, why is this approach used so rarely in health policy analysis? The discussion of this questions falls into three parts. The first part deals with invalid objections to the technique. The second part deals with more fundamental or more basic conceptual objections. The third part concerns the feasibility of valid measurement of willingness to pay relative to measures of effectiveness.

Probably the most common objection to willingness-to-pay measures is the thought that such valuations may be positively correlated with wealth or income. This is much less of a problem when the budget is not fixed than when it is. Suppose the budget is not fixed, and some programs to benefit higher-income persons will pass the cost–benefit test. Similar programs that primarily benefit lower-income persons may not pass the test if benefits are limited to direct benefits to recipients.[6] Providing the program that benefits higher-income people, if financed by the users themselves, will provide net benefit to the users and need not harm anyone else – if no one else is asked to pay for it. So this program should be enacted. If the program for lower-income persons does not pass the cost–benefit test, there is no good reason why it should be enacted. If we want to provide benefit to low-income people, a more efficient approach would be to use the money that would have been spent on the program to make a direct money transfer to them, since the money will benefit low-income people more than the program would. In this case, providing the program, as opposed to making a direct money transfer, is worse for both lower-income people and the rest of the community. If the community decides not to make the money income transfer, it must not have attached high value either to low-income persons' health or to their overall welfare.

The analysis is less satisfactory when there is a fixed budget big enough only for one program. Then, undertaking the program that benefits higher-income persons precludes a program, possibly one saving more lives, that benefits lower-income persons. It will still be true, however, that higher-income persons may be willing to make a money transfer to lower-income persons to obtain their consent to give up their program. Higher-income persons may then be willing to undertake their own program. That is, there would be a way, with transfers, to make both groups better off by implementing the higher-income program.

Even if transfers are not made, however, it is not obvious that the cost–benefit approach is inappropriate. Saying that society prefers the program that saves more poor lives, even when those lives have lower aggregate value, is equivalent to saying that society would regard benefits to poor people worth a given dollar amount as of greater value than a program with larger money benefits that helps rich people. In effect, dollars of benefit to poor people are of higher social value than dollars of benefit to rich people. Indeed, one suggested compromise in cost–benefit analysis is to weight money benefit differently depending on the income level of the recipient (Stiglitz 1988). But if a dollar's worth of benefits to poor people were worth more to society than a dollar's worth of benefits to rich people, it follows that society should be redistributing more income from rich people to poor people. If we observe, however, that society, whichever decision it makes, does not seem disposed to make further transfers from rich to poor, then we are not justified in asserting that the same society would value health benefits of a given money value more if they go to poor people than to rich people.

To be sure, an analyst's personal preference might involve more redistribution to the poor. But it is not legitimate to doctor the books in cost–benefit analysis in order to bring about by subterfuge what would not be tolerated in the standard political process.

A more conceptually valid way of looking at redistributive elements in cost–benefit analysis harks back to the discussion earlier in this chapter. If one is trying to plan a decision rule for deciding on public health programs in a future where one's own situation is unknown – that is, when one is behind the constitutional veil – one might prefer that government adopt a cost–benefit rule, regardless of the distributional consequences, rather than be given the power to make arbitrary decisions weighting benefits more for the poor. There is an alternative model, however. If we look at constitutional choice as picking a kind of insurance policy, one might prefer to weight dollars in the poor state as having greater marginal utility than dollars in the rich state. It is, however, the dollars of net benefit, not the dollars of gross benefit, that should be so weighted.

In a practical sense, many programs and medical services do not have a wealth bias, so the distributional objection to cost–benefit analysis is often a red herring. When some programs benefit the poor, then adding the benefits to others to the benefits to the direct user will permit one to undertake cost–benefit analysis without apologies.

Another potentially valid conceptual objection comes from those who do not feel that individual preferences *should* be a guide to resource allocation. It is surely possible to reject welfare economics as a guide to welfare; welfare economics is based on strong postulates that some may choose not to accept. But if one rejects part of the welfare analytic model, there is no compelling reason to seek to apply the remaining part. For instance, costs need not be measured by marginal social opportunity cost; one would be justified in weighting costs in different ways, depending on the income level of the person who pays the cost and, perhaps, that of the person who receives the money. The main point, as has been noted in connection with so-called merit goods, is that using individual preferences as a basis for judging welfare is at the heart of welfare economics. Jettison individual preference, and one might as well toss out the rest.

A third conceptually valid objection relates to the presumed utilitarian basis of cost–benefit analysis. In aggregating benefits across individuals by summing willingness to pay, one makes the specific assumption that the happiness or well-being of the community is the sum of individual well-beings measured and added in this way. Some aspects of equity can be taken into account in the choice of the initial distribution of income, so the use of cost–benefit analysis is not an endorsement of the laissez-faire distribution of welfare. But cost–benefit analysis does imply that one can find welfare weights and then use those to add up monetary values. This is, however, a postulate with which some may disagree.

By definition, there is no arguing about postulates. At base, the cost–benefit approach endorses all projects and products that can, in principle at least, be provided in a way that makes everyone better off. However, the real test of the cost–benefit approach is not whether it is flawless when held up against some ideal standard but rather whether it is better than other feasible alternatives. Viewed in this light, the method holds up rather well. It automatically and almost painlessly answers questions that have roiled cost–effectiveness analysis in recent years, such as whether future QALYs or other physical measures of benefits should be discounted (Keeler and Cretin 1983; Chap. 7, this volume). If benefits were measured in money terms, no one would object to discounting; yet the money measure is just a transformation of the physical measure and not a new concept. Reasons that are sometimes offered against discounting, such as growing income or the possibility that one's quality of life may vary with age (Parsonage and Neuberger 1992), disappear as issues in discounting and become merely questions of valuing the effects that are to be discounted. Or consider Mehrez and Gafni's (1990) assertion that "healthy year equivalents" are to be preferred to QALYs. Mehrez and Gafni's objection comes down to the idea that utility may not be linear in QALYs. But if the benefits of a project are valued directly in willingness-to-pay terms, any of the risk aspects of the project, and the beneficiary's attitude toward risk, are automatically embedded in the money measure. No recourse to a new lexicon is needed.

Even if cost–benefit analysis is conceptually preferable to cost–effectiveness analysis, there may be measurement difficulties in implementing it. Can these difficulties be so severe as to lead to a preference for cost–effectiveness analysis? The most straightforward method for generating a willingness-to-pay measure for some health invention ought to involve asking respondents about a carefully described listing of the consequences of the intervention. For an intervention that affects both life expectancy and the quality of life and that has a variety of potential side effects, the probabilities attached to each outcome would be described, as would the final consequences.

In some studies that deal with more general interventions, simplified versions of possible scenarios are often used. For instance, a respondent might be asked, "What would you pay for a cure for your arthritis?" Alternatively, a set of respondents might be asked whether they would pay $X for a cure for arthritis, and the set of answers would be used to construct a measure of the average maximum willingness to pay (or reservation price). It is generally believed that this second method, despite its need for a larger number of respondents, generates less strategic answering on the part of subjects (Johannesson, Jönsson, and Borgquist 1991).

In all cases, however, the most direct method imposes no a priori restrictions on individual preferences or utility functions. However, respondents combine various dimensions of outcomes, and those combinations are reflected in this "all-of-a-piece" measure of willingness to pay.

In contrast, all measures for generating QALYs for purposes of cost–effectiveness analysis are known to impose simplifying restrictions on utility functions. Such restrictions are necessary because respondents are asked about trade-offs between various dimensions of outcomes; some tractable functional form must be chosen to express those trade-offs. Although there is evidence that simplifying assumptions do represent preferences on average (Chap. 3), such restrictions are in general undesirable.

A potential strength of the QALY methods, however, is the simplification of the description of health programs into a limited number of clearly defined characteristics. Respondents may well have difficulty in understanding the complex combinations of probabilistic outcomes represented by the all-of-a-piece model. It may be easier to understand the terminal effects used in the QALY approach and to understand artificial but simplified efforts to measure risk premiums. This leads to the conclusion that, as a practical matter, cost–effectiveness analysis may be preferred to all-of-a-piece cost–benefit analysis.

Compromises are possible, however. Respondents could be asked about their willingness to pay for a QALY. For reasons discussed elsewhere in this chapter, the weighting of outcomes embodied in a QALY is likely to represent, at least on average, the same weighting that would be based on willingness to pay. The problem, of course, is that a QALY is an artificial concept and does not represent direct experience. However, QALYs can be analogized to "years of good health" and can perhaps be valued by respondents in this way.

An alternative, and perhaps better, strategy would be to develop willingness-to-pay measures for the components that are assembled to make up QALYs. With such money measures, one could develop a "constructed" measure of the willingness to pay for any health intervention. For instance, willingness to pay for the ability to perform certain functions could be determined. This money measure would have two strong potential advantages. It would be based on questions subject to much more testing for reliability and construct validity than the all-of-a-piece measure. In addition, willingness-to-pay measures could be assembled for new programs with new combinations of outcomes without the need for new surveys. Instead, the measures would literally be constructed by adding together the willingness to pay for the various parts of the description of the complete outcome.

The trade-offs here are obvious but not especially easy to decide on an a priori basis. The constructed measures are less subject to respondent mis-understanding than are the all-of-a-piece measures and can easily be assembled for new interventions. On the other hand, they involve more simplifying assumptions about utility functions, assumptions that may not be realistic.

A highly valuable empirical study would be one that compared these alternative methods for generating monetary values. Do they yield different answers? We have no standard by which to judge validity, but we could learn a substantial amount.

Insurance and cost–benefit analysis

If a person is asked about willingness to pay for a program or product, the risk characteristics associated with that choice will be important. The simple rule of thumb here is to associate with the product the risk characteristics that will actually prevail. For instance, if a pharmaceutical product is to be sold in a market without insurance, the person should be asked the maximum amount he or she is willing to pay for the product. In contrast, if the bill for the product is fully covered by insurance, this must be taken into account. As Gafni (1991) has recently argued, one would ask the maximum amount the person would be willing to pay for insurance that would fully cover the cost of the product. If insurance will provide partial coverage, for example, with 20 percent coinsurance, then the relevant willingness-to-pay measure is the sum of the maximum willingness to pay for an insurance that covers 80 percent of the cost of the product plus the maximum willingness-to-pay coinsurance, conditional on paying for the insurance policy in the first place.

In general, if the presence or absence of insurance does not affect the nature of the care delivered, risk-averse persons would be expected to pay more for insurance to cover the price of a product than for the product without insurance. For instance, suppose there is a 50 percent chance of needing a particular product and the maximum amount a person would be willing to pay for the product, given that he or she is in the illness state for which it is needed, is $X. Then the amount per capita that a population of risk-neutral people would be willing to pay for the product is $0.5X. However, if people are risk averse, they would be willing to pay more than this expected value for insurance that fully covers a $X cost. Indeed, the difference between willingness to pay with and without insurance is the well-known risk premium.

Conclusion

The conceptual arguments for measuring benefits in money terms are strong, at least to economists. There is so much skepticism about cost–effectiveness analysis, however, that asking policymakers to swallow the additional assumptions behind cost–benefit analysis may be difficult. When will the time be ripe for cost–benefit analysis?

There are two auguries to watch. One has to do with acceptance of the need for rationing. As long as policymakers believe that the main challenge to health policy is to find those new programs that will enable them to lower costs without reducing benefits at all, they will not be eager to measure benefits in monetary terms; they will not even need to measure benefits in monetary terms. After all, if one program provides more physical benefits but has lower cost than another, there is no need to quantify those benefits to decide that the program is preferred. The assumption (or the wish) that there are large amounts of waste in the health care system makes it possible to avoid confronting programs that do some good at high cost; it is only in this case that we really need to quantify how much good is done.

One guess is that we are fast moving toward the recognition of true shortage, but that it will be a bitter pill for policymakers to swallow. An integral part of this debate is the view about equity that becomes acceptable. If higher than average health benefits for those willing to pay for them with their own money are regarded as unfair – unless all are able and willing to pay for similar benefits – then the welfare economics-based measure will not be acceptable. The United States generally seems to accept a minimum benefits view of equity, but other countries are alleged to take a view that spending one's own resources on more medical care for oneself or one's family is socially undesirable.

The other stimulus to cost–benefit analysis is the emergence of private insurance coverage in a managed care setting. Such managed care plans, by necessity, must decide which programs are worth the cost. They explicitly eschew letting resource allocation decisions depend solely on agreement between physician and patient. But the measure of benefit a managed care plan must confront is essentially and intrinsically monetary. Especially for programs or products such as drugs that sometimes do some good but at high cost, the plan must ask whether the benefit from the program can be collected in the form of higher premiums. Cost–benefit analysis, in a very literal sense, will tell the HMO's marketing manager whether this is so – although if he or she had commissioned a conjoint analysis from a marketing consultant, much of the same information would have been obtained, salted with a different jargon. In any case, the fact that markets in competitive health plans ultimately return market choice to medical care settings means that they will return a concern for the money value of benefits as well.

When is cost–effectiveness analysis more appropriate than cost–benefit analysis? The simple answer to this question is that cost–effectiveness analysis is more appropriate when the decision maker wants to value health outcomes relative to each other and to other things people value in a way different from the way people value them. European countries who take the absolute view of equity and decision makers who want to be paternalistic will therefore not accept the willingness-to-pay approach.

There is, however, a nonpaternalistic explanation for what governments seem to prefer. Overall, social welfare is maximized in all cases by following the cost–benefit rule. As already noted, "benefit" surely includes the willingness to pay of direct beneficiaries of health programs, but it also includes the altruistic value others in the community place on health benefits received by a particular person. It would be useful to conduct empirical studies of taxpayer willingness to pay for such benefits, but the ultimate "market" in which such public good preferences are decided must be the political process.

What, then, is a reasonable way to pose the question of political or social evaluation? The best way may be to define those values in terms of social or community willingness to pay per QALY. For this to be true, the following would be required of any proposed QALY measure:

1. It captures all the aspects of health program outcomes that matter to taxpayers.
2. The relative weights attached to aspects of the quality of life reflect the weights that concern altruistic taxpayers.
3. Taxpayers should be concerned with the simple sum of QALYs added by a program.

If a program satisfies these conditions, the social value of any program can be derived by multiplying the number of QALYs produced by a program by the taxpayer value per QALY.

If this social value is large and the value of the willingness to pay of the beneficiaries of the program is small, then it may be appropriate to use the cost–effectiveness measure because the direct user's willingness to pay has little to do with the final decision, since it is swamped by the political willingness to pay. In contrast, for those programs that primarily benefit persons who are not objects of altruistic concern at the margin, it will be crucial to obtain direct user willingness-to-pay measures. The reason is that imprecision in measurement of willingness to pay may result in forgoing a program that beneficiaries value more than the program's cost.

It is plausible to suppose that altruistic concern is greatest for low-income people but may be minimal, at the margin, for people who are middle income or above facing relatively small medical costs. Cost–effectiveness analysis plus an accepted cutoff value would therefore give approximately the right answer for programs whose beneficiaries are primarily low-income people. In contrast, programs that benefit the middle class will need cost–benefit analysis. Roughly speaking, cost–effectiveness analysis is most suited for Medicaid, and cost–benefit analysis should be used for private insurance or Medicare for middle-income elderly.

The other set of circumstances in which cost–effectiveness analysis may be preferred, even for nonpoor people, is when people really do have approximately the same tastes, preferences, and incomes. Middle-income Americans caricature Scandinavians in this way. Perhaps the affection policymakers appear to have had for QALY-based cost–effectiveness analysis suggests that the caricature has some applicability for the United States. In general, however, for heterogeneous countries such as the United States, the cost–benefit approach will be more appropriate.

CHAPTER 7

Discounting health effects
for medical decisions

W. Kip Viscusi

> The set of virtually unanswerable questions includes the discount rate used for future
> health status.
>
> Lester Lave, *The Strategy of Social Regulation*

In any decision-making context in which effects of decisions are generated over time, it is necessary to establish some relative weight on deferred outcomes as opposed to immediate impacts. The task of converting future effects into present dollars by discounting them at some rate of interest is not a process unique to medical decision making. Indeed, all economic decisions in which resource allocations involve an intertemporal element entail some weighting of the effects at different points in time. The main economic question is what weight impacts should have at different times. In particular, how much more highly should current, as opposed to future, impacts be weighted?

Intertemporal aspects are inherent in the medical decision making context as well.[1] The entire notion of investment in human health implies some concern with future well-being. Although strategies for treating headaches and the common cold involve remedies with imminent payoffs, most major medical decisions involve a long-run element (see, among others, Edelson, Tosteson, and Sax 1990; Weinstein and Stason 1977). The communicable nature of AIDS, for example, means potential future beneficiaries. Pharmaceutical products, such as those for treating hypertension and cancer, have long-run effects on future earnings and individual health that require some discounting process (Shibley et al. 1990; Kawachi and Malcolm 1991). Choice of diet, exercise patterns, and smoking behavior clearly have long-run effects on physical well being. Ailments such as heart disease and cancer are often the result of a long period of individual decisions. Some of these effects are cumulative, and others occur with a lag.

Intertemporal elements also are intrinsically involved in almost all major surgical decisions. Patients contemplating back surgery must decide whether relief of immediate pain warrants back surgery. An operation offers the promise of improved health in the long run but at the cost of increased risk of complications at the time of surgery. Thousands of back patients annually must confront the decision to undergo back surgery and make some trade-off involving expected future health effects, current costs, and potentially substantial losses associated with immediate surgery.

Intertemporal aspects are also an inherent part of societal decisions. In the case of the drug Taxol, the U.S. government had to trade off the present benefits of saving lives against long-run environmental consequences of destroying the Pacific yew trees used to make the drug (Box 7.1). To what extent, then, should the government allocate health sector resources to promote the welfare of the citizens presently alive as opposed to future generations? Future generations may be more affluent and value health more than those now alive, but transferring resources to them without some means of compensating those now alive would be regressive. Moreover, because good health is an economic good, it may be more desirable to confer good health status and other in-kind transfers, such as a clean environment, than simply to raise future welfare levels.

Substantial pressures are often brought upon the medical research establishment because of the temporal dimension of research breakthroughs. The AIDS lobby has exerted a strong influence on AIDS research because a large identifiable population who might benefit immediately from research breakthroughs will not survive to benefit later. Since this research has highly uncertain prospects, and since time may be an important part of the research process (allowing for dissemination of early research results, etc.), the degree to which this research should be accelerated is not clear.

Because of the central role of research and development in the medical industry, companies involved in producing products related to medical decisions necessarily must place weights on outcomes over a period of time. The classic case in which a substantial research effort is expended is that of the pharmaceutical industry, where companies invest years in research and supervised testing of drugs before bringing them to market.

If companies were only concerned with immediate rewards and acted, in effect, as if the rate of interest used to discount future benefits were infinite, then they would never undertake research involving any lag time. The only concern would be how to achieve the greatest possible profit from products currently on the market. At the other extreme, if companies acted as if they had a zero rate of interest, then effects far into the future would receive the same weight as current profits. Considering the greater affluence and larger market

Box 7.1 Intertemporal trade-offs: the case of Taxol

A classic example of the intertemporal choice trade-off arose in 1991 with respect to the drug Taxol. The 1992 Food and Drug Administration (FDA) approval of this drug for use in treatment of cancer of the ovary, breast, and lungs has heightened the controversy. Using the bark from the Pacific yew tree, scientists were able to develop a drug that appeared to be effective in treating several kinds of cancer, such as breast cancer. The main problem is that obtaining the bark involves destroying 100-year-old trees, which cannot be readily replaced, at least in the near term. To produce enough Taxol to treat a single cancer patient requires the bark of as many as six trees of diameter of at least ten inches.

From a societal standpoint, a question arose as to how fast the trees should be chopped down for use in production of this drug. Exploitation of the bark now offered the promise of immediate rewards, but a slower depletion of the stock of Pacific yew trees would enable scientists to better understand the effects of the drug and perhaps perfect it so that more lives would be saved in the future. Should we deplete the stock of trees now or do so over time, and at what rate?

This decision was complicated even further by the prospect of developing synthetic substitutes for the drug that, in the long run, might make it unnecessary to cut down the trees. Moreover, environmentalists raised the issue of trade-offs other than those involving health. Society was also sacrificing a scarce resource, Pacific yew trees, so that it could promote individual health. The ability to use hybrid yews cultivated by Weyerhaeuser eases these environmental concerns but does not eliminate them.

The trees soon had their advocates. A group known as the Native Yew Conservation Council formed a lobby to protect them. Rather than fending off lumberjacks eager to make boards, these environmentalists sought to preserve trees that were being used to save lives. The stakes had escalated enormously, particularly considering that the tree involved is one that few Americans knew even existed.

Almost all of the issues involved in this policy debate have a strong intertemporal aspect. Preservation of natural resources necessarily entails that weight be given to the effects on future generations, and the assessment of the merits of using the bark from the Pacific yew tree for medical purposes hinges on one's assessment of the likely developments with respect to the use of this bark as well as the development of substitute drugs. Unless one is willing to place weights on the effects that occur at different points in time, one cannot even begin to think about such decisions, much less make them. The FDA ultimately decided to save lives rather than trees, but the development of semisynthetic Taxol from the wild yew trees promises to ease the long-term harvesting of the Pacific yew.

of future generations, companies would have little incentive to develop pharmaceutical products for those now alive. Their efforts would shift to likely consumers of their products in the distant future.

In practice, pharmaceutical companies have not gone to either extreme. The evidence suggests that in their research and development decision-making process, pharmaceutical companies use a real rate of interest of 9 percent in converting future effects into present value.[2] This is not, however, a riskless rate of return, since it embodies a return for some of the uncertainty in pharmaceutical research. This rate will consequently exceed the rate of discount that should be used for discounting health effects. Pharmaceutical companies have undertaken an appropriate response to the wishes of the current stockholders. The same kinds of intertemporal concerns that stockholders evidence in their other economic decisions will be reflected in their stock purchases as well.

This chapter focuses primarily on why one should choose to discount in the health context, and what discount rate one should use. From an economic standpoint, raising this question may be belaboring the obvious. However, government policy frequently prevails in this arena, by no means recognizing the need for universal discounting. In assessing the merits of its health-enhancing regulations, the U.S. Environmental Protection Agency (EPA) frequently assumes that deferred effects, such as reduced cases of cancer resulting from diminished asbestos exposure, need not be discounted. This chapter will be concerned not only with the need to discount but how one should approach discounting in the context of medical decision making.

The next section provides an overview of the rationale for discounting in medical contexts. Why do we discount in the health area, not simply for costs but also for nonfinancial effects? The third section motivates the rationale for discounting even further by indicating some of the problems that can arise by failing to discount. The fourth section explores analytically some of the ramifications of discounting for optimal experimentation strategies with respect to new drugs. The fifth section presents the multiperiod choice problem that involves discounting health effects influencing mortality and it summarizes the existing evidence on the magnitude of these discount rates. The sixth section concludes the chapter.

The rationale for discounting

Health as an investment

Discounting deferred impacts is an essential concern in almost any context where there is investment activity. The basic task is to convert future effects into terms that can be compared with present impacts. Using an interest rate of r, the value of \$1 received n years from now is $1/(1 + r)^n$.

Present-value calculation used in financial contexts can be applied to other contexts as well. For example, a standard practice in policy analysis is to discount both the benefits and the costs using such a discount rate. At the present time, the U.S. Office of Management and Budget (OMB) requires that all federal agencies evaluate government regulations using a real (i.e., net of inflation) discount rate of 10 percent, although agencies are free to show the present value of their policies using other discount rates as well.

To abstract from the role of inflation, all the discount rates referred to in this chapter will be in real terms.[3] One rationale for discounting future dollar amounts is that the purchasing power of this money will be less in the future than it is today because of inflation. However, one can account for the role of inflation directly in the assessment of benefits and costs. This approach is generally preferable, because there is no reason to believe that inflation rate patterns over time will differ from those of interest rates. Inflation rates for medical care, for example, have been much higher than those for the economy as a whole, with 6–9 percent inflation for the past decade. One would want to incorporate the effect of such inflation directly into any analysis, rather than assuming that the same discount rate including inflation will be pertinent in medical contexts as in other situations.

Even in an inflation-free world, there is a preference for having resources now rather than later. Money can be invested and earn a rate of interest. This real rate of interest available to investors establishes the opportunity cost of capital. In addition, economists such as Marglin (1967) have suggested that an important factor is the social rate of time preference. Capital market interest rates may not be a perfect guide, because these markets are not perfect. Society's collective interests in transferring resources across generations may not be fully expressed in private actions, whereas social decision making may yield quite different results. For example, if society wished collectively to transfer certain kinds of resources to the future in greater measure than is reflected in private decisions, then private levels of savings would be too low and observed interest rates too high. A lower rate of interest could be used to reflect this social rate of time preference in situations in which there was a desire to foster a greater shifting of resources to the future than is provided by private market forces.

Although there is a substantial literature on the selection of the rate of discount, the choice of the discount rate continues to be a matter of substantial debate.[4] Most estimates of the current real risk-free rate of return to capital range from 1 to 3 percent. What is clear is that the rate of discount is not zero. Moreover, it appears to be substantially below the real rate of interest of 10 percent that the OMB requires for policy assessments.

In situations in which individuals advocate a substantial rate of time preference, one should also take into account the fact that these high rates of time preference may affect benefit values as well. In particular, the principal factor driving the real rate of interest is the rate of productivity in the economy. Higher rates of productivity in turn will raise per capita income. Since there is a positive income elasticity of demand for health, higher income levels imply higher valuations of health status.[5]

Estimates reported in Viscusi and Evans (1990) suggest that the income elasticity of the implicit value of job injuries is approximately 1.0. The value of job injuries is the value workers require to bear the risk of one statistical injury. Thus, if the annual wage premium for risk were $30 for an injury risk of 1/10,000, the value per statistical injury would be $30,000.

An income elasticity of 1.0 implies that the $30 compensation amount rises proportionally with one's income. If this value is applied to other valuations of health impacts as well, and if income grows at some percentage growth rate g and an implied interest rate of r, then the appropriate net rate of discount that is applicable is not $1/(1 + r)$. Rather, one should net out the growth and the benefit values so that the net rate of discount becomes $1/(1 + r - g)$. The underlying rationale for incorporating income growth in the discounting process is that the value of income Y after n years of growth is $Y(1 + g)^n$. When brought to present value, this amount is $Y(1 + g)^n/(1 + r)^n$, which is approximately $Y/(1 + r - g)^n$. In effect, one should reflect the effect of growth in income on unit benefit values in the analysis.

Although the cost–effectiveness literature for medical decisions has devoted far too little attention to the role of discounting, in other contexts economists have made discounting a central matter of concern. As one would expect, a substantial debate exists over the extent to which society should transfer resources to future generations. A higher discount rate reflects a greater present orientation and a low discount rate reflects a greater orientation toward future benefits and rewards.[6] One can expect continuing debate over the choice of the parameter that in effect drives the relative weight on present and future outcomes. However, it is important to recognize that whereas the debate over the magnitude of the discount rate is legitimate, the concept of discounting at a nonzero discount rate is not controversial.

What is being discounted

Although there may be debate over the correct rate that should be used, discounting costs and other dollar expenditures is straightforward. However, bigger problems arise in discounting health effects. For example, are we discounting statistical lives, years with different morbidity effects, or similar health effects? Quality-adjusted life years (QALYs) certainly should take into account the discounted value of the life years saved and not treat them symmetrically. When discounting such health effects, what is the rationale for using the same discount rate as that for monetary effects?

This controversy can be muted by establishing a financial bridge between the health effects and their financial counterparts. In particular, one can first convert these health effects into a monetary equivalent and then discount these valuations.

For example, consider mortality-reducing efforts. Although some medical contexts involve the likelihood of certain life and certain death, what is usually at risk is a statistical life rather than a certain life. The issue then becomes the dollar value of a statistical life (see Chap. 5 for further elaboration). Based on evidence using labor market data, the value of a statistical life to the workers at risk is in the range of $3–$7 million.[7] Workers who face an annual mortality risk of 1/10,000 receive extra wage compensation for risk ranging from $300 to $700.

The value of a statistical life reflects individual attitudes toward life extension. Individuals should not be expected to have the same attitudes toward life and death any more than they should be expected to have the same valuations of standard economic commodities, such as food and housing. Some of these differences are systematic. More-affluent individuals generally place a higher value on a statistical life.[8]

In social decision contexts concerning life and death, it is useful to assume that what is being discounted is the implicit value of the statistical lives that will be saved in different years. The discount rate is applied to a monetary willingness-to-pay figure rather than to a number-of-lives-saved amount. We continue to discount money, as in the case of costs, and there is no need to discount health effects per se.

More generally, what is being discounted is the utility stream associated with certain health effects rather than the health effects themselves. It is no more controversial to discount utility streams in which health status is an argument of the utility function than it is to discount utility streams more generally. The fundamental source of all discounting stems from an economic model in which an individual maximizes the present value of a stream of utility over time, subject to an intertemporal budget constraint.

Health as a commodity

Although one can convert health into willingness-to-pay amounts, as well as subsume it within utility functions, health does differ from money in a number of ways. Most important, one cannot trade health either across time or across individuals. I am limited in terms of how I can exchange my health. I can purchase medical care and other inputs that may have a probabilistic effect on my health. But if my health were to deteriorate significantly, it might be difficult to restore it. Many health outcomes are irreversible in character.

This irreversibility also makes it difficult to trade in health status across time. If we value our health at forty-five but do not at twenty-five, then we cannot simply shift health status across time in the same way that we would shift monetary resources. Deterioration of one's health at twenty-five may prevent one from reaching forty-five, or if one does live that long, health deterioration may have a permanent effect on one's well-being at that age.

Although these different aspects of health status do make it a very distinctive commodity, health nevertheless enters utility functions of individuals in much the same way as do other objects of choice.[9]

Present versus terminal value

Even if one is reluctant to discount health effects or the monetary values associated with health effects, the rationale for the discounting process is clear-cut.[10] Moreover, one can establish the validity of discounting even without converting deferred health effects into their present value by converting the immediate expenditure of costs into their terminal value. Thus, one can compare the terminal value of the health effects with the value of the costs after they are converted to their future value, taking into account the interest that can be earned (Box 7.2).

Social versus private rates of discount

Selecting the appropriate discount rate depends in large part upon the decision maker. As a general rule, the appropriate discount rate for decisions is the intertemporal rate of trade-off that reflects the value to the decision maker of the effects being considered. Attitudes toward risk should be handled separately from discounting through appropriate valuation of the payoffs, since the premium one demands for risk may not have the same time pattern as would be imposed by incorporating it into the discount rate. In the case of private decisions, the appropriate reference point is the private decision maker's rate of trade-off and his or her relative valuation of the future effects. In the case of social decisions, one would want to use the social rate of time preference, although many economists have suggested that private opportunity cost of capital provides the most reliable guideline for this social rate of discount.

As a practical matter, these discounting decisions should be made either using the private rates of interest as the reference point or on a decentralized basis by an individual decision maker who will apply whatever discount rate he or she believes is appropriate. For example, government decisions to invest in different kinds of medical research will be governed by social rates of discount.

Private decision makers within pharmaceutical companies and other businesses will be influenced by market forces. Consequently, private decision makers' decisions will reflect a cognizance of prevailing private rates of interest

Box 7.2 Reluctance to discount health effects not a valid reason for not discounting

Consider the following example. Suppose that in year 10 we will save two statistical lives through the introduction of a new drug. The cost of doing so is an expenditure in year 0 of $8 million. Let V be the value of life in year 10. Under what circumstances will the benefits of introducing the new drug exceed the costs? First, instead of converting the benefit values into their current amount, let us assess the attractiveness of this policy ten years from now. The benefit of saving two statistical lives in year 10 will be $2V$. The costs associated with this policy in year 10 will be $8 million plus the accumulated interest that we would have been able to earn over the ten-year period had we invested it. Thus, the pertinent cost figure in terms of its terminal value is $8(1 + r)^{10}$. In this situation, one will conclude that the benefits of introducing the drug will exceed the costs provided that

$$2V > 8(1 + r)^{10}.$$

Note that the health effects are never discounted.

Suppose that instead of converting the amounts into the terminal values we assess their present value. The present value of the $8 million cost allocation is simply $8 million. The present value of the lifesaving effects with a ten-year delay is $2V/(1 + r)^{10}$. We will conclude that the benefits of introducing the drug exceed the costs, based on a present value calculation, provided that

$$2V/(1 + r)^{10} > 8.$$

Straightforward rearrangement of terms shows that the terminal value requirement and the present value requirement are mathematically equivalent. One can achieve the same results as would occur under a present value calculation in which health effects are discounted by converting the monetary expenditures into their terminal value.

Although this calculation becomes more complicated in situations with multiple health effects in different time periods, the underlying economic rationale is the same. Shifting the reference point in this manner does not alter the relative attractiveness of the policies. The real issue is not whether health effects will be discounted. The fundamental question is whether one will appropriately recognize that economic effects at various points in time should be weighted differently to reflect the opportunity cost of capital.

and the private cost of capital. Private decision makers also will be affected by intertemporal resource constraints. Because of capital market imperfections, the market borrowing and lending rates may not be identical. Moreover, the private rate of interest may not always be the same as the social rate of discount. These differences are not irrational. They simply reflect the fact that opportunities may vary across individuals for transferring resources across time, and these differences in opportunities may be manifested in the rates of time preference that are applied.

Problems with the failure to discount

Notwithstanding the compelling economic rationales for discounting, discounting in health contexts remains controversial.[11] In some cases, the failure to discount is an oversight. In others, the lack of any discounting of future effects reflects a conscious decision to treat all health effects symmetrically across time. For example, in the controversial case of the EPA's asbestos regulation, the effects of the regulation on reducing cancer cases occurred with a substantial lag of two decades or more. A required discount rate of 10 percent implies that a dollar in benefits received in twenty years has a present value of only fifteen cents. The long time lag, coupled with such a high rate of discount, greatly depresses the attractiveness of this regulatory proposal. Rather than seeking a more rational discount rate, such as 2 percent, which would have led the present value of $1 in twenty years to be sixty-seven cents, the EPA objected more generally to the discounting process.

Although discounting at a zero rate frequently makes health investments appear more attractive, this is often misleading, as examples in the following section indicate.

Policy deferral

Suppose that we have a situation in which there are two policy options. Policy A costs $1 million and will save ten lives next year. Policy B also costs $1 million but will not begin until next year and will save ten lives two years from now. In a world without discounting of health effects, each of these policies will save ten lives and the fact that one policy saves ten lives one year from now and the other saves ten lives two years from now is a matter of indifference. Although the $1 million monetary cost of the policies is identical, Policy B will always be more attractive from a financial standpoint, since at a 5 percent rate of interest an investment of approximately $950,000 will yield $1 million a year from now. A current outlay of $950,000 will generate the saving of ten lives in two years, whereas a current outlay of $1 million is required to generate a saving of ten lives next year. The current allocations required to save ten lives next year will be higher than those for saving ten lives the following year. When policies that save the same number of lives at different time periods are available and costs do not change over time, it will always be desirable to defer these policies when health effects are not discounted.

The role of affluence

Over time, society has become richer. Because of the positive income elasticity of the valuation of health status, this increase in income over time will increase the value placed on health outcomes. Recognition of this increased valuation over time when assessing Policy A and Policy B will simply enhance the desire to defer expenditures and to focus on efforts like Policy B. The farther in the future the lives are saved, the more highly these lives will be valued, since future generations will be more affluent. Wholly apart from the fact that Policy B will entail lower cost allocations than Policy A, there will be an advantage to deferral because the health effects generated by the policy will be more highly valued if they are generated farther into the future than if they are generated today.

Although the impetus in a zero discount rate world to defer policies will be quite strong, it is questionable whether this will be advocated as a rational policy. Clearly, the transfer of some resources to future generations is desirable. For example, there is some societal value to decreasing genetic damage and decreasing the rate of communicable diseases that will affect future health status. However, our generosity toward the future does have limits, as the public's resistance to incurring an extra nickel per gallon gas tax to promote energy conservation has demonstrated. Most public demand for pharmaceutical research is for products related to ailments that affect those now alive or that can potentially affect the current population. This emphasis is true of government-sponsored research as well.

If future generations will be more affluent and live longer, one would ideally like these more affluent future generations to compensate their poorer counterparts who must undertake actions now to protect the future. Unfortunately, such transactions are not feasible. Moreover, if intergenerational markets like this did exist, the prevailing rate of interest for such intertemporal rates of transfer would not be zero. Weighting the present value of $1 in health effects equally with $1 in health effects a century from now will lead to a substantial income redistribution to the more affluent future generations. It is doubtful that once the full implications of such a policy were understood, any of the advocates of the zero discounting of future health effects would pursue it.

Technological change

An analogous influence arises within the context of technological change. Suppose that Policy C cost $1 million in 1993 and will save ten lives in 1994.

This policy may appear attractive when viewed in isolation. However, other potentially more attractive alternatives may emerge in the future. Medical technologies, pharmaceutical products, and other mechanisms for enhancing individual health have become increasingly effective in enhancing mortality and reducing morbidities and will continue to do so.

Suppose that Policy D takes advantage of a modest technological improvement in how this $1 million could be spent so that an allocation of $1 million in 1993 would lead to the saving of eleven lives in 2094. In a situation in which there is no discounting, Policy D will be preferable to Policy C.

Current resources can be parlayed into substantial future gains if we simply invest the money and then wait for the benefits of technological change to accrue. Spending money to save lives at the current time simply makes no sense whatsoever in a world in which the value of health effects is not discounted. More productive means for allocating medical resources will make it desirable to shift resource expenditures from the present to the future, where greater dividends will be reaped.

This is one of the trade-offs embodied in the Taxol example already mentioned. Using the Pacific yew tree bark now may save lives next year, but if we defer use of the bark until the properties of Taxol are better understood, then we may be able to save more lives utilizing these trees in the future than if we deplete this resource now.

The permanent cost slam dunk

One of the most fundamental problems arising from a failure to discount is that it places one in a situation in which one would never accept a risk of permanent harm in return for present gains. Suppose that society could defer by a decade all deaths that would take place in the world this year for an expenditure of $1 per year forever. Every person who would have died this year will have an extra ten years added to their lives. In a situation in which there is no discounting, one would never undertake such an effort, because an infinite $1 expenditure stream would impose an infinite loss that would dominate any finite benefits associated with the current lifesaving gains.

Discounting and medical decisions under uncertainty

The classic problem surrounding uncertain medical decisions involving a sequence of trials has come to be known as the two-armed bandit problem. Consider a situation in which a sequence of trials involves two different drugs. Drug A offers a probability p of leading to a successful outcome in each period. The value of p is, however, uncertain, since the properties of this drug are not yet known. In contrast, drug B offers a known probability q of success with each trial that is known with precision. If a patient is engaged in a sequence of trials, what is the optimal selection of drugs in each period? If all we are concerned with is the patient's own welfare and not how this experimentation will affect our ability to treat other patients, how should we proceed? Is drug B always superior to drug A; is $q > p$?

What drives this particular class of problems is its multiperiod aspect. If one were only concerned with a single period choice problem, the only issue would be whether or not p was greater than q. However, because of the potential gains from experimentation, the benefits of which are necessarily deferred, the problem assumes an intertemporal nature. Discounting consequently plays a fundamental role, since the discount rate determines the weight that will be placed on the gains from experimentation and how much one can learn about the properties of the drug with uncertain effects.

This section explores different models of testing drugs, focusing on two different classes of models. The first class consists of those in which there are lotteries on life and death. In this model, success means that the patient survives, and failure means that the patient dies. In such a situation, adverse experimental outcomes with a drug that has unfavorable properties will have dire consequences. In the second class of models, which is more akin to the classic two-armed bandit model structure, continued experimentation after an adverse outcome can occur. To keep the models amenable to analysis and to obtain closed form solutions, this discussion will focus on two-period models. Within the context of two periods, one can analyze the role of learning and the potential gains from experimentation, while at the same time not overly complicating the model in a manner that would make it unwieldy.

Experimentation with lotteries on life and death

A cancer patient might be given a drug with known properties or a drug with uncertain properties. The probability that the patient will die in the initial period is higher for the unknown drug. Which drug should the patient pick? This class of experimentation models can be solved, yielding some potentially surprising conclusions.

Consider a situation of experimentation in which two outcomes are possible in each period. The first outcome is that the patient survives, which we will assume has a payoff of 1. Alternatively, the patient may die, which has a payoff of 0. For von Neumann and Morgenstern utility functions, one can establish a metric of this type with no loss of generalizability.[12] In the second period, should the patient survive, the initial lottery is repeated, with a payoff structure that is the same as before. Rewards received in period 2 must be discounted to put them on the same basis as the expected payoffs in period 1. For purposes of this calculation, it is assumed that the patient uses a discount factor β, equal to $1/(1 + r)$, where r is the rate of interest.

Trials with the uncertain drug A offer an initial probability of success of p.

However, if the patient survives the trial in period 1, then after a Bayesian updating process, the assessed probability of success in the second period becomes $p^* > p$. The key element of structure of the problem is that it terminates after an unfavorable outcome in the first period so that there is no need to take into consideration the downward revision of the probability following an unfavorable outcome.

Uncertain drug A offers an expected utility EU_A over the two periods given by

$$EU_A = p + pp^*\beta, \tag{7.1}$$

and drug B, which has known properties, offers the discounted expected rewards given by

$$EU_B = q + q^2\beta, \tag{7.2}$$

Because of the learning process and the influence of the upward revision of p in equation (7.1) but with no effect of a downward revision following an unfavorable trial, experimentation with an uncertain drug A will generally be preferable to selection of a drug B whose properties are more precisely understood and that offers an expected immediate probability of success of q. Viewed somewhat differently, the uncertain drug A offers the prospect of long-term survival. If the drug proves to have a favorable effect, then the patient can continue with it, with an expected probability of continued success in excess of the initial value p.

The key concern here is the effect of the discount factor β on the relative attractiveness of experimentation. Clearly, if the value of β is zero or the interest rate is infinite, one will be concerned only with the immediate payoffs in the first period so that the decision will turn solely on whether or not p is in excess of q. For finite values of β, the value of experimentation assumes a critical role. One measure of the effect of β on the relative attractiveness of experimentation is to assess the effect of β on $EU_A - EU_B$, yielding the following equation:

$$EU_A - EU_B = p(p^*)(1 + \beta) + p(1 - p^*) - q^2(1 + \beta) - q(1 - q)$$
$$= \beta(pp^* - q^2) + p - q. \tag{7.3}$$

Hence,

$$pp^* - q^2 \leq 0 \quad \text{implies} \quad p < q. \tag{7.4}$$

In that case, differentiating with respect to β to find the effect of the discount factor on the value of the experiment, one obtains

$$\frac{\partial V}{\partial \beta} = pp^* - q^2. \tag{7.5}$$

Increasing β raises the relative attractiveness of experimentation. This result is true even if the decision maker has biased risk perceptions, as shown in this chapter's Appendix.

Experimentation with nonfatal outcomes: case 1

In situations in which the lotteries facing the patient do not involve life and death, there is a chance of survival after an unfavorable trial in the first period that has a payoff of 0. Two possible situations can prevail. First, it may be optimal to continue experimentation with the uncertain drug after an unfavorable outcome in the first period. This would be the case if the drug's properties are such that it offers an expected probability of success in excess of q even after an adverse outcome on the first trial. Alternatively, it may be desirable to switch to drug B following an adverse outcome with drug A if the assessed probability of success with drug A is lowered sufficiently by an adverse trial in the first period. In this section, I will consider the strategy X, in which the patient switches to drug B after an unfavorable trial with drug A in the first period. I will then address the situation in which there is no drug switching.

Under this scenario, the individual begins experimentation with drug A in the first period and either switches to drug B after an adverse trial in the first period or continues with drug A after a successful trial in the first period. Assuming a value of failure of 0, this leads to a discounted expected utility for strategy X of

$$EU_X = p + (1 - p)q\beta + pp^*\beta. \tag{7.6}$$

The discounted expected utility associated with drug B is simply given by

$$EU_B = q + q\beta. \tag{7.7}$$

It will never be optimal to switch from drug B to drug A once started on drug B, since the gains from experimentation are necessarily deferred and the attractiveness of drug B never decreases over time.

The main issue of interest is the relative attractiveness of strategy X as compared with taking drug B in the first trial and this value is given by the difference between EU_X and EU_B, or

$$V = (p - q) + \beta p(p^* - q). \tag{7.8}$$

Again, if $p^* \leq q$, then $p < p^* \leq q$; strategy X can be optimal only if $p^* > q$.

Differentiating with respect to the discount factor β to determine the effect of discounting, one finds that

$$\frac{\partial V}{\partial \beta} = p(p^* - q) > 0. \tag{7.9}$$

Increasing the discount factor β will increase the value of experimentation.

Experimentation with nonfatal outcomes: case 2

If drug A offers a sufficiently high probability that even after an unfavorable trial in the initial period, the assessed probability of success exceeds that associated with drug B, then it will always be optimal to utilize drug A. Thus, in this situation, the discounted expected utility for drug A is given by

$$EU_A = p + p\beta, \tag{7.10}$$

and the discounted expected utility for drug B is given by

$$EU_B = q + q\beta, \tag{7.11}$$

The difference in the discounted expected utility between the two drugs is

$$V = (p - q)(1 + \beta). \tag{7.12}$$

Increasing the value of the discount factor β will necessarily boost the value of experimentation, since

$$\frac{\partial V}{\partial \beta} = p - q > 0. \tag{7.13}$$

Modeling and estimating rates of discount for health

One's immediate inclination in framing policy analyses of long-term health decisions is simply to employ financial rates of discount within the context of health decisions. Although this approach may be correct, a useful exercise is to determine whether or not implicit discount rates for health are in fact comparable to the implicit rates of discount used in financial contexts.

In a series of papers, Michael J. Moore and I have used labor market data in which workers are making long-term decisions with respect to their well-being, which is influenced by the fatality risks they face on the job (Moore and Viscusi 1988, 1990a; Viscusi and Moore 1989). Based on the wages workers receive to bear greater fatality risks, one can impute the rate of discount that they display with respect to the years of life that are at risk (Box 7.3).

The main implication of three quite different empirical models estimated using a variety of econometric assumptions is that the implicit rate of discount for life is in the range of 1.0 to 14.2 percent. Although double-digit discount rates are clearly too high, the confidence intervals for these estimates are sufficiently broad that prevailing market rates of interest are generally included within them. Thus, generally one cannot reject the hypothesis that the implicit rate of discount that individuals place on years of life equals prevailing financial rates of return. Given such evidence, it would seem that the presumption should be that the same rates of discount used to discount financial impacts should be applied within the context of medical decision making as well.

Box 7.3 Deriving implicit rates of discount from wage data

The most simplistic approach is to assess the discounted expected years of life that will be gained or lost. Within the context of the labor market models that have been used to estimate risk–dollar trade-offs, one could consequently estimate the wage premiums workers receive for the expected life years lost because of a job.

To calculate this amount, let R be the remaining years of life, r be the rate of interest, and p the annual probability of death. The expected years of life lost based on working on a risky job for one year is given by

$$\frac{1}{r}(1 - e^{-rR})p. \tag{7.14}$$

This approach neglects the fact that if one were to repeat this job choice over time, then the lifetime at risk would not be R, but would be something less than R which would accommodate the future fatality risks the worker faces.

Using this simple framework, if one includes the discounted expected years-of-life-lost term in a wage equation and estimates the implicit rate of discount that workers display for years of life, one obtains an estimate of the rate of discount that the workers have of between 9.6 and 12.2 percent, depending on the particular empirical specification used.

A more detailed approach that reflects the fact that a repetition of risky job choices affects one's current, as well as future, well-being is to formulate a Markov decision model to capture this choice process. In particular, suppose that the worker must select a fatality risk p in each period, where there is a probability p of death and a probability $1 - p$ of survival. The worker is paid a wage rate $w(p)$ for the risky job, from which he or she derives a utility $U[w(p)]$. For time-invariant probabilities and wages, the worker's choice problem takes the form

$$\max_{p} V = (1 - p)U[w(p)] = \beta(1 - p^2)U[w(p)]$$
$$+ \cdots + \beta^{t-1}(1 - p)^t U[w(p)] + \cdots \tag{7.15}$$

or

$$\max_{p} V = U[w(p)](1 - p)\sum_{t=1}^{\infty}[\beta(1 - p)]^{t-1}. \tag{7.16}$$

One can solve this optimization problem leading to a wage equation based on the structural decision problem facing the worker. This approach yields an implicit rate of discount of 10.7 percent (Viscusi and

Moore 1989). In addition, one could estimate variants of this model in which one places restrictions on the market opportunity locus based on estimated wage equations, makes different simplifying assumptions when going from the Markov decision model to the estimating equation, or adds a bequest term explicitly to the analysis. These variants of the model yield implicit rates of discount of 1.0 percent, 1.0 percent, and 14.2 percent, respectively (Moore and Viscusi 1990b).

A final variant of the fatality risk problem is to assume that instead of leading to a period-by-period risk of death, the fatality risk simply shortens the path of life one has. Some common descriptions of smoking, for example, suggest that each cigarette shortens your life by a certain number of minutes. In reality, the risk does not work in that fashion. The years of life lost may not simply come from the tail but instead may involve premature death at, for example, fifty years of age. Thus, the life-cycle approach has the virtue of simplicity, but it sacrifices realism to the extent that one could lose years of life in the interim that would not be reflected by simply shortening the path of life in response to the risks that are faced. The main advantage is that it leads to a simple functional form. In particular, if an individual has T years of life left that are a function of the fatality risk p on the job, the worker's objective is to select the job risk that will maximize

$$\max_{p} V = \int_{0}^{T(p)} U[w(p)]e^{-rt}dt. \tag{7.17}$$

Based on this approach, Moore and Viscusi (1990a) have derived estimates of the discount rate of between 1.6 and 2.0 percent.

The range involved in the estimates of the discount rates for health may appear to be substantial, but when compared to other discount rate estimates that have appeared in the literature, this range is actually quite tight. Consider, for example, the implicit rate of discount that individuals have revealed through their decisions to purchase household appliances. If one has a low rate of time preference, the value of the deferred energy savings associated with energy-efficient appliances will appear to be substantial when compared to the initial outlay associated with the energy-efficient appliances. Thus, one can use consumers' choice of the degree of energy efficiency and the associated price that they pay for their appliances to infer the implicit rate of discount that they have with respect to appliance-related financial savings.

Studies of these decisions have yielded perhaps surprising estimates of the implicit rate of discount. Hausman (1979) reports a series of estimates for refrigerator purchases, where these discount rates are close to 20 percent and, in some cases, much higher. Gately (1980) performed a similar study of appliance efficiency and found that the implicit rates of discount range from 45 to 300 percent. Thus, at least in this context, the estimates of the rates of discount are implausibly high. Indeed, if these estimates do in fact reflect actual behavior, they suggest that individuals may display a kind of temporal myopia with respect to energy-efficiency choices. In contrast, there appears to be no evidence of substantial temporal myopia with respect to fatality risk decisions stemming from job hazards.

The estimates based on worker decisions also appear to be in a more reasonable range than those based on survey evidence. Fuchs (1986) undertook an exploratory study of discount rates in health contexts and found, based on survey responses, that individuals often reported discount rates around 30 percent. If one actually encountered a medical decision-making context in which the patient indicated an implicit rate of discount of 30 percent, presumably the first task would be to ascertain whether the patient understood the particular choice that was being made. In particular, rather than accepting an extremely high discount rate at face value, one should determine whether the respondent understood the consequences of these intertemporal decisions for his or her own well-being.

Corporate executives appear to display discount rates in a much more reasonable range, since survey evidence suggests that their discount rates are on the order of 15 percent.[13] Moreover, as indicated, pharmaceutical companies display a rate of discount of 9 percent. These corporate rates may embody a premium for risk that should not be included when computing the discount rate, which should pertain to riskless decisions. In particular, attitudes toward risk should be addressed through proper valuation of the payoffs.

Conclusion

An examination of the intertemporal choices in the medical decision-making context suggests that discounting is important. Many health decisions involve a substantial investment component. The choices we make now, both in our daily lives and with respect to medical care decisions, have a long-term effect on our future welfare. Indeed, the irreversible nature of many health-related decisions ensures that discounting will remain a prominent concern.

Discounting of monetary effects is an essential and widely accepted procedure for reflecting the terms of trade for individual welfare across different periods of time. The discounting of health effects has been more problematic. A failure to discount health effects altogether by employing a zero rate of discount may appear to be more farsighted in terms of its emphasis on the future, but in practice this no-discounting approach may have the opposite result. In particular, it may lead one to defer decisions in a manner that will enhance the well-being of future generations rather than those now alive. Similarly, discount rates that are excessively high are not ideal.

Discount rates have a fundamental effect on the character of decisions in terms of their temporal orientation, particularly within the context of experimentation. Situations in which there is learning and acquisition of risk information, as in most sequential trials, are strongly affected by the rate of discount. In particular, higher rates of time preference imply a lower weight on future benefits and will reduce the gains from experimentation. Experimentation is similar to prevention in that it is a form of investment.

Because there are no markets for explicitly trading health status across time, the choice of the appropriate discount rate for health status has remained a substantial subject of debate. Estimates based on workers' job risk decisions with respect to fatality risks indicate that the implicit rate of discount individuals apply to welfare at different years in their lives is not significantly different from prevailing financial rates of return. Indeed, the estimates of the discount rates displayed in this context appear in many respects to be more reasonable than the implicit rates of time preference that analysts have found with respect to other individual decisions, such as appliance efficiency choices.

As a practical matter, many cost–effectiveness studies currently use a real rate of discount of 5 percent. Although this approach is not unreasonable, real rates of return of 3 percent, or even less, appear more in line with U.S. economic performance in the past decade. In most contexts, the medical decision will not be sensitive to reasonable variations in the discount rate. Sensitivity analyses using discount rates ranging from 1 percent to 7 percent would be of assistance in identifying the degree to which the discount rate estimate must be refined within that range.

There is no question that health is special as an economic commodity. Individual health status has many unique characteristics, not the least of which is its ability to derive welfare from any other expenditures we might make. Nevertheless, the appropriate way to recognize the special status of health is through appropriate benefit valuation of one's health status in different periods of time. One should not distort intertemporal rates of time preference in an effort to boost the intertemporal rate emphasis a particular policy might have on health.

Appendix: Experimentation contexts with biased risk perceptions

It is useful to contrast the properties of rational experimentation with the outcomes that would prevail if there were biased risk perceptions. This bias pertains to the situation in which the decision maker (possibly the physician, not the patient) has biased probabilistic beliefs. A large literature in psychology and economics has documented a variety of such biases, such as the tendency to overassess low probability risks and underassess large risks.

Consider the case where an unfavorable trial leads to the patient's death. For concreteness, assume that individuals' probabilistic beliefs can be characterized by a beta distribution, where γ corresponds to the precision of the individual's prior beliefs. In particular, the decision maker acts as if he or she has observed trials from a Bernoulli urn, of which a fraction p are successful and a fraction $1 - p$ are failures. With this formulation, the assessed probability p^* following a favorable trial of the drug in period 1 will equal $(\gamma p + 1)/(\gamma + 1)$. With a rational Bayesian formulation such as this, the probability that the decision maker will survive for both periods, which is the key component determining the value of the experiment in equation (7.3), is given by

$$pp^* = p\left(\frac{\gamma p + 1}{\gamma + 1} \right) = \frac{\gamma p^2 + p}{\gamma + 1}. \tag{7.18}$$

It is useful to contrast this probability of survival over both periods with the perceived probability given biased risk perceptions. Although individuals may act in a rational Bayesian fashion, a variety of studies have suggested that there are systematic biases in risk perceptions. In Viscusi (1989) I formulate a model that I call "prospective reference theory" in which individuals, in effect, act as if they have some underlying prior information regarding the decision context. Instead of treating the new information as if it had an implied probability p with an associated precision γ, they also act as if they have prior information that the probability is s with precision ξ.

This formulation is in many respects a linearized counterpart of Kahneman and Tversky's (1979) prospect theory model, in which the risk perceptions flatten out. The main difference is that the prospective reference theory formulation predicts a wide variety of forms of deviations from standard expected utility maximization. In particular, this model predicts the Allais Paradox, the overweighting of low-probability events, the existence of premiums for certain elimination of risks, and the representability heuristic. In short, a large class of the paradoxes that have been identified in the choice-under-uncertainty literature can be predicted using this quasi-Bayesian formulation. As a result, I will use it here as a reference point for assessing the impact of inadequacies in risk perceptions on experimental behavior.

More specifically, under a prospective reference theory model, individuals act as if the perceived probability $\pi(p)$ associated with any stated probability p is somewhat different in that it takes on the functional form

$$\pi(p) = \frac{\xi s + \gamma p}{\xi + \gamma} \tag{7.19}$$

and the assessed probability after a favorable trial in period 1 assumes the form

$$\pi(p^*) = \frac{\xi s + \gamma p + 1}{\xi + \gamma + 1} \,. \tag{7.20}$$

The perceived probability of survival over both periods is no longer given by equation (7.19). Instead, it is the product of the perceived probabilities, and it appears as

$$\pi(p)\pi(p^*) = \frac{\xi s + \gamma p}{\xi + \gamma} \, \frac{\xi s + \gamma p + 1}{\xi + \gamma + 1} \,. \tag{7.21}$$

The main issue from the standpoint of optimal experimentation, judged from the perspective of the risk perceptions of the decision maker, is whether the perceived probability of survival over both periods is greater given the biases in risk perceptions than when the probabilities are assessed as in the standard Bayesian learning case. In particular, is

$$\pi(p)\pi(p^*) >, <, \text{ or } = pp^*? \tag{7.22}$$

One can rewrite this condition substituting from equations (7.20) and (7.18) as follows:

$$\frac{\xi s + \gamma p}{\xi + \gamma} \, \frac{\xi s + \gamma p + 1}{\xi + \gamma + 1} >, <, \text{ or } = \frac{\gamma p^2 + p}{\gamma + 1} \,. \tag{7.23}$$

As can be seen by inspection, the effect of the biases in risk perceptions hinges on two sets of parameters. First, it matters whether the individuals act as if they have some prior information implying a chance of success s before being told that the associated chance of success with drug A is p. Higher values of s, which imply greater chances of success, will necessarily enhance the attractiveness of the experimental drug. The second key parameter is ξ. Even if the value of $s = p$, it is of consequence that individuals act as if they have more information about drug A than is simply dictated by the precision γ. In effect, this additional prior information tightens the probability assessments in a manner that will reduce the value of information and the informational content provided by a successful trial on the first experiment. Reducing this value in turn will decrease the importance of the deferred effects influenced by the discounting process.

The role of biased risk perceptions for the nonfatal outcome experimentation model case 1 is fairly similar to that for fatal outcomes. The condition that p^* $> q$ can be rewritten as

$$\frac{\xi s + \gamma p + 1}{\xi + \gamma + 1} > q \,. \tag{7.24}$$

The key issue here is whether this condition is more or less demanding and hinges on the value of p and the associated precision ξ. Increasing the value of p makes experimentation more attractive. The effect of increasing the precision of the reference probability p depends to some extent on the value of s that enters in equation (7.24). If the value of $s = p$, then the net effect is to make the probabilities tighter, thus reducing the potential gains to experimentation in terms of how much the experiment will alter the probabilistic beliefs.

From the standpoint of biased perceptions in the nonfatal outcome experimentation model case 2, what matters is not the effect on perceived probabilities following success but rather the assessed probability in the initial period. Using the prospective reference theory model, the assessed probability π of p is given by

$$\pi(p) = \frac{\xi s + \gamma p}{\xi + \gamma} . \tag{7.25}$$

As before, the main parameters of interest are ξ and s, and their influence follows the same patterns.

CHAPTER 8

Statistical issues in cost–effectiveness analyses

John Mullahy and Willard Manning

Most of the literature on cost–effectiveness, cost–benefit, and program evaluation has focused either on what should in principle be included in costs,
benefits, and effects of programs or on the empirical implementation for specific treatments and programs. The rest of this book discusses many of those
issues. In Chapter 2, Allan Detsky examined issues related to the evidence of
effectiveness for a treatment based on the nature of a study's design. Among
other issues, he discussed the relative merits of randomized controlled trials
(RCTs) and various observational study designs. In Chapter 4, David Dranove
examined issues of measuring economic or opportunity costs in cost–effectiveness studies. In this chapter, we will concentrate on a number of statistical
issues that arise in comparing alternative treatments. Part of our discussion
provides the rationale for a preference for randomized over observational
studies. The majority of our discussion, however, applies in differing degrees
to RCTs and observational studies.

Our basic concern is that the statistical modeling or analysis must mirror an
understanding about how the behavior came about *and* what process generated
the data, whether the data are observational or experimental. Observational
behavior and data, especially in clinical or claims databases, did not come about
at random. One has to understand the process that generated the treatment
choices by physicians, the care seeking and compliance of patients, and the data
reported to adequately understand whether the observed associations among the
treatment, costs, and outcomes are really causal or merely an artifact of the
correlation between the treatment and some other latent or unobservable causal
factor. Even in randomized studies, compliance, refusal, and attrition can raise
the same methodological issue: when is association equivalent to causality?

The central idea is summarized as follows. "True" effectiveness[1] and "true"

149

cost each have a systematic component and a random ("noise") component. The "cost–effectiveness ratio," therefore, consists of both systematic components and noise. The basic objective of statistical analysis in this regard is to obtain unbiased and/or consistent estimates of the central tendencies (mean, median) or some other parameters of the statistical distributions of effectiveness, of cost, and/or of the cost–effectiveness ratio. The key issue confronting analysts is whether the "experiment" – clinical, natural, or otherwise – that generates the data is sufficiently well structured that such parameters can indeed be estimated in an unbiased or consistent manner.

The concern for what generated the observed data and behavior involves three major areas:

1. To the extent that analysts rely on data from nonexperimental settings, for example, from prospective studies or retrospective analyses, the estimation of program/treatment parameters may be biased because of omitted factors confounded with the treatment variables. Individual patients and their providers do not make purely random choices. Those choices may reflect tastes, unobserved case mix, or other factors that have their own separate influences on outcomes and costs. This is a problem of omitted variables or selection bias.
2. Attempts to control for case mix differences are likely to be incomplete because of measurement error. If the case mix measure is confounded with treatment, then case mix adjustment will reduce but not eliminate the bias in estimated treatment effects.
3. When studies rely on patient medical records or claims data, many possible biases can arise. These data sets were created for nonresearch purposes and may not provide data of the level of detail, accuracy, and reliability attainable with prospective designs or other research methods.

Once consistent estimates have been obtained, the next issue is how much confidence can be placed in the estimates so obtained. Because the available data are based on one sample or, more generally, on a finite number of samples, the analyst must account for sampling variation in the parameter estimate(s). The cost–effectiveness ratios from observational data and randomized trials alike are based on estimates of cost and effectiveness. As a result, the estimated cost–effectiveness ratio is a point estimate, not a ratio of population parameters. The degree of sampling variation, that is, the estimated parameter's standard error, then offers guidance as to how much confidence should be placed in the ratio estimate so obtained.

Much of what follows focuses on problems encountered in observational studies. Although many of the best cost–effectiveness studies are based on RCTs, not all studies can share that design.[2] Some studies are based on natural experiments or rely on naturally occurring variations in treatment and choice. Even in cases where RCTs have been employed, the issues addressed here may differ in degree, rather than kind, due to unavoidable threats to the validity of the study when human subjects voluntarily participate. Such threats include refusal to participate, attrition, and compliance problems. In a real sense, an RCT falls between observational studies and Fisher's (1926) ideal of an experiment in agricultural settings. The RCT reduces, but may not completely eliminate, many of the biases found in observational studies.

Further, RCTs may suffer from limitations of their own: (a) they may not provide an economically feasible method for studying rare adverse reactions or side effects; (b) time frames may be too limited to ensure a full accounting of either benefits or costs; and (c) the sample sizes may be adequate for assessing efficacy but not for obtaining reasonably precise estimates of costs.[3] When adverse outcomes occur only rarely, use of observational data is unavoidable, as illustrated by the examples of pertussis and rubella vaccines in Box 8.1. In these instances, data from trials may be augmented by adverse reaction and cost data from nonexperimental sources, including expert panels. This raises the prospect that the denominator in the cost–effectiveness ratio (the assessment of efficacy) is unbiased by randomization but that the numerator (the cost) may not be because it is observational.

In this chapter, we first discuss what is meant by causality and effectiveness from a statistical point of view. We then examine why some research designs will generate biased estimates of program or treatment effects and why case mix adjustments are unlikely to eliminate the biases. We briefly explore how and when pre–post designs can address these concerns. Then we discuss the problems inherent in using administrative data. We conclude with a discussion of inferences using cost–effectiveness ratios.

To make all of these discussions much more concrete, most of what follows will be carried out in the context of the familiar linear regression model. Although this sacrifices some generality, many of the fundamental issues can be described quite simply with this model.[4]

Estimation issues

Objectives of statistical analyses

Applied statistical analysis has two major but related objectives. First, and perhaps most fundamental, is hypothesis testing. Clinical or social science suggests some refutable null hypothesis: data are gathered that can in principle be used to refute the null hypothesis; a statistical significance level (α-level) is

Box 8.1 Why observational data are sometimes unavoidable:
assessing adverse outcomes of pertussis and
rubella vaccines

Where adverse effects of treatments are suspected, it may not be economically feasible to rely on expensive clinical trials to detect rare adverse outcomes. The job here is often more that of the statistical detective who must piece together observational evidence about the suspected relationships between the treatment and the observed adverse outcomes. This is a difficult task in any event but is particularly so when the adverse outcomes occur only rarely. In a nutshell, one can perhaps readily gather population evidence on probabilities $Pr(E)$ (E = effect) and $Pr(C)$ (C = Cause). However, since

$$Pr(E) = Pr(E|C)\,Pr(C) + Pr(E|\text{not } C)[1 - Pr(C)],$$

and since evidence on $Pr(E|C)$ and $Pr(E|\text{not } C)$ is what is of interest, it may be difficult to shed light on such issues when both $Pr(E|C)$ and $Pr(E|\text{not } C)$ are quite small (i.e., the adverse outcomes are rare), especially since both may be nonzero. The fact that outside experimental settings C is likely to be self-selected makes matters all the more complicated, as we will discuss later. In attempting to determine whether pertussis and rubella vaccines might be causal factors for any of a set of plausible "adverse events," an Institute of Medicine (1991a) study had to deal with just such circumstances. Alluding to several themes that will be discussed at length in the remainder of the chapter, the IOM committee summarized the difficulties inherent in any such investigation:

> The adverse events under consideration . . . are, in most instances, rare in the exposed population. They are known to occur in the absence of vaccination, are clinically ill-defined, and are generally of unknown causation in the general population. The exposures – pertussis and rubella vaccines – are very widespread in the population, so that the absence of exposure may itself require an explanation in the interpretation of comparative studies. (Institute of Medicine 1991a, 1–2)

specified, and statistical tests are undertaken that either will or will not provide enough evidence against the null hypothesis to refute it in favor of some alternative hypothesis. The second related but distinct objective is measurement. Analysts are often interested in understanding the magnitude of some relationship among covariates/treatments, and statistical analysis can provide estimates of such relationships and the confidence in those estimates. Because estimates of magnitude are instrumental in testing hypotheses of interest, the two objectives are closely related.

Whether hypothesis testing or measurement is of greater concern, central in most statistical analyses is the issue of causation. Does some treatment or procedure cause some outcome to occur relative to what would have happened in the absence of that treatment? The relationship of causation to understanding something about the efficacy of the treatment or procedure is apparent.

Cost–effectiveness analysis is by its very nature concerned with both hypothesis testing and measurement. Consider, for instance, a clinical trial setting where the "effectiveness" of some procedure or treatment is fundamentally assessed by whether one can reject the null hypothesis that the treatment results on average in the same outcome as does the placebo (or other control), versus the alternative hypothesis that the outcomes of the treatment are on average better than those when a placebo is administered. In causal terms, does the treatment cause a better outcome to occur?

Rejecting such a null hypothesis does not by itself, however, inform one as to "how much better" the treatment is than the placebo. Because procedures and treatments are costly, knowledge of "how much better" is essential in inferring something about the cost–effectiveness of various alternative procedures or treatments. In such settings, it is useful to bear in mind that statistical significance does not necessarily imply that the magnitudes of the impact are economically or clinically significant.[5]

Although readers may be most familiar with discussions of effectiveness in clinical terms relating to the results or consequences of some drug treatment or medical procedure, the discussion here applies more broadly to effectiveness of both biomedical interventions (drugs, medical procedures) and public policy interventions (regulations and taxes). In clinical terminology, the concern is with understanding something about the effects of "treatments," but treatments should be thought of quite broadly.

Causality, effectiveness, efficacy, and treatment effects

In the RCT literature, Sommer and Zeger (1991) draw an important distinction between "effectiveness" and "efficacy," and in this context "efficacy" may be a more appropriate term than "effectiveness." "Efficacy" describes the outcomes of treatment in a strictly controlled randomized environment with full compliance on the part of subjects. In contrast, "effectiveness" (or "programmatic effectiveness") allows for the possibility of less than full compliance (also, see Chap. 2, this volume). Either way, the terminology itself suggests something about "effect," which in turn suggests something about causation (see Box 8.2).

Box 8.2 Defining efficacy in routine pediatric care

Wagner, Herdman, and Alberts (1989) have argued that there is scant empirical evidence to support claims for the efficacy of the American Academy of Pediatrics guidelines for well-child physician visits (those for immunizations and health supervision) that suggest thirteen visits through age six. These researchers find no solid empirical evidence to suggest that well children's health is improved as a result of the *additional* physician contacts beyond those visits in which immunizations are administered.

Lack of empirical evidence does not necessarily indicate that efficacy is in fact absent, and Wagner et al. indicate that a part of the problem is that efficacy studies with high power and validity are difficult to conduct in the pediatric care sphere. Moreover, they suggest that cost–effective delivery of well-child care may ultimately involve less traditional well-child care but more services for high-risk children. Without empirical evidence, however, the bottom-line question remains: "The 'logical' question, then, is not whether any well-child care visits should be provided, but *how many* visits should young children receive?" (Wagner and Herdman 1990).

Indeed, it can be argued that understanding cause and effect is at the core of much applied statistical analysis. Clinical trials have at their core the notion that the treatment or procedure being investigated causes some outcome to occur; structural models in econometrics are typically interpreted as causal models (see Hausman and Wise 1985); path analysis in sociology is inherently concerned with causal relationships.[6] Accordingly, it is of some importance to appreciate the characterizations and implications of causality in the context of applied statistical analysis.

Philosophers have debated for centuries what can and cannot be learned about causation from empirical observation.[7] Much of modern statistical analysis views the issue of cause and effect in the context of a model developed by Rubin (1974).[8] The heart of the statistical problem of inference is the inability to do empirically what we want to do theoretically. The theoretical concern is the difference between what would happen if everyone received treatment A versus treatment B, holding all other things constant. The empirical analysis requires the comparison of different populations (or of the same population at different times) under different treatment regimes. When does such a comparison provide an unbiased estimate/answer to the theoretical question? At the core of Rubin's model is a counterfactual argument that has at least two key implications. First, it provides a reasonable characterization of causation. Second, because of its counterfactual character, the model is inherently incapable of being applied directly to empirical data, regardless of whether the data have been obtained by randomized methods. Since the publication of Rubin's model, a central concern of analysts working with it has been the nature and stringency of the assumptions required in order to identify interesting parameters of the model, given that the model in its purest form is not identified because of its counterfactual nature.

A brief overview of the model and of some of the assumptions invoked in practice to identify and estimate it is useful at this juncture. For any given individual unit j at time t,[9] the model postulates a set of scalar response variables (such as health status or costs) $y_r(j, t)$, where r indexes the treatment regimes that are available to j at t, that is $r \in R = \{1, \ldots, S\}$.[10] By "treatment regime," we mean any intervention for dealing with the patient, whether it be diagnostic, management, or medical, surgical, or pharmaceutical care. At t, each individual j in the group being studied[11] will be in one and only one of the S available treatment regimes. To be concrete, it may be that $S = 2$ and r indexes whether the individual has received drug ($r = 1$) or placebo ($r = 2$), or it may be that, for $S > 2$, r indexes strength of dose.

The counterfactual character of the model is shown as follows. The variable $y_r(j, t)$ measures the response of j at t that would be observed if j received treatment r at t. However, of the S variables $y_r(j, t)$ that have been defined, only one (that corresponding to the treatment actually received by j at t) will actually be observed; the remaining $S - 1$ response variables will be latent (e.g., unobserved) variables, corresponding to the $S - 1$ counterfactual states of the world of what would have happened under the other treatment regimes had they occurred. It is central to the analysis that all S response variables are well defined even though $S - 1$ of them will be latent for j at t.

What does all this imply insofar as cause and effect are concerned? At this point, the analysis is simplified by assuming that there are only two possible treatment regimes, $r \in \{T, C\}$, where T denotes actual treatment with drug or procedure, and C denotes control, whether by placebo or other method.[12] It will be useful to define a variable $d = d(j, t) = 1$ if j receives treatment at t and $d(j, t) = 0$ if j is in the control group at t.

Following Holland (1986), the "causal effect" of the treatment on j at t is defined as

$$CE(j, t) = y_T(j, t) - y_C(j, t); \tag{8.1}$$

that is, the treatment causes the "effect" $y_T(j, t) - y_C(j, t)$ to occur. Ideally, one would like to know both $y_T(j, t)$ and $y_C(j, t)$. In light of the earlier discussion, using such information as collected for some representative sample would be an excellent way to learn something about the central tendency and other parameters of the statistical distribution of effectiveness. Alas, what Holland calls the "fundamental problem of causal inference" is that for j at t, either $y_T(j, t)$ or $y_C(j, t)$ is observed, but not both, because the patient can receive one and only one of the treatment regimens. As such, $CE(j, t)$ is not observable. As Holland (1986) notes, $CE(j, t)$ or properties thereof are typically estimated in practice by some form of averaging of the observed $y_r(j, t)$ over meaningfully defined subpopulations (subsamples). This strategy is based on the notion that it may be interesting for analysts to know the *average* causal effect at t,

$$\text{ACE}(t) = E[y_T(j, t) - y_C(j, t)], \tag{8.2}$$

where the expectations are taken with respect to some relevant probability distribution.[13]

Before discussing details of the methods and strategies that have been proposed for "estimating" $CE(j, t)$, $\text{ACE}(t)$, or certain parameters thereof, it is instructive to think a bit about the processes that generate the $y_r(j, t)$. The $y_r(j, t)$ can be thought of as arising from very general models that depend on $x_r(j, t)$ (vectors of observed exogenous [fixed] covariates that are thought to affect the $y_r(j, t)$); $\eta_r(j, t)$ (scalar random variables summarizing all unobserved determinants of $y_r(j, t)$); and $\rho_r(j)$ (vectors of unknown parameters that may vary over the population, i.e., over j).[14]

Given covariates that vary over j, a first question to consider is whether the analysis will proceed unconditionally or be conditional on the $x_r(j, t)$. As will be seen, in some instances (e.g., perfect randomization) this distinction is unimportant; in other applications, however, the distinction is crucial. In either event, it is useful to define a conditional-on-x analogue to the ACE as the conditional average causal effect for j at t, or what has come to be called (Manski 1990) a "treatment effect" or "average treatment effect":[15]

$$\text{TE}(z) = E(y_T|z) - E(y_C|z), \tag{8.3}$$

where the conditioning is made explicitly on some variables z that may or may not coincide with the x-vector specified in practice by the analyst.

Although it is sometimes possible to nonparametrically identify and estimate treatment effects of interest, most applied research is still basically parametrically oriented. And although many interesting applications of parametric treatment effects models involve structures that are nonlinear in the parameters, such as logit/probit models for qualitative outcomes and Poisson models for count outcomes, for present purposes it is useful to illustrate our main points in the context of linear regression models.[16] Except where noted, our results will generalize to other statistical models as well.

The linear model that will be used to frame most of our discussion is

$$y = d\delta + x\beta + dx\gamma + \varepsilon, \tag{8.4}$$

where the possibility of interaction between treatment and covariates is admitted by allowing for nonzero γ. For example, the effectiveness of medical versus surgical intervention may depend on which blood vessels are occluded, and how badly. Interactions are also potentially important in assessing effects of smoking cessation programs (Box 8.3).

Given the simplifying assumptions made in equation (8.4) and others (see note 16), it is straightforward to see that δ represents the treatment effect in this model, where treatment (d) for simplicity is measured as a (0, 1) variable:

$$y_C = x\beta + \varepsilon, \tag{8.5a}$$

$$y_T = \delta + x\beta + \varepsilon, \tag{8.5b}$$

and

$$\text{TE}(x) = E(y_T|x) - E(y_C|x) = \delta, \tag{8.5c}$$

for the moment assuming no interaction effects.

A central result of regression analysis is that as long as this is the correctly specified model and as long as d and x are uncorrelated with ε, then least squares estimates of the parameters $\theta = (\delta, \beta, \gamma)$ will generally be consistent in large samples and unbiased conditional on d and x.

In developing these ideas in the context of a linear model, it is useful to keep in mind the distinction between the model's *linear predictor*, $\eta = d\delta + x\beta$, and the model's *link function*, $\eta = g(\mu)$, where $\mu = E(y|x, d)$ (McCullagh and Nelder 1989). The discussion to follow focuses mainly on the implications of various statistical issues for estimation of the models linear predictor, assuming the link

---

Box 8.3 Interaction effects in smoking cessation programs

Smoking cessation programs provide an interesting example where interactions between treatments and other covariates, or among multiple treatments, are potentially important. The central hypothesis here is that the efficacy of pharmacological treatments, like transdermal nicotine patches and nicotine polacrilex gum, depends on whether or not patients are concurrently involved in counseling programs (Tønnesen et al. 1991; Transdermal Nicotine Study Group 1991). Several studies to date that have claimed such nicotine replacement therapies to be effective have made such claims based on data where subjects were all involved in some type of counseling program. Accordingly, what has been identified is the combined (interaction) effect of drug therapy and counseling, not the main effect of drug therapy alone.

function is linear, but proper specification of the link function is no less important an issue to address.

For example, a common assumption is that binary dependent variables are generated by a logit probability model. However, in most instances there is no a priori reason to maintain a logit probability model. For a given linear predictor, which link function is appropriate is generally an empirical matter. Tests for goodness of fit and goodness of link can be taken to determine whether a maintained link function is suitable for the application at hand, assuming that the linear predictor is properly specified (see McCullagh and Nelder 1989 for discussion).

The comparison of alternative statistical models for medical care (Duan et al. 1983) illustrates how sensitive the estimates can be to modifications in the specification of the model, including the link functions. Duan et al. (1983) used data from a randomized trial of health insurance. Estimates of differences among randomized treatments varied appreciably across model specifications.

Unobserved variables

Most statistical problems encountered in estimating treatment effects can be characterized as cases where measured regressors are correlated with unobservables. This phenomenon is very likely to generate biased estimates in observational studies but, for reasons to be discussed later, can also cause biased estimates in various contexts in RCTs. Accordingly, it is useful to sketch some general implications of a regression where unobservables are correlated with observables. Suppose the data are generated by the following process:

$$y = d\delta + x\beta + \varepsilon, \tag{8.6}$$

where d and/or x (for reasons to be discussed later) may be correlated with the unobservable component ε, and x is a scalar regressor.[17] If ordinary least squares (OLS) is used in estimation, the point estimate of δ is

$$\hat{\delta} = \delta + [(m_{xx}m_{d\varepsilon} - m_{dx}m_{x\varepsilon})/(m_{xx}m_{dd} - m_{dx}^2)], \tag{8.7}$$

where

$$m_{RS} = N^{-1} \sum_{i=1}^{N} R_i S_i$$

are the sample product moments. The large-sample central tendency of this estimator is given by its probability limit (plim) as

$$\text{plim}(\hat{\delta}) = \delta + [(\sigma_{d\varepsilon} - \sigma_{dx}\sigma_{x\varepsilon})/(\sigma_{dd} - \sigma_{dx}^2)], \tag{8.8}$$

where the σ_{RS} are the large-sample limit values of the corresponding m_{RS} and where, without loss of generality, units of x are redefined such that $\sigma_{xx} = 1$. The denominator of the bracketed term is necessarily positive. Thus, the sign of the large-sample least squares bias is determined by the sign of the numerator.

At least since Fisher (1926), it has been recognized that sound experimental data (i.e., data generated via randomization) give, by design, orthogonality (at least approximately) between regressors and unobservables and therefore provide the ideal solution to the omitted variables problem. Clinical as well as social experiments have been designed to generate data that are in principle capable of testing hypotheses in instances where reliable testing with nonexperimental data is difficult. For reasons to be suggested later in the chapter, however, experimental data may not be a panacea but may, rather, present problems that, although perhaps different from those that attend the use of nonexperimental or observational data, affect hypothesis testing. Indeed, there is some consensus that conducting observational studies within experimental studies could be fruitful (especially if compliance is of major concern), and that the effect of assignment to a particular treatment is important (see Rubin's comment on Efron and Feldman 1991).

Specific statistical issues

Unmeasured characteristics confounded with the treatment variable can be manifested in many ways. Here, we will focus on three potentially major problems that can arise in both experimental and observational studies when estimating efficacy or effectiveness: nonrandom selection into or out of the sample, errors in measurement; and latent fixed effects. The basic message is that individuals make choices and their choices will often have implications for the structure of the data that are generated by the experiments and the kinds of inference for which such data can be used. Moses (1985) referred to this phenomenon as "personal choice as a confounding variable." While clinicians view this as problematic and economists view it simply as rational choice in action, the applied statistician must confront the issue and assess its implications and/or control for it as best as possible. In addition, we address several statistical issues that may be problematic insofar as estimation of cost functions are concerned.

Nonrandom selection into and out of study samples: Although we tend to associate adverse selection biases in the estimates of treatment effects with observational studies, where we expect patients and providers to self-select their treatments, RCTs can also suffer from the same threats to validity. A study is truly randomized if and only if the assignment to and participation in the treatments in the study are random. Any of the following events could threaten that validity of the ex ante randomization in an RCT.[18] First, although the subjects may have been randomized as to treatment, they may selectively refuse to participate if recruited into some particular treatment. Second, those willing to participate in the overall study may not be representative of the population at large, or of interest, even if there is no differential bias among the subpopulations enrolled in individual treatments. Third, individuals may self-select out of the study population (attrition) at different rates across treatment groups, leaving the groups unbalanced ex post.[19] Fourth, in some studies, eligibility has been based on endogenous characteristics.[20] Similar issues arise in the recruitment for smoking cessation and problem drinking treatment studies. Fifth, there may be selective compliance with the treatment regimens. We will return to these specific issues later.

The fundamental idea can be summarized briefly as follows. Because individuals are (at least to some degree) free to choose whether or not to be studied (or how well to comply with the treatment regimen), there is in addition to the structural model relating treatments to outcomes

$$y = d\delta + x\beta + dx\gamma + \varepsilon, \tag{8.9}$$

a second model describing the individual's propensity to be observed or to participate,

$$p = f(d, x) + u, \tag{8.10}$$

where the individual participates only if p exceeds some threshold p^*. The essential problem is that the expected outcome conditional on participation will not generally be the same as the unconditional expected outcome (Heckman 1979; Heckman and Robb 1985; Heckman and Hotz 1989; Moffitt 1991); that is

$$E(y|d, x, p > p^*) = d\delta + x\beta + dx\gamma + E(\varepsilon|d, x, p > p^*). \tag{8.11}$$

Unless ε and u are independent, $E(\varepsilon|d, x, p > p^*)$ will generally be nonzero, even when $E(\varepsilon|d, x) = 0$ is a reasonable assumption. Heckman's (1979) now well known insight is that in trying to infer something about treatment effects from self-selected samples of participants, a regressor, $E(\varepsilon|d, x, p > p^*)$, is missing that will in general be correlated with both d and x. Therefore, the correct specification has an overall unobserved component

$$\varepsilon = E(\varepsilon|d, x, p > p^*) + w, \tag{8.12}$$

where $E(w|d, x, p > p^*) = 0$. Because the observed regressors d and x are generally correlated with ε, the basic omitted variable problem sketched above applies. Box 8.4 provides examples from the polio trials and alcoholism treatment fields.

Another phenomenon that can affect the inferences drawn about efficacy from observational data is known as allocation, or channeling, bias (Petri and Urquhart 1991). The basic idea is that the way treatments are prescribed in practice is correlated with characteristics of the recipients that are known to the physician but perhaps only in part to the data analyst. In describing channeling bias, Petri and Urquhart used the example of a new drug prescribed to patients

---

Box 8.4 Self-selection in polio vaccine trials and substance abuse treatment

A classic example of the effects of self-selection into the study group is the large-scale polio vaccine trials of 1954 (Hausman and Wise 1985). Evaluation of these trials found that rates of reported cases of polio were higher in placebo/control groups than among those who refused to participate. The general conclusion has been that those relatively more likely to benefit from an effective vaccine (e.g., those children or families having or suspecting relatively higher likelihoods of contracting polio) were more likely to participate than those less likely to benefit from such a vaccine.

Consider another example. Claims for the efficacy of alcoholism treatment programs like Alcoholics Anonymous (AA) have been questioned by observers who suggest that those problem drinkers participating in AA are those who (for whatever reason) are relatively highly motivated to recover in the first place (Fingarette 1988; Heather and Robertson 1989). Indeed, a recent randomized assignment to alcoholism treatment modalities (Walsh et al. 1991) has cast some doubt on AA efficacy relative to that of other treatment settings.

---

who have not responded to existing treatments (Box 8.5). In this context, it is apparent that the recipients of the two treatments (new versus old) are, on average, not the same. In this case, channeling will lead to an underestimate of the efficacy of the new drug. In a nutshell, the implications for statistical analysis are that, in observational data, d may be correlated with the other covariates observed by the analyst (x) and with factors known to the physician but not observed by the analyst (ε) (which is likely to be problematic for the reasons already suggested unless such correlation is somehow controlled by methods like those discussed later in this chapter).[21]

Payment differences may also exert a subtle but important bias in comparisons of treatments. To the extent that providers and patients react to the structure of the insurance plan and the reimbursement policy, they may select treatment regimens that are neither the most effective clinically nor the most cost–effective from a social point of view. If prescriptions are not as well covered as curative care, or if medical interventions are less generously covered than surgical ones, then many providers and patients may select a less efficacious approach. Observational data will then generate biased comparisons of the potential effectiveness of alternative treatments.

> **Box 8.5 Channeling bias in asthma treatment**
>
> Petri and Urquhart (1991) discuss a case of channeling bias in drug treatments for asthma. First-line treatment is typically one of three beta agonists (albuterol, terbutaline, or fenoterol), and more-severe cases are followed up with inhalational steroid treatment. Using a large pharmacy-based data set, Petri and Urquhart demonstrate that the users of the first-line therapies differ as to their propensities to also use inhalational steroids (23.0% of albuterol recipients, 35.4% of terbutaline recipients, and 42.4% of fenoterol recipients also used inhalational steroids) and suggest that the greater propensity of fenoterol recipients to also use inhalational steroids is consistent with the likelihood that fenoterol is channeled to patients with more severe cases of asthma.

Measurement error: Measures of variables of interest may contain measurement error (error in variables) for a number of reasons: blood pressure is labile; today's health status imperfectly measures health status over the last several weeks; respondents may give socially desirable responses to questions rather than truthful ones; or patients may not adhere completely to the prescribed medical regimen.

In observational studies, some adjustment must be made for differences in case mix (e.g., severity of illness or comorbidities) or other factors among the subgroups being compared if the analysts are to avoid the omitted variable selection biases discussed earlier. Unfortunately, the inclusion of case mix variables and measures of other factors may reduce but not eliminate the bias in the estimates of the treatment effects. The problem is the unavoidable measurement error in the control variables. The bias from measurement error in the variables that control for differences among groups is not limited to those variables. The bias can also be transmitted to the estimate of the treatment's effect δ if the treatment variable d is correlated with the measured control variables (the x's).

To show either of these situations, let us reformulate equation (8.4) (assuming $\gamma = 0$). The true relationship is given by

$$y = d\delta + x^*\beta + \varepsilon, \tag{8.13}$$

where x^* is the true value of sickliness or case mix. Because one cannot observe the true value x^*, the analyst substitutes the observed value $x = x^* + v$, which yields the following observed relationship:

$$y = d\delta + x\beta + (\varepsilon - v\beta). \tag{8.14}$$

Although the error term ε in the true relationship is uncorrelated with x^* and with the treatment d, the error term $(\varepsilon - v\beta)$ in the equation for observed variables is correlated with the observed x. And if x is correlated with d, then the error term in the observed equation is correlated with the treatment variable d. The large-sample bias in the estimate of δ will be:

$$\text{bias} = \text{plim} \, (\hat{\delta} - \delta) = \frac{\sigma_{dx}}{\sigma_{dd}} \, \frac{\sigma_{vv}}{(\sigma_{xx} - \delta_{dx}^2)/\sigma_{dd}} \, \beta. \qquad (8.15)$$

The first term in the bias is the probability limit of the auxiliary regression of the observed x on the treatment variable d. The numerator of the second term is the variance of the measurement error in x. The denominator is the variance in the observed x times 1 minus the square of the multiple correlation coefficient between d and x. Because the denominator is positive, the sign of the bias depends on the signs of σ_{dx} and β.

Thus, the greater the correlation between the treatment d and the observed sickliness x, the greater is the measurement error in x; and the lower the variance in x, the greater is the bias in the estimate of δ. (For an example involving health and air pollution, see Box 8.6.) As we will discuss later, administrative data have the additional problem that their information on case mix and sickliness may be systematically biased. Such a bias exacerbates the bias from measurement error, because v may be systematically related to x^* and hence to d.

A well-designed RCT avoids both these problems because the expectation of m_{xd} is zero and v is uncorrelated with d by randomization – so long as the parameter of interest is the main effect δ of the treatment, and the compliance problem is not an issue. Owing to randomization, d is (approximately) uncorrelated with all other right-hand side variables in the model in equation (8.11), including the observed and actual other covariates (x and x^*), the measurement error (v), and the error term (ε). Hence, the probability limit of the RCT's estimate $\hat{\delta}$ of the treatment effect δ is δ because the σ_{dx} term is zero by design.

One clinically important form of measurement error that plagues both RCTs and observational studies involves the failure of subjects to follow the prescribed treatment regimes: imperfect compliance or noncompliance (Efron and Feldman 1991; Horwitz et al. 1990; Sommer and Zeger 1991). Two recent examples where compliance has been a substantial issue are the beta blocker trials and nicotine patch trials (Box 8.7). Imperfect compliance implies that the level of treatment or dose (in general, the measured level of the dose) that is administered may not be the dose taken by the patient. The measured dose d is related to the true dose d^* by $d = d^* + v$, where v is the measurement or compliance error. The compliance error v may simply be random noise, or it may be that the probability distribution of v may depend on observables (x) and/or unobservables (ε).

Box 8.6 The effects of measurement errors in models of health and pollution

Covariate measurement error can transmit bias to the treatment effect estimate if treatment and covariates are correlated. In other contexts, the main focus is on the statistical effects of mismeasurement of treatment or dose itself (the example of compliance behavior discussed in Box 8.7 can be interpreted in this context). In such cases, it is important to recognize that even if treatment or dose is measured reasonably well, substantial bias in the estimate of treatment effect can still arise if σ_{dx} is nonzero and x is correlated with unobservables, as it would be, for instance, if x itself is measured with error (as shown).

For example, in studies relating health outcomes to ambient pollution, a central concern is how well the pollution measures obtained for the analysis correspond to the actual pollution "doses" received by the subjects in the sample. Klepper, Kamlet, and Frank (1993) formally studied this issue using as examples two earlier studies that had analyzed how ozone pollution and lead exposure affected various health outcomes. Klepper et al. demonstrated that the treatment effect bias problems were more severe in the lead exposure study (where reasonably good pollution [treatment] measures were coupled with relatively poor measures of covariates of x that had significant correlations with pollution) than in the ozone exposure study (where the pollution measurements were themselves considered relatively poor but where the correlation between pollution and x was low).

If compliance is an issue, then d in an RCT will measure the true treatment with error, and the RCT's estimate of δ will in general be biased. If there is also interest in the interaction γ of the treatment d with a covariate x, as in equation (8.4), then measurement error in x will lead to an inconsistent estimate of γ even in an RCT. Measurement error is one instance in which the general conclusions from linear models may not apply to other estimators. In probit and logistic regression, measurement error in some other covariate x can lead to inconsistent estimates of the treatment effect δ, even if the data are from an RCT where x is orthogonal to d and compliance is not an issue (Carroll 1989).

If these measurement or compliance errors have some systematic component, then understanding the process of compliance itself becomes very important. Why are some patients compliant and others not? Noncompliance may result because of unpleasant or other side effects of treatment, but the process

---

Box 8.7 Compliance behavior: examples from propranolol treatment in beta blocker heart attack trials and nicotine polacrilex gum treatment in smoking cessation

Horwitz et al. (1990) found in their analysis of data from the beta blocker heart attack trials that individuals who were poor compliers to either propranolol (the treatment) or to the placebo had increased risk of death relative to good compliers. Poor adherence was not statistically explained by severity of heart attack, by observable sociodemographic factors, or by other observed characteristics.

In another setting, the Transdermal Nicotine Study Group (1991) suggested that nicotine transdermal patches might be a useful substitute for nicotine gum for those patients who have had difficulty complying with nicotine polacrilex gum treatment. Compliance to the nicotine gum treatment, it is suggested, has been limited by "special chewing requirements, gastrointestinal side effects, and social prohibitions."

---

of compliance may be related in important ways to outcomes apart from the effects of compliance on actual dose.

Compliance behavior is thus akin to the model of the participation propensity (p) discussed earlier. Following Efron and Feldman (1991), one could postulate a behavioral compliance model $c = f(d, x) + u$, $0 < c < 1$, and relate the true dose to the measured dose by a multiplicative measurement error relationship $d = cd^*$. In any event, the analyst must then explicitly deal with the observational character of the data so generated.[22]

The main statistical implication of the compliance problem is that the measured covariates will be correlated with unobservables. Unless this can be controlled or modeled, consistent estimates will be elusive.

Estimates of the reliability of the measure can prevent or reduce the measurement error problem in observational and randomized studies.[23]

Latent- or omitted-variable bias: For any number of reasons, both experimental and observational data sets may be missing data on at least some variables for at least some cases.[24] The important issues for researchers are the determination of why the data are missing and what the implications are of having missing data. As already noted, the critical issue for regression analysis comes down to whether the covariates observed for the sample are uncorrelated with unobservable determinants, including, of course, the decision to be an observation, a participating, complying, nonattriter of the outcome of interest, y.

A problem plaguing observational studies that attempt to causally link one or more exposures to one or more outcomes is the failure to have measurements on key covariates that also are likely to affect the outcomes. For instance, many observational studies finding statistically significant correlations between coffee consumption and cardiovascular problems (Grobbee et al. 1990) have variously failed to control for factors like smoking, job stress, family structure, and any number of other covariates that could plausibly be related to coffee consumption. Box 8.8 discusses the negative association between education and smoking in this light.

Statistical issues in cost estimation: Chapter 4 surveyed the main themes in measuring costs. In addition to the topics surveyed there, however, some particular statistical issues arise in the estimation of cost functions that should be briefly noted here.[25] First, much of the literature on cost function estimation assumes that firms are "quantity takers"; that is, output is determined exogenously for the firm. This assumption may be reasonable in some health care settings, such as in hospital emergency rooms in public hospitals, but it is clearly tenuous in other settings, such as admissions, especially discretionary ones (see Breyer 1987). If output is determined endogenously, as it would be under many models of producer behavior, then regressing costs on quantities will in general lead to biased estimates of cost function parameters.

Second, the assumption of cost–minimizing behavior that is prevalent in the literature may also be tenuous. Whether or not the reasons that firms may fail to minimize costs are under the control of the firm, firms will in general fall

---

Box 8.8 Smoking, health, schooling, and omitted variables

It is widely recognized that the propensity to smoke and schooling are strongly negatively correlated. Does greater educational attainment *cause* a reduction in the propensity to smoke? Or is there some unmeasured "lurking variable" that affects both schooling attainment and smoking behavior?

Farrell and Fuchs (1982) tested these hypotheses using data on smoking propensity at various points during individuals' schooling careers and found that additional schooling did not elicit corresponding changes in smoking behavior. They concluded that the missing-variable hypothesis is more reasonable than the hypothesis that schooling is a causal determinant of smoking behavior and suggested that factors like family background and time preference may be among those lurking in the background as the key missing variables.

short of the minimum cost frontier due to allocative and technical inefficiency (see Bauer 1990 for a survey of these issues). Whether analysts should attempt to estimate the determinants of the cost frontier or should instead attempt to determine the cost structure corresponding to actual practice is an issue analogous to whether efficacy or effectiveness is most appropriate to analyze on the effect side of the equation.

Finally, to underscore themes discussed in greater detail in Chapter 4, it is imperative that researchers be sensitive to certain model specification issues particularly germane to health care costs. These issues include, but are not limited to, controlling for differences in providers' case mixes, specifying cost functions to account for the multiple output nature of hospital production, and measuring all important inputs and/or their prices (see Grannemann, Brown, and Pauly 1986). The last issue in this list is particularly vexing as far as physicians' time and wage rates are concerned.

Alternative estimation strategies

A common attribute of all the issues discussed to this point is that measured regressors, whether the treatments themselves or other control covariates in the model, may have nonzero correlation with the unobserved components of the model. At least in principle, several possible solutions exists to the under-identification that arises when regressors are theoretically or behaviorally likely to be correlated with unobservables (Moffitt 1991). We will discuss three commonly used or espoused alternatives: (1) longitudinal data methods that allow the individual to act as his or her own control; (2) instrumental variables to purge estimates of the bias; and (3) control function approaches that attempt to model the selection process directly. The strategy chosen in practice, of course, will be dictated by the nature of the available data, but it is useful to summarize here three important options that might be available to researchers.

Longitudinal data: If the doctor has selected the treatment that he or she believes is optimal for the patient, then there is a very strong presumption that the treatment variable d is confounded with characteristics not observed by the analyst. To avoid or reduce these biases, the analyst can employ longitudinal or panel data methods. If the part of the unobservable correlated with the measured regressor(s) has a time-invariant or fixed effect character, then by using longitudinal data in conjunction with appropriate statistical methods, one may be able to obliterate these fixed effects by differencing or conditioning (Hsiao 1986; Chamberlain 1980; Hausman, Hall, and Griliches 1984; Heckman and Hotz 1989; Heckman and Robb 1985; Maddala 1971, 1983, 1987) using a pre–post design with a contemporaneous control group (Campbell and Stanley 1963; Cook and Campbell 1979).

The following simple example illustrates the method. Alter the model in equation (8.4) so that

$$y_{i,t} = d_{i,t}\delta + x_{i,t}\beta + \mu_i + \varepsilon_{i,t},$$ (8.16)

where ε is independent and identically distributed (iid) across observations i and time period t. The unobserved individual's propensity μ_i may not be independent of either $d_{i,t}$ or observed $x_{i,t}$. If μ_i is correlated with $d_{i,t}$, then the least squares estimate of δ will be biased.[26]

However, a fixed-effects estimator can provide consistent estimates. With the fixed-effects estimator, we take each observation as a deviation from the mean for that variable for that individual and regress the deviation in the dependent variable on the deviations for the independent variables.[27] The average of the observations for the ith individual is

$$\bar{y}_{i.} = \bar{d}_{i.}\delta + \bar{x}_{i.}\beta + \mu_{i.} + \bar{\varepsilon}_{i.}.$$ (8.17)

Subtracting equation (8.17) from equation (8.16) yields

$$y_{i,t} - \bar{y}_{i.} = (d_{i,t} - \bar{d}_{i.})\delta + (x_{i,t} - \bar{x}_{i.})\beta + (\varepsilon_{i,t} - \bar{\varepsilon}_{i.}),$$ (8.18)

which is purged of the correlated error component $\mu_{i.}$. As long as there is (within cluster) variation in the $d_{i,t}$ or $x_{i,t}$ for some individuals i, the model will be full rank and can be estimated by OLS. A pre–post comparison provides the necessary variation in d within the observations on an individual, whereas cross-sectional data are prone to the omitted-variable bias discussed earlier. The inclusion of a contemporaneous control group guards against the omitted-variable bias from secular changes that are correlated with $d_{i,t}$.

Alternative estimation methods that control for a stable selection effect μ_i, include pre–post (post–pre) comparisons, or that use preintervention values as explanatory variables. The last approach is briefly described in Box 8.9.

Differencing or conditioning will eliminate the problem of regressors correlated with unobservables only if the model has a special structure (Heckman and Hotz 1989). Differencing works when the unobserved effects correlated with regressors are additively separable in models linear in parameters.[28] Accordingly, even if good panel data are available, special care must be exercised to ensure that the model structure to which differencing is to be applied is sensible for the problem at hand.

Another critical assumption in this model is that μ_i is a constant, time invariant parameter for each individual i. If this is not the case, then the fixed-effects model may reduce the bias from the confounding of μ and d, but it will not eliminate it. Kaplan and Berry's (1990) discussion of one evaluation of the Head Start program provides an example where this model would be inappropriate because the groups were selected in such a manner that regression to the mean would be confounded with treatment. In a medical context, the

---

Box 8.9 Cimetidine treatment for duodenal ulcer

Geweke and Weisbrod (1981) used panel data on medical claims from the Texas Medicaid program to study the effect of cimetidine treatment for duodenal ulcer on health care expenditures. Although the study did not have access to data on many of the costs discussed in Chapter 4, it does illustrate how a pre–post longitudinal database can be used.

Geweke and Weisbrod found no demographic differences between the cimetidine and the control groups. However, they found substantial and statistically significant differences in preperiod use of general (but not duodenal ulcer) health care. (The preperiod for those receiving cimetidine was the twelve months prior to the prescription being filled for the individual. For the control group it was the first occurrence of an ulcer in the time window studied.) To correct for the potential selection bias, they split the groups into three subpopulations based on health care use from months −12 through −2 of the preperiod. Their results indicated that cimetidine reduced health care expenditures only for those who had low prior use of the health care system.

---

concern would be that the provider knows something about the course of the disease, as distinct from its severity at a point in time or its average severity. Geweke and Weisbrod's (1981) study could be subject to this risk because they selected the cimetidine group at the onset of that treatment pattern, whereas the control group was already under treatment (see Box 8.9).

A further obstacle to applying longitudinal statistical methods to interesting problems in cost–effectiveness analysis is likely to be the data themselves. Large (with "large" defined in terms of the number of subjects or cross-sectional units) longitudinal observational databases are still somewhat rare, and small longitudinal databases may not permit analysts to precisely estimate parameters of interest. Although use of panel databases is becoming more prominent in applied social science research, applied longitudinal research is probably still in its infancy and, in any event, has certainly not yet caught up with the rich statistical methods that have been developed for analyzing such data.[29]

Instrumental variable estimation: Instrumental variable (IV) estimation is an alternative strategy that can be used with single cross sections or with longitudinal data. IV estimation combines the idea of experiments (natural or clinical) with certain a priori restrictions on which right-hand-side variables are included in a model. The assumptions required for IV estimation to provide consistent parameter estimates are somewhat stringent. In particular, the key identifying restriction is that there is a set of instrumental variables z properly excluded from the model itself that is correlated with the "problematic" included variable d and is uncorrelated with the unobservable ε (Hansen 1982; Amemiya 1985). In determining which variable or variables are IV candidates (i.e., which variables can be properly excluded from the model of interest and are uncorrelated with unobservables), the analyst must look beyond the data and appeal to some other criterion to judge the propriety of excluding such variables from the model. The legitimacy of any candidate IV is determined only with reference to a priori assumptions or theory about the process generating the data. A study on the relationship between maternal smoking, a smoking cessation program, and infant birth weight provides an example of the use of IVs (Box 8.10).[30]

If experiments cannot provide the requisite relationships between candidate IVs, measured regressors, and unobservables, some other basis for maintaining the necessary "identifying restrictions" must be found.[31] In many applications, however, the specific IV strategies used are based on ad hoc assumptions about the relationships between the IVs and the unobservables. Nonetheless, certain restrictions are a priori probably "more reasonable" than others, and with a minimum of two competing sets of estimates (one using IVs and one not), one can perform specification tests or sensitivity tests.

Finally, it should be obvious that the utility of IV estimation hinges critically on the relationships between the IVs and both the included measured regressors and the unobservables. Even if it is reasonably maintained that the IVs are uncorrelated with the unobservables, determining a strong relationship with the included problematic regressor is also crucial. If the latter correlations are weak, then the bias of the IV estimator can be considerable (see Nelson and Startz 1990; Maddala and Jeong 1992).

"Control function" approaches for controlling for selection bias: The longitudinal data and IV methods attempt to get around the omitted variable term in equation (8.11) by either making the term an incidental parameter or removing it by instrumentation. In contrast, the control function approach tries to use some information on the nature of the selection process to explicitly model selection and to remove its effect from the estimates. Often the control function approach to correcting for selection bias has taken the form of a parametric correction to the "omitted variable" in equation (8.11), where additional information allows one to explicitly specify $E(\varepsilon \,|\, d, x, p, > p^*)$. Depending on the maintained self-selection process, the correction has often been based on an assumption of joint normality of the errors ε and u. In the simplest case, the correction consists of estimating a probit model for the participation decision and then using the resulting estimate of the inverse Mill's ratio ($\hat{\lambda} = \hat{\phi}/\hat{\Phi}$) as the

---

Box 8.10 Instrumental variable estimation of a model of birth weight and smoking

Although IV methods have probably been used far more in economics than in other areas of applied statistics, recognition of the potential usefulness of IV methods has recently entered the biometrics literature with the study by Permutt and Hebel (1989), and an example from that paper serves to highlight the key issues in IV estimation. Permutt and Hebel consider a model of how maternal smoking behavior relates to birth weight in the context of a randomized smoking cessation intervention. A two-equation recursive model was specified:

$$s = a_1 + b_1 d + \varepsilon_1$$

and

$$b = a_2 + b_2 s + \varepsilon_2,$$

where s measures smoking behavior, d is the $(0, 1)$ intervention or treatment indicator, b is birth weight, the a_i and b_i are parameters, and the ε_i are such that ε_1 and ε_2 may have nonzero correlation. If $\sigma_{\varepsilon_1 \varepsilon_2} = 0$, then there is no inconsistency in estimating the parameter of primary interest (b_2) from least squares regression of b on s and a constant term; otherwise, the least squares estimate of b_2 will be biased and inconsistent.

The authors argue that it is unlikely that $\sigma_{\varepsilon_1 \varepsilon_2} = 0$, and propose IV methods to circumvent this problem. By design, the intervention was uncorrelated with ε_1 and ε_2 and was also designed to be unrelated to any other determinants of birth weight. Thus, so long as the intervention has some effect on smoking behavior (i.e., $b_1 \neq 0$), then d satisfies the requirements of being a valid IV. Given these assumptions, some substitution shows that regressing b on d and a constant term recovers a slope parameter that consistently estimates the product $c_{12} = b_1 b_2$; regressing s on d and a constant term consistently estimates b_1; and dividing $\hat{c}_{12}$ by $\hat{b}_1$ provides a consistent estimate of the parameter of interest, b_2.

"correction" term, that is, as an additional regressor in equation (8.11). Corrections associated with more complicated selection processes are discussed in Heckman and Robb (1985) and Heckman and Hotz (1989).

The potential problems associated with the use of this parametric approach are now well known. Without exclusion restrictions, the model is not likely to be identified in an econometric sense.[32] In addition, the parametric assumption of an iid bivariate normal distribution may be incorrect, and if it is, the resulting corrected estimates will be inconsistent. The estimates are not robust to minor departures from normality and may not be numerically well behaved even when other distributional assumptions hold (see Manning et al. 1987 for an example). Some semiparametric approaches have recently been proposed, but their usefulness in applications is still largely unexplored. Even if the parametric assumptions are feasible, however, our experience is that the regression model of interest is still in some sense underidentified, even with a statistically appropriate selection correction (if there is not at least one significant determinant of participation apart from d and x; that is, if there is not at least one variable that would be a legitimate instrumental variable in a linear model context).

Heterogeneous populations

One of the more vexing problems involved in applied statistical analysis is determining when it is reasonable to describe individual "units" by the same statistical model. That is, when can subsamples be pooled? It is common practice in applied social science research for analysts to present separate estimates for males and females, whites and nonwhites, young and old, and other categories of people. The rationale is that, on the basis of some statistical test (e.g., likelihood ratio, Wald), the relevant subpopulations are characterized by models sufficiently different that pooled estimates might be misleading. The biased inferences that may result from inappropriate pooling are often referred to as aggregation bias (Theil 1971).

A classic example of misleading inferences resulting from inappropriate pooling is Simpson's Paradox. Although the paradox is commonly demonstrated using conditional probability algebra, it can also be shown quite readily in the context of the linear model that we have been using here. Suppose there are two distinct subpopulations: A and B. The $(0, 1)$ response of each to a $(0, 1)$ treatment variable is thought to be characterized by a simple linear probability model:

$$y_{ij} = \beta_i + \delta_i d_{ij} + \varepsilon_{ij}, \qquad i = A, B, \tag{8.19}$$

where y_{ij} and d_{ij} are, respectively, the outcome and treatment indicators for the jth individual in the ith subpopulation. In Simpson's Paradox, each subpopulation could have $\delta_i > 0$. However, if the parameters in the two subpopulations are not identical, it is possible that pooling the two subsamples and estimating a pooled version of the model without interactions,

$$y_j = \beta + \delta d_j + \varepsilon_j, \qquad j = 1, \ldots, N_A N_B, \tag{8.20}$$

will result in a negative point estimate of δ, suggesting that treatment is harmful rather than effective,[33] as illustrated by a study of discrimination in admissions to college (Box 8.11). The result in this example may be extreme, but the implications for applied researchers are nonetheless meaningful: if there is reason to suspect heterogeneity across subpopulations that are definable on the basis of exogenous characteristics, then it is probably worthwhile to test for the possibility that responsiveness (i.e., treatment effect) is heterogeneous. However, to make such a correction possible, it is necessary to include all (major) groups. The recent concern about adequate inclusion of women in RCTs is essential in this regard.

A related, yet distinct, phenomenon is Lord's Paradox (Lord 1960, 1967, 1969; Kaplan and Berry 1990). In studying changes over time for subpopulations, for example, boys and girls, Lord's Paradox states that one can find evidence of differential rates of change across the subpopulations even when no changes have actually taken place. Much of the concern in applications where Lord's Paradox is encountered is with measurement error on the baseline characteristics whose rates of change over time are the subject of study.

Although both Simpson's and Lord's Paradoxes are probably more likely to affect observational studies than RCTs, they cannot be ruled out as possible "accidents" in a trial, especially when the trial is small.

Box 8.11 Simpson's paradox in admissions

Freedman, Pisani, and Purves (1991) provide an example of Simpson's Paradox using data on graduate admissions to the University of California at Berkeley. During a specific period, 44% of the male applicants, and 35% of the female applicants were admitted. On the face of it, these data indicate that women were significantly less likely to be admitted ($p < .001$) and may have been discriminated against.

However, an examination of admissions by majors indicates a more complex story. For the six largest majors, accounting for a third of the cases, the fraction of women admitted to each was approximately the same as the fraction of men admitted, except for one that admitted appreciably more women. But over all six majors, more men were admitted. The discrepancy is due to two "facts." Most of the men applied to the two departments with the highest acceptance rate. Most of the women applied to the four departments with the lowest acceptance rates. By omitting variables for department and interactions between department and gender, the simple comparisons yield a biased estimate of the true gender differences.

Another perspective on heterogeneity may be useful. Implicit thus far in most of the discussion is that mean or average effects are the analyst's primary concern. Identification and consistent estimation of a parametric conditional mean function most fundamentally informs analysts about the partial derivatives of $E(y|x)$ with respect to the elements x_j; these are simply the $\hat{\beta}_j$ in a linear regression setting. Although this may be a perfectly reasonable focus in many contexts, it should be stressed that the mean is just one property of the conditional distribution $f(y|x)$. The distribution $f(y|x)$ has an infinite number of properties beyond simply its low-order moments, and estimates of some of these additional properties could be quite useful in applied cost–effectiveness analysis.

Earlier it was noted that one of the strong assumptions implicit in the standard linear regression model was that of homogeneity of response, that is, the model is not a varying-parameter model or analysts are concerned only about mean responses. However, concern has been expressed in the literature about the implications of heterogeneous responses to treatments (Brook et al. 1983) and to health policies more generally (Shepard and Zeckhauser 1982). Consider a population that has heterogeneous responses to some treatment. Suppose, for concreteness, that, for some continuous outcome variable y, a proposed treatment has zero efficacy for 80 percent of the population having measurable characteristics x but that the efficacy for the remaining 20 percent of the population with these characteristics is substantial. Then, it may be that the mean treatment effect is quite small, and it is certainly true that the median treatment effect is zero. If focus is restricted to either of these parameters, then the efficacy of the treatment might be judged to be too small to merit further consideration despite the fact that, for the upper quintile of this distribution, the efficacy is considerable.[34]

Standard varying-parameters models are one way to approach the problem of heterogeneous responses. An alternative approach is quantile estimation (Box 8.12).[35]

A key implication of heterogeneity is that it forces the analyst to recognize that the statistical estimand implies something about the loss function or social welfare function (Manski 1988). To date, neither cost–effectiveness nor cost–benefit analysis has been used to compare the "worth" of a treatment with low mean efficacy that benefits a small percentage of the population dramatically with that of a treatment with somewhat higher mean efficacy but no such dramatic effects (see Shepard and Zeckhauser 1982).

Problems in using administrative data

In many cost–effectiveness studies, time, money, or ethical constraints (e.g., the possibility of severe adverse reactions to a new drug) will often render in-

Box 8.12 Quantile regression analysis

The recent literature on conditional quantile estimation offers one approach to quantifying and estimating such potentially important parameters as treatment efficacy in the upper α-quantile of a given population. One way to conceive of a varying-parameters model is as a heteroscedastic linear regression model with no interactions:

$$y = d\delta + x\beta + (\zeta d + x\xi)\varepsilon.$$

Define $Q_\alpha(\varepsilon)$ as the α-quantile of the probability distribution of ε, $F(\varepsilon)$. It follows that the αth conditional quantile of y given x is

$$Q_\alpha(y|d, x) = d\delta + x\beta + (\zeta d + x\xi)Q_\alpha(\varepsilon).$$

As suggested, in regression analysis the usual focus is on the treatment effects or dose–response relationships like δ or the partial derivatives $\partial E(y|x)/\partial x_j = \beta_j$, both of which are based on expectations. However, one can consider more generally effects like the partial derivatives $\partial y/\partial d = \delta + \zeta\varepsilon$ or $\partial y/\partial x_j = \beta_j + \xi_j\varepsilon$. As such, it is reasonable to speak of these slopes $\partial y/\partial(d, x)$ as themselves having probability distributions whose quantiles are given by

$$Q_\alpha\partial y/\partial d = \delta + \zeta Q_\alpha(\varepsilon) \equiv a_\alpha$$

and

$$Q_\alpha\partial y/\partial x_j = \beta_j + \xi_j Q_\alpha(\varepsilon) \equiv b_{\alpha j}.$$

Thus, it is possible that the response of y to (d, x) is heterogeneous in the population, if the corresponding ζ and γ_j are nonzero. The interpretation of the $c_\alpha = (a_\alpha, b_\alpha)$ is that they summarize the partial response between y and (d, x) at the αth quantile of the distribution of the unobservables ε. It is these "coefficients" that are estimated by the regression quantile estimators, $\hat{c}_\alpha$ (Koenker and Bassett 1982). By reference to parameters $\hat{c}_\alpha$ for various values of α, the analyst is in a position to determine whether the response of individuals at one quantile of the population distribution of unobservables differs from the response at some other quantile; in terms of the earlier example, it would enable the analyst to determine that the response in the upper quintile differs substantively from that at the mean, median, or other lower quantiles.

Manning et al. (1991) used quantile regression to see if heavier drinkers were more or less responsive to the price of alcohol than other drinkers. They found that the price elasticity varied appreciably by consumption levels. The decision to drink at all during the last two weeks exhibited a price elasticity of $-.56$, whereas drinking by the median drinker exhibited a price elasticity of -1.2. However, the heaviest drinker's price elasticity was not significantly different from zero. These estimates were significantly different from each other ($p < .05$).

feasible an RCT that would, if it could be conducted, be the ideal method for assembling data for addressing the question of interest or for assembling a major primary collection for observational data. In recent years, there has been a substantial interest in using large clinical and claims databases to examine variations in the use and efficacy of alternative treatments or procedures. A large research initiative in patient outcomes from the U.S. Agency for Health Care Policy and Research is predicated on the use of existing, observational databases and past observational and clinical trials to assess various treatments. Administrative databases are appealing because they are relatively inexpensive to use compared with primary data collection for an observational study or RCT. In addition, the sample sizes can be quite large, and they offer information on patients receiving a number of alternative treatments.

When using such data, however, one must be aware of possible dangers, including (1) the traditional concerns with any observational study (sample selection and omitted-variable bias, systematically missing data) and (2) the risk that the results of such analyses could be an artifact of how the data were generated or collected. In the following, we outline some of the problems that can arise from such data.

The most important point to remember about such administrative databases is that they were not generated for research purposes. Research using these data asks the database to do something it was never intended to address. Therefore, if the data are to be used in research projects, the researchers should know how the data were generated and what the implications are for the analysis. Here we will discuss issues of selection biases, omitted and missing variables, and measurement errors that may arise in the use of administrative data.

Selection biases

Administrative data are on users of a particular system or sets of systems. Because the allocation of patients across systems is unlikely to be random, analyses based on administrative data may be prone to sample selection biases. First, the populations covered may not be representative of the population at large or subgroups of clinical or policy relevance. The elderly and the insured nonelderly may be overrepresented; the poor, the uninsured and working near-poor, children, and minorities may be underrepresented unless they are sick enough to merit public insurance (Medicaid, Medicare, or general assistance). Potential patients in areas with relatively plentiful providers may be better represented than those in areas where access is more limited.

If the data are based on patients, then, to the extent that the less ill are less likely to visit a provider, the healthy will be underrepresented or may be missing altogether. In many insurance claims databases, only the employee is known, as well as any dependents who were covered and used a service. Such data will tend to be more comprehensive in areas that require some main-tenance treatment or where treatment is believed to be effective. Samples based on who used a provider during a window of time overrepresent frequent users and people in the midst of treatment; at a minimum, one may have to reweight for the sample selection procedure.

Clinical databases are collected on encounters between a specific provider (or set of providers) and his or her patients. These data do not include data on nonpatients, on patients' use of alternative providers, or, in some cases, the use of providers to whom the patient was referred. For example, health main-tenance organization (HMO) administrative data exclude out-of-plan utiliza-tion generated by the patient's self-referral (e.g., to a fee-for-service provider because of lack of coverage in the HMO or delays to the appointment) and cases referred to other providers but paid for by the HMO.[36] The same applies to Veterans' Administration and public hospital data.

Claims data are generated for payment or reimbursement of services. They exclude nonusers, users below their deductible or beyond the upper limit on covered services, users of noncovered providers (e.g., users outside the pre-ferred provider option), and use not filed for or excluded from the benefit package.

Missing data and omitted variables

Administrative data may pose missing data and omitted-variables problems for both dependent and independent variables. Such databases generally contain only information useful for reimbursement. If a physician cannot be reimbursed for taking a patient's blood pressure, such information may not be recorded. If comorbid diagnoses needed for case mix adjustment (to avoid an omitted-variables bias) are not a part of the payment mechanism, they may not be recorded at all, or only rarely. Further, providers may use euphemisms or artful coding to circumvent restrictions on benefits or to mask conditions involving possible stigma, such as treatment for mental health problems or substance abuse.

Missing-data problems are particularly vexing in administrative databases. Data may be missing either at random or in a highly selective manner. Should missing data be treated as "inapplicable" or as missing at random due to eccentricities of individual providers? For example, the absence of test X on a patient with disease Y might arise because the test may not be conducted; the record may have been lost; the test may not be recorded because it is not a reimbursed service (e.g., taking blood pressure); the patient may be too healthy to merit that service; or the physician does not conduct the test under the same circumstances as does another physician.

Some items are missing because the data collection instrument, a claim, for example, does not include sufficient space for it. Some systems collect a limited amount of data on procedures and/or diagnoses. Hence, records tend to be complete on patients with few procedures and diagnoses and incomplete on the more "intensively treated" and sicker patients. This could lead to an under-adjustment for case mix in the statistical analyses because the data are most incomplete for the sickest patients or the ones who have experienced the most adverse events. Neither clinical nor claims databases will have data on con-ditions treated outside the usual system: workers' compensation, free clinics, self-help groups, and care provided directly at the work site.

Measurement error

Data in administrative databases are not consistently or reliably coded; nor are they consistently provided. Providers vary in the thoroughness of describing what was provided. They may not all follow the same definitions of what constitutes a particular diagnosis or treatment. Unlike a highly formalized trial or prospective study with stringent protocols, there are very few standards as to what constitutes a particular procedure or diagnosis. To further complicate matters, what consensus there is will evolve over time as diseases like AIDS (see Ellenberg, Finkelstein, and Schoenfeld's 1992 discussion of AIDS trials) are better understood and procedures are developed. The dissemination of the *Diagnostic and Statistical Manual of Mental Disorders* (3d ed.) for mental health, for example, is widely believed to have increased the reliability and validity of psychiatric diagnoses and coding. Laparoscopic cholecystectomy, with its lower morbidity and cost, became quite widespread before procedure codes were introduced that allowed analysts to distinguish between it and the conventional treatment. Even where there have not been shifts over time, some data are notoriously unreliable. Misclassifications in diagnoses of nearly 40 percent can occur (Safran 1991). This raises the serious risk that the population being studied does not in fact suffer from the disease or did not receive quite the treatment indicated in the record. The resulting biases could be substantial.

The problem of controlling for comorbidities illustrates the dilemma in administrative databases. To avoid a potential omitted variables bias or a selection effect, the analyst will want to adjust the results for comorbidities. However, using the data on comorbid conditions can lead to biased estimates. In a study of comorbidities and death, Iezzoni et al. (1992) found that many conditions that one would expect to increase mortality, such as diabetes and previous myocardial infarction, had the opposite observed association in a data set that allowed for a substantial number of diagnoses. They argued that the bias against coding of chronic and comorbid conditions could generate this perverse finding. Jencks, Williams, and Kay (1988) found a similar result but attributed it to the limited number of fields allowed for additional diagnoses (see Jencks

1992 for a further discussion of this issue). Another interpretation is that what information is provided contains substantial measurement error, some of which may be systematically related to other factors included in the model.

Despite their many flaws, administrative data can provide an inexpensive data source, often on relatively large samples. As such, they provide useful input for exploratory analyses or analyses where RCTs and observational studies are too expensive. Because of their flaws, however, such data must be carefully analyzed and cautiously reported.

Inferences in cost–effectiveness analysis

Many analysts act as if they know the actual effectiveness and cost of treatment alternatives when they announce their optimal choices. Unfortunately, such certainty about incremental costs and effectiveness is unwarranted. At best, the analyst can hope to have unbiased or consistent estimates of the costs and effectiveness from a well-designed RCT or observational study. As with any other point estimate, the use of the estimated cost–effectiveness ratio requires some indication of what confidence can be placed in it. For instance, what would happen if the true cost per case was somewhat higher or lower than the mean estimate?

Sensitivity analyses

Many of the articles in the literature deal with this uncertainty by doing sensitivity analyses. Weinstein and Stason (1977) argue that sensitivity analyses are fundamental to cost–effectiveness analysis. Some critical component in the calculation is changed by a meaningful amount or to a worst case, and the cost–effectiveness ratio is recalculated. The resulting difference in the ratio provides some indication of how sensitive the results might be to a major, but not implausible, change in that parameter. In some studies, the values have been altered by plus or minus one standard deviation (Goldman et al. 1991). Where the analysts have had to make some assumption to carry out the calculation, alternative assumptions can also be tried. This is frequently done for the discount rate, because of the lack of consensus on the true or relevant real rate of discount for policies and treatments that have consequences over a number of years.[37]

Such an exercise is extremely useful because it indicates which, if any, parameters in the model are critical to the results. If the source of the problem is lack of understanding of the underlying process or lack of a precise measure of a variable, then sensitivity results may indicate an area where further investigation is required before a decision can be made.

Although very useful, such univariate sensitivity analyses are inadequate.

Looking at one source of uncertainty at a time in the model provides an incomplete and overly optimistic estimate of how uncertain the estimated overall cost–effectiveness ratio actually is. There are two problems to be considered here: (1) the numerator and denominator probably include multiple parameters, and (2) the cost–effectiveness ratio is a ratio of two random numbers.

Multiple parameters

The typical cost–effectiveness analysis is based on multiple parameters, not just a "cost" and an "effect." For example, the cost in the numerator may depend on the volume of drugs, the number of visits and hospitalizations for the treatment, and subsequent adverse reactions. Thus, the estimated costs depend on the following estimates: the amount of drugs in the original treatment, the number of visits and hospitalizations required, the unit prices of each of these goods and services, the probability of an adverse reaction or iatrogenic effect, the costs of treating the adverse reaction or iatrogenic effect, and the impact of the treatment on subsequent survival. The total variability in our cost example depends on the variability in each of the components *and* the correlation among these variables. Looking at one component at a time may thus grossly understate the overall variability. Ignoring the correlation could have the same effect; later, we return to this issue with an example.

There are several ways to deal with this variability. One is to use bivariate sensitivity analysis (Christianson and Bender 1982; Vogel and Christianson 1986). Another is to simulate the model with assumptions about the variability in each of the parameters (see Dittus, Roberts, and Wilson 1989 for a discussion and citations). A third is to use the delta method (Rao 1973) to calculate the variability in the composite measure.

As an example of the third approach, consider a case where one is interested in the total cost of outpatient medical treatment but only the price per visit (p) and the number of visits (v) are observed from separate samples; the product (pv) is not observed directly on the same population. If the estimates are independent, then the overall variance is given by

$$\text{Var}(\overline{pv}) \sim \overline{p^2}\,\text{Var}(\overline{v}) + \overline{v^2}\,\text{Var}(\overline{p}), \tag{8.21}$$

which is based on a Taylor's series approximation. In general, if there is a vector of parameters Θ in a function $f(\Theta)$, then the variance of the average of f is approximately

$$\text{Var}(\overline{f}) \sim \overline{\left(\frac{\partial f}{\partial \Theta}\right)}\,\text{Var}(\hat{\Theta})\,\overline{\left(\frac{\partial f}{\partial \Theta}\right)}, \tag{8.22}$$

where Var($\hat{\Theta}$) is the variance–covariance matrix for all of the parameters in Θ. See Table 8.1 for a derivation. This approximation may not be very well behaved. Nevertheless, it does provide some indication of the overall variability of either the cost or the effectiveness.

Ratio problems

In calculating a cost–effectiveness ratio (= Δ cost/Δ effect), incremental efficacy of a treatment enters as a reciprocal.[38] Many studies are designed to provide reasonable power to detect a clinically meaningful difference between two or more treatments. Thus, there is a real probability that the true value of the change in effectiveness is close to zero, and thus, its inverse can range from very small to quite large. We were unable to find an asymptotic distribution for the cost–effectiveness ratio when the components were multivariate normal.[39]

Table 8.1. *Ratio Summary*

		95% confidence interval		
NUMT	Correlation	Lower	Upper	Prob. < 0
2	−0.5	−0.26	8.90	<5
	0.0	−0.48	6.46	<5
	0.5	−0.37	4.14	<5
3	−0.5	0.24	3.89	<1
	0.0	0.31	3.11	<1
	0.5	0.43	2.29	<1

Note: The numerator and denominators are normal with mean 1 and std. err = 1/NUMT and correlation as specified. Derivation of the delta method: Consider a function $f(x, y)$. If we take a first order Taylor's approximation around x_0 and y_0, we get

$$f(x, y) \approx f(x_0 \, y_0) + f_x \cdot \Delta x + f_y \cdot \Delta y.$$

$$\text{Var}(f) = E[(f - \bar{f})^2] \approx E(f_x \cdot \Delta x + f_y \cdot \Delta y)^2,$$

where Δx indicates the deviation from x_0. The last equation can be written as

$$\text{Var}(\bar{f}) = f_x^2 \, \text{Var}(x) + f_y^2 \, \text{Var}(y) + 2f_x f_y \, \text{Cov}(x, y).$$

For the ratio, let $r = x/y$. The $\partial f/\partial x = 1/y$, and $\partial f/\partial y = -r/y$. If we evaluate the ratio at $x = y = r = 1$, $\text{Var}(x) = \text{Var}(y) = 0.25$, and $\rho = -0.5$, then the $\text{Var}(r) = 0.25 + 0.25 + 2*0.5*0.25 = 1.0$, and the 95 percent confidence interval is [−0.96, + 2.96]. By comparison, the actual is [−0.26, + 8.90], which is quite different.

To further complicate matters, the estimates of the incremental costs and efficacy are probably not independent.[40] The magnitudes and directions of such covariances between costs and effectiveness are an empirical matter. Rarely is there sufficient structure to know a priori whether they are positively or negatively related. Nevertheless, one might suspect that the two are negatively correlated, because cases with adverse effects are very likely to be more expensive than average.

Results of a simple simulation shed further light on the last point. Consider a case where incremental cost and effectiveness are distributed as bivariate normal with sample mean for both cost and effect of 1.0, correlations $\rho = -0.5$, 0, or +0.5, and the standard error of the mean either 1/2 or 1/3. These standard errors correspond to t-statistics of 2 or 3 for the incremental cost or effectiveness being different from zero. The 95 percent confidence interval for each of the combinations is shown in Table 8.1. As the results indicate, the ratio is much more variable than either of its two constituent parts would suggest. One cannot rule out the possibility that the true cost–effectiveness ratio is several times or substantially less than the calculated value. The ratio may not be significantly different from zero, even when its components are individually significantly different from zero. Further, as the correlation between the numerator and the denominator becomes more negative, the confidence interval for the ratio increases.

The delta method does not work well in the case of a ratio, because the first order approximation does not adequately capture the nonlinearity in the inverse of the effectiveness.[41] In all of the cases in Table 8.1, the delta method estimate of the 95 percent confidence interval includes substantially more negative lower limit values and underestimates the upper limit.[42]

Thus, the only safe strategies for calculating the confidence interval for the cost–effectiveness ratio appear to be (1) simulation from summary statistics and (2) bootstrapping the estimate of the interval. The latter is particularly appealing if the sample sizes are modest and either the numerator (cost) or the denominator (effectiveness) is skewed. Generally, the costs of medical care are quite skewed. A third possibility may work under certain conditions. If cost and effectiveness can each be modeled as linear models under a logarithmic transformation, or if the incremental costs and efficacy are much larger then zero and quite statistically significant, then one may be able to calculate the logarithm of the cost–effectiveness ratio and its confidence interval directly. However, such an approach requires a level of statistical modeling well beyond that typical of cost–effectiveness analyses.

Conclusion

The statistical evaluation of alternative treatment regimens requires a thorough understanding and modeling of the process that generated the physician's and patient's behavior as well as the data collection effort. In observational studies, there is a strong presumption that the choice of treatment did not occur at random but was the result of a conscious selection process. As a result, unobservable characteristics, that is, case mix, of the patient may be confounded with treatment and lead to biased estimates of the efficacy (effectiveness) and cost of the treatment. Attempts to correct for case mix may be incomplete because of measurement error in the case mix variables. As a result, we believe that observational analyses are more difficult to perform in a statistically consistent manner. Nevertheless, such studies are essential in the early stages of exploring a research issue or in cases where randomized trials are unethical (e.g., the effects of smoking), too short term, or impractical for finding rare events (e.g., adverse reactions). But an observational study will not generally be a good substitute for an RCT if the RCT is feasible.

The statistical problems resulting from adverse selection due to individual and provider choices, measurement error, and latent or omitted variables are not limited to observational studies. Refusal to participate, attrition, and differential compliance can also threaten the validity of a randomized trial. If severe enough, they can reduce the quality of the study to that of an observational one.

This should not be construed as an indication that the addition of one part statistician or econometrician for each two parts of data will solve the issues raised here, especially in the case of observational studies. There are, for example, research designs that reduce the risk from latent differences among populations, estimators that can be used for selection models or endogenous explanatory variables, "fixes" for measurement error *if* some extraneous data on the error process are available. Because such methods require the analyst to know a great deal about the data-generating process, often at levels of detail beyond what is available, we should not expect that the use of sophisticated statistical methods ("omnimetrics" in Green and Byar's 1984 terminology) can protect us from the statistical problems we have discussed. These methods are not infallible, and the results may not be robust or unbiased to deviations from the assumed structure of the process. The estimates may still be biased because the adjustment was not comprehensive enough to resolve all problematic issues.

In this chapter, we have also stressed the importance of going beyond simple univariate sensitivity analyses to understand how much confidence one can place in the estimated cost–effectiveness ratio. Sensitivity analysis does indicate which parameter values will have a dramatic effect on the conclusions, but it fails to capture all of the variability in the ratio that results from the estimation of multiple parameter values. The full confidence interval is useful for at least two reasons: hypothesis testing and decisions about further research. The first is obviously one of the major reasons for the research. But the second is important as well. If the estimate of the cost–effectiveness ratio is as imprecise as our simulated example would suggest, then the proper conclusion of many of the studies in the literature should have been that the sample size was insufficient to provide clinically and economically meaningful power to choose among the treatments. These studies should have concluded that what is needed is further study, larger sample sizes, meta-analysis, etc.; see Weinstein (1991) and Hay and Robin (1991) for examples of the logic for deciding to do additional study.

Finally, analysts need to be reminded that failure to reject the null hypothesis when treatment A is not significantly different from treatment B does not imply that the two are equivalent in any sense. All too often, the null finding is attributable to a fundamental defect in the study (such as inadequate size for detecting meaningful effect), not failure of the treatments to be different.

CHAPTER 9

Decision trees and Markov models in cost–effectiveness research

Emmett Keeler

This chapter shows how decision trees can be used to structure analyses of choices involving drug treatments. The choices can be either at the individual level of deciding which treatment is best for a particular patient or at the policymaking level of influencing how classes of patients are treated. Such policy choices are faced by insurers in deciding which treatments to cover, by quality reviewers, by managers or consensus panels of health maintenance organizations (HMOs) in deciding which treatment options to allow or promote for various classes of patients, and even by the U.S. Food and Drug Administration or its counterparts in other countries in deciding whether drugs are safe and effective for a particular use.[1]

The chapter begins by showing how decision trees display the choices and uncertainties involved in diagnosis and treatment decisions. In this method, management alternatives are judged on the basis of the value of expected costs and health outcomes. Typical alternatives for treatment might be using the current standard drug versus using a new more expensive and more powerful drug. Typical diagnostic alternatives are deciding treatment immediately versus getting more information before deciding. Predicting the immediate outcomes of treatment is usually straightforward, but predicting long-run impacts can be more difficult.

Many models have been used to predict the long-run outcomes of treatment. The second half of the chapter discusses these models (in order of increasing complexity): formulas for life expectancy, Markov chains, Markov processes, and simulations.

Decision trees

Decision trees are a simple way to structure problems of decision making under uncertainty. As an example, consider the question of whether to give prophylactic antibiotics after cesarean section.[2] Antibiotics are given to reduce the probability of postpartum infection, in particular, endometritis. Many cost–effectiveness analyses of the use of various antibiotics for this treatment have been published (Iams and Chawla 1984; Ford, Hammil, and Lebherz 1987). A decision tree captures the essence of this decision (Fig. 9.1).[3] The leftmost node is connected to two branches that specify alternative actions. By convention, *choice nodes* are rectangular. At a choice node, the decision maker can pick whichever branch is better. The upper branch, "prophylaxis," represents the strategy of giving antibiotic prophylaxis (after the baby is delivered and the cord clamped). The lower branch, "no prophy," represents the strategy of not giving antibiotics. In analyses comparing various antibiotics, there would be a branch for each drug: "prophylaxis with ampicillin," "prophylaxis with cefoxitin," etc.

Allergic reactions by the new mother are a rare side effect of the antibiotics. The uncertain possibility of an allergic reaction is represented by a *chance node* (the circle after "prophy") leading to the branches "reaction" and "no reaction." Under the reaction branch is the probability p(react) with which it will occur. The other branch following prophylaxis indicates the much more probable case that there is no reaction. The branches coming from a chance node should partition the set of possibilities. That is, each possible result should lie in exactly one of the branches so that the probabilities of all the branches sum to 1. The symbol # on the last branch of a chance node conventionally means the probability of all other possibilities, in this case $1 - p$(react). Following the no reaction branch, another chance node reflects the uncertainty of infection. The mother will either have endometritis, with probability p_1(endo), or not.

The no prophylactic branch avoids a drug reaction, so it is followed immediately by the chance of infection node. The disadvantage of no prophylaxis is that the probability of infection, p_2(endo), is higher than when drugs are given prophylactically. The end of each terminal branch displays the outcome measured in terms of the financial and health costs. The outcomes and probabilities are used to compute the expected dollar costs and health costs for each choice or some weighted sum that reflects the relative values put on health versus dollars.[4]

The decision tree describes the major factors involved in decision making. For decision making, estimates of the parameters are needed: the costs or benefits and health outcomes of the various branches and the probability of their occurrence. Analytic techniques for obtaining these estimates have been discussed in other chapters. However, once the estimates have been made, simple calculations as shown in Box 9.1 suffice to combine them.

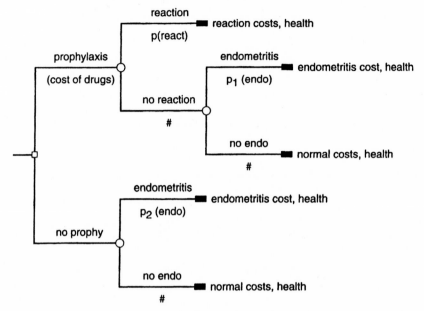

Figure 9.1. Decision tree for antibiotics after cesarean section.

Trees of screening and testing decisions

Decision trees provide a useful picture for simple clinical situations, but they are even more useful in clarifying diagnostic workup decisions about whether to secure more information on patients prior to treatment. Modern medical treatments are very powerful, entailing large financial costs and even potential health costs. If those who would benefit from treatment were known in advance, only those people would need to be treated, and the costs of treatment of the others could be saved. Decision trees have been widely used to model screening and testing decisions. Examples are given in the Appendix.

Management of a sore throat, a common decision in pediatric care, provides a concrete illustration of use of decision trees. The three alternatives are to give antibiotics to all, to test for strep throat and give antibiotics to those with positive cultures, and to give antibiotics to none (Fig. 9.2).[5] Computations with such trees reveal that, for screening to be effective, the test has to discriminate fairly well between those with and without treatable disease. For simplicity, assume the test perfectly identifies the patients who need antibiotics. With a perfect test, the best strategy for a particular patient depends on the initial probability that he or she has strep,[6] the costs of the test, the costs of the antibiotic, and the health consequences of untreated strep. In one

Box 9.1 Computing the best strategy

Suppose for simplicity that health is measured by days in the hospital and that the chance of a reaction is negligible, that is, assumed to be zero. Assume that the prophylactic drug costs $300 per mother and endometritis adds four days of hospital morbidity and $8,000 dollars to the cost of the cesarean section. With no infection, the mean length of stay in the hospital is three days at a cost of $7,000. Further assume that the probability of infection is 8 percent with this antibiotic, and 25 percent without. All these assumptions are listed at the bottom of the tree. We work backward from the tips of the tree to find average cost (0.08 × [$8,000 + $7,000] + 0.92[$7,000] = $7,640) at the branch "no reaction." Because we have assumed the chances of reaction are zero, the branch "prophylaxis" costs $300 + 1.0($7,640) = $7,940. For the "no prophylaxis" branch the dollar costs are 0.25 × ($8,000 + $7,000) + 0.75($7,000) = $9,000.

A similar calculation shows prophylaxis leads to 3.24 hospital days on average, while no prophylaxis leads to 4.0 days on average. In this case, prophylaxis is better on both costs and health grounds and would be recommended (assuming that the objective of society or the patient involved is to minimize mean cost and mean length of stay). If the drug cost $2,000 per mother, and there were no cheaper substitutes, the expected cost of the prophylaxis strategy would be $9,640. Then spending the extra $640 would save the mother from 4.0 − 3.24 = 0.76 days of hospital morbidity on average, and someone (physician, mother or payer) would have to decide whether the health gain was worthwhile.

In this example, the consequences of treatment are immediate, and so computing the expected consequence of each strategy is straightforward. Indeed, most of the cost–effectiveness analyses of this issue correctly computed average cost of each strategy without using a decision tree. Some of these analyses used the extra cost of infection as the criterion. To do so, they subtracted out the three days and $7,000 associated with cesarean section without infection from all outcomes, making the extra cost and health consequences of the "no endometritis" branch be zero, and of the "no prophylaxis endometritis" branch be 0.25 × $8,000 = $2,000, and 4 × 0.25 = 1 extra day. In this example and in general, any uniform changes in costs have no effect on choices, which are driven by the differences in the costs of each strategy.

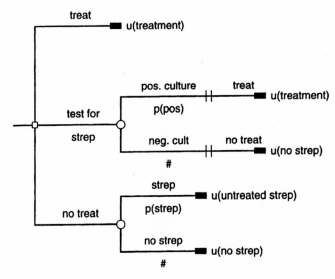

Figure 9.2. Decision tree for managing sore throat.

analysis, treating was optimal for initial probabilities above 20 percent, testing was optimal for probabilities from 5 to 20 percent, and no treatment was optimal for initial probabilities below 5 percent (Tompkins, Burnes, and Cable 1977).

Bayes' theorem can be used to analyze decisions with imperfect tests (Box 9.2). Using previously gathered information on test performance, analysts can estimate the expected proportion of "false positives," or people that the test indicates have the disease who do not, and use this information to decide whether to treat without testing, to test, or to neither treat nor test.

The problem of false positives is most severe when the initial probability of disease is low. This is a well known flaw in many screening programs. Consider the misguided policy of screening schoolchildren with or without sore throats using the throat culture test, giving antibiotics to those with positive cultures. If the prevalence of strep is 1/1,000 in such children, less than 1/220 of the children who test positive will have strep and potentially benefit from the antibiotics.

Modeling long-term consequences

The simplified decisions just discussed were easy because the consequences of treatment were immediate. Treatment decisions with long-term consequences

Box 9.2 Imperfect tests and Bayes' theorem

In fact, few tests are definitive, and the problem of combining various kinds of imperfect information is central to decision theory. A full analysis of the decision to culture needs data on how well the tests identify patients in practice who could benefit from antibiotics. Such information is normally collected by testing a spectrum of people with sore throats, keeping track of the proportion of those who fall into each of the four cells in a 2 × 2 box. Some hypothetical data are shown in Table 9.1.

The test identified 90/100 = 0.9 of the patients with strep correctly and 160/200 = 0.8 of the patients without strep correctly. Individuals that the test indicates have disease are called positives, so in this population there were 130 positives, of whom 40 were "false positives." Of the 170 test negatives, 10 actually had disease and were false negatives. Such data depend on a "gold standard" determination of whether people really have strep against which the proposed test is rated. Bayes' rule assumes that the current patients with and without strep are similar to those previously tested. So the conditional probability of test results given disease status is unchanged, for example, the conditional probability that a patient with strep in the test series had a negative culture, p(neg. test|strep), is 10/100. This conditional probability is assumed to hold for the current patient. Simple probability theory is then used to compute the probability that a current patient has disease, conditional on the prior estimate of the probability of disease, and on the test results. Suppose prior to a test, there is a 15 percent probability the patient has strep, but the patient's culture shows no strep. From the meaning of conditional probability,

$$p(\text{strep}|\text{neg. test}) = \frac{p(\text{strep and neg. test})}{p(\text{neg. test})} \tag{9.1}$$

$$= \frac{p(\text{strep and neg. test})}{p(\text{strep and neg. test}) + p(\text{no strep and neg. test})}$$

Substituting in equation (9.1), p(strep|neg. test) = (0.15 × 0.1)/(0.15 × 0.1 + 0.85 × 0.8) = 0.02. The probability of a negative test is the denominator, which is 0.695. With the same patient, p(strep|pos. test) = (0.15 × 0.9)/(0.15 × 0.9 + 0.85 × 0.2) = 0.44. These calculations are needed to fill in the probabilities on the strep tree with this imperfect test (Fig. 9.3). Figure 9.3 has further choice nodes after the test results, because one cannot assume that test results should be followed blindly by treatment. If the initial probability of disease is high enough, even a negative test result will not reduce the probability enough to make treatment a bad idea. To take an extreme case, if the prior probability were 100 percent (i.e., if a patient certainly has strep), then any negative culture must be a false negative. In such situations where management will not be affected by any possible test result, the test should not be given. Similarly, if the initial probability is low enough, even a positive test result should not lead to treatment, as it is probably a false positive.

Table 9.1 *Hypothetical results of test on previous patients with sore throats*

Test results	Patient Had		
	Strep	No strep	Total
Strep (positive)	90	40	130
No strep (negative)	10	160	170
Total	100	200	300

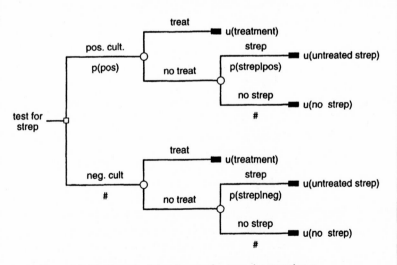

Figure 9.3. Test branch of decision tree for managing sore throat.

are harder to analyze. For example, many people have studied the effectiveness of high blood pressure or cholesterol drug treatments in modifying risk factors so as to reduce the probability of patients developing cardiovascular problems. A sketch of a tree that could be used to study the costs and effects of drug treatments to reduce mild hypertension is shown in Figure 9.4. The first part of the tree is straightforward: a patient is given drug treatment or not, a chance node indicates the possible amounts of risk factor modification, and a box marked lifetime outcomes gives the value of the outcomes of interest (discounted costs, life expectancy, disease free years, or quality-adjusted life years [QALYs]).[7] The figure begs the question of how to fill in the box.

Some analysts have avoided predicting long-term outcomes by assuming that the benefits of a drug are proportional to some intermediate outcome that predicts the long-run outcome. In primary prevention studies, they have used the change in the risk factor as such an intermediate outcome. Schulman et al. (1990) compared the "pharmacological" effectiveness of a variety of cholesterol-lowering drugs, showing that niacin had an average cost over five years of $139 per percentage reduction in low-density lipoprotein (LDL), low dose lovastatin cost $177 per percentage reduction, and cholestyramine $347 per percentage reduction. If the amount of cholesterol reduction is the same with different drugs, or if benefits are linear with the reduction in cholesterol, then niacin is also the most efficient approach for purchasing extra discounted years of life and can be recommended as better than cholestyramine, everything else being equal. However, unless the magnitude of lifesaving from a 1 percent reduction in cholesterol is known, for particular patients or on average, it is hard to compare these treatments to cheaper treatments, such as diet modification, smaller LDL reductions, or other health interventions.[8]

One approach to filling in the box of long-term outcomes is to build decision trees. In theory, complex trees could be built with proliferating chance nodes for what happens each year. Values at each of the resulting thousands of end branches would be determined by accumulating (discounted) costs and QALYs along the branches leading to that end. These values could be averaged back to the treatment date. In fact, with simplifying assumptions, analysts may be spared from working with enormous trees.

When using trees with more than a few branches, one of the standard decision tree software packages may be used (see the Appendix to this chapter for brands). These packages are practically necessities for construction and analysis of trees. First, they provide a simple way to draw and display larger trees. Usually, larger trees contain subtrees with the same structure in many places. For example, a subtree for one of the lifetime outcomes boxes in Figure 9.4 might look roughly like Figure 9.5.

This figure shows, for each five-year period, the probability of staying well or contracting heart disease. It contains the disease consequences box, which

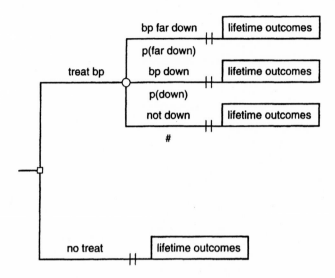

Figure 9.4. Decision tree for managing hypertension.

might contain a different subtree. The only difference between the subtrees attached to various levels of risk factor modification might be in the probabilities of disease, which the software allows to be altered. The software allows the analyst to define these groups of branches once and then paste them where needed onto the tree. The resulting tree is easier to enter into the computer, to visualize, and to revise. The software also has advantages for analysis and presentation of results. Various analyses, such as threshold analyses and two- and three-way sensitivity analyses, of key parameters may be conducted. These analyses can be displayed numerically and graphically.

The lifetime consequences of alternative courses of action may be split into several parts (Figs. 9.4 and 9.5). Most of the major models of prevention or screening and treatment do this. For example, the Coronary Heart Disease Policy Model (Weinstein et al. 1987) consists of three submodels: an epidemiological model of the chances of getting coronary disease (chd), a bridge model that describes what happens in the first thirty days after people develop disease if they do so, and a disease history model that deals with the rest of their lives.

In the rest of the chapter, four approaches for computing outcomes for the rest of patients' lives are discussed. The first approach, directly computing a single number representing discounted life expectancy from formulas based on characteristics of patients and their disease, is the simplest and cheapest. The

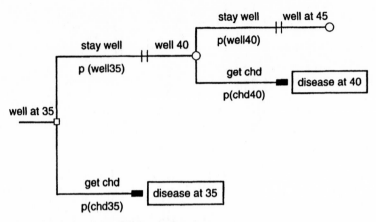

Figure 9.5. Piece of deep lifetime outcome tree.

other three approaches – Markov chains, Markov processes, and simulation – progressively allow more complexity and make weaker assumptions about the long-term consequences of disease.

Formulas for life expectancy after disease

The simplest approach to dealing with "the rest of their lives" is to invoke formulas for life expectancy after disease as a function of age, sex, and disease severity. These formulas are based on survival analysis.

Given data on survival of a cohort of individuals after the onset of severe disease, two functions of t, the time since onset, can be computed: $S(t)$, the proportion surviving to time t or longer, and $h(t)$, the "hazard," or survivors' proportional rate of dying, defined by $dS(t)/dt = -h(t)S(t)$. In general, some of the deaths are caused by disease, but some are due to other causes. Benefits of prevention or treatment can be assessed using the life expectancy for a variety of other people from the time they contract the disease. The simplest technique for directly computing life expectancy for people with disease assumes the hazard of dying from disease and of dying normally are both constant. This technique, called the DEALE, is described in Box 9.3 (Beck, Kassirer, and Pauker 1982; Beck et al. 1982).

In fact, the hazard of natural death is not constant, but exponentially increases with age (Gompertz 1825), and so the DEALE overestimates the probability of early death and systematically underestimates life expectancy with disease. Much more accurate, but more complicated, formulas for life expectancy with disease are given in Keeler and Bell (1992). However, the

---

Box 9.3 The DEALE

In the DEALE, the hazard of dying normally and of dying from severe disease are both assumed to be constant, and the combined hazard is assumed to be the sum of the two. It is easy to show that if the hazard of dying is a constant h, then $S(t)$ is $\exp(-ht)$ and life expectancy is $1/h$. For example, if 1 percent of survivors of a certain kind of cancer die each month, life expectancy is approximately $1/0.01 = 100$ months. The first step of the method uses the literature to compute the hazard of dying from severe disease. Suppose a cohort of sixty- to sixty-five-year-old women lived five years on average after contracting the disease. From the U.S. life tables, their normal life expectancy is about twenty years (DHHS 1989; Sox et al. 1988, 373). Assuming the hazard of dying normally is constant, it would be $1/20 = 0.05$, so $1/(x + 0.05) = 5$ years can be solved for x, the hazard of dying from the severe disease, obtaining $x = 0.15$. Now for another person contracting the disease whose normal life expectancy is L, the assumed hazard for normal death is $1/L$, and so the life expectancy by the DEALE approximation is $1/(0.15 + 1/L)$. The DEALE assumptions make it easy to discount future life years; exponentially discounting future years of life at a rate d is formally equivalent to adding a constant hazard d. Thus in the above example, if the discount factor for future years is 0.06, the discounted life expectancy is $1/(0.15 + 1/L + 0.06)$.

---

inaccuracies in the DEALE rarely lead to bad choices (Beck, Kassirer, and Pauker 1982; Beck et al. 1982). Imagine a formula that consistently underestimated life expectancy by a year. In any comparison of treatments, the error would cancel out, and the choice would be the same as with correct estimates.[9]

Markov chains

Most of the large models used for computing long-term outcomes in the literature are Markov models. These models are a technique for analyzing events that repeat, such as headaches (Leviton et al. 1980) or mental health treatment (Keeler, Wells, and Manning 1987), or events that play out over an extended period of time, such as the HIV–ARC–AIDs sequence (Cretin and Larson 1991), the progression of cancers (Eddy 1980), or heart disease (Weinstein et al. 1987). The basic idea of a Markov model is that individuals at any time are in one of a finite set of states of health, and that health changes from state to state according to a set of transition probabilities.[10]

In the simplest form, called a Markov chain, the transition probabilities are constant. A Markov chain could be used to model changes in health status of patients with kidney failure who are on dialysis. Here the two states are life on dialysis and death (for simplicity, ignore the possibility of transplants). In each period, living people die (transition to death) with probability p and survive with probability $1 - p$. Dead people stay dead (in "non–Stephen King" models). In specialists' jargon, death is an absorbing state because once entered, it is never left. Two common ways of depicting this Markov model are shown in Figure 9.6.

Suppose that 10,000 people enter the system at time zero and 10 percent of the people on dialysis die each year. Then at the end of the first year, 9,000 people are alive; at the end of the second year, 8,100 are alive. Life expectancy can be calculated by first summing the geometric series of how many people are alive in each year – $(10,000 + 9,000 + 8,100 + 7,290 + \ldots)/10,000 = 1/(1 - 0.9) = 10$ years – and then subtracting 0.5 years to get 9.5 years, assuming that people die on average in the middle of the year.[11]

The transition matrix P is another way of describing the dialysis Markov chain (Table 9.2).[12] The rows represent states at time t, and the columns the destination states in time $t + 1$. The matrix entries are the transition probabilities. Because everyone must end up in some state, the row probabilities add to 1.

If $a(t)$ is the row vector of the number (or proportion) of people in each state at time t, then the Markov chain follows the rule

$$a(t + 1) = a(t)P. \tag{9.2}$$

By applying this rule repeatedly,

$$a(n) = a(0)P^n. \tag{9.3}$$

The complete history of any initial cohort $a(0)$ can be predicted simply by repeating P. In fact, one can use simple matrix algebra to calculate parameters of interest, such as the mean and variance of the time spent in each state (Box 9.4).

Some analyses do not involve death as an outcome but rather the proportion of time people are in a particular state, or the length of time on average it takes to go from one state to another. To study the effects of health insurance on mental health treatments, Keeler, Wells, and Manning (1987) used Markov chains for people who had some treatment over the first three years of the Rand Health Insurance Experiment. In the model, time was measured in months, and the states were "under treatment" (defined as some treatment in that month) and "not under treatment" (no treatment in that month.)

The transition matrix for monthly mental health spending P is given by Table 9.4 (Keeler, Wells, and Manning 1987).

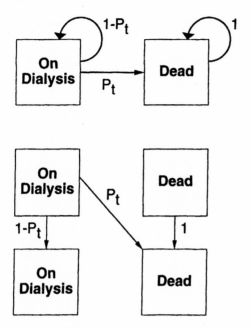

Figure 9.6. Two ways to depict the Markov process for dialysis.

Table 9.2. *Dialysis transition matrix*

	Next Period	
This Period	Dialysis	Dead
Dialysis	$1 - p$	p
Dead	0	1.0

The rows correspond to the state currently occupied, and the columns to the next period's state. Thus the figure 0.215 shows that 21.5 percent of those under treatment this month will not be so next month. The three statistics of most interest are the average length of treatment episode and of remission and the long run proportion under treatment, which again can be computed using simple matrix algebra (Box 9.5).

Box 9.4 Results on Markov chains with death

The canonical form for a matrix P with an absorbing state death is

$$P = \begin{vmatrix} Q & R \\ 0 & 1 \end{vmatrix},$$

where Q is the absorbing-states-to-nonabsorbing-states part of the transition matrix, and R is the column vector of absorbing states to death transitions. The matrix P in Table 9.1 is in canonical form, with Q the 1 × 1 matrix $(1 - p)$. The fundamental matrix $N = (I - Q)^{-1} = I + Q + Q^2 + Q^3 + \ldots$ where I is the identity matrix with the same dimension as Q. The fundamental matrix for P of Table 9.1 is thus $N = [I - (1 - p)^{-1}] = 1/p$. If n_{ij} is the entry of N in the ith row and jth column, then n_{ij} is the average number of steps that someone starting in state i spends in state j before dying. The variance matrix of the elements of N is $V = N(2N_{dg} - I) - N_{sq}$, where N_{dg} is the matrix whose diagonal elements are those of N and whose off-diagonal elements are zero, and N_{sq} is the matrix whose entries are the square of those of N. See Kemeny and Snell (1960, Chap. 3) for proofs and related results. These calculations are conditional on the assumed values of P. If the elements of P are measured with error, then those errors propagate into the variance. One can use sensitivity analysis to see whether estimation error or stochastic model error predominates.

Suppose that the first year of dialysis is a particularly critical time in which 15 percent die, but after the first year only 10 percent of survivors die in any year. The transition probabilities do not appear to be constant, but increasing the number of states to three – new dialysis, continuing dialysis, dead – results in the Markov chain transition matrix shown in Table 9.3.

Table 9.3. *Revised dialysis transition matrix*

	Next Period		
This period	New dialysis	Continuing dialysis	Dead
New dialysis	0	0.85	0.15
Continuing dialysis	0	0.90	0.10
Dead	0	0.00	1.00

In the revised dialysis matrix,

$$(I - Q) = \begin{vmatrix} 1 & -0.85 \\ 0 & 0.1 \end{vmatrix}, \quad \text{and} \quad (I - Q)^{-1} = \begin{vmatrix} 1 & 8.5 \\ 0 & 10 \end{vmatrix}.$$

Thus, people entering the system will live 1 year as a new dialysis and an average of 8.5 years as a continuing dialysis, for a total of 9.5 years. A person who is continuing dialysis can be expected to live 10 more years on average. The variance matrix that gives the variance of each estimate in N is

$$V = \begin{vmatrix} 1 & 8.5 \\ 0 & 10 \end{vmatrix} \times \begin{vmatrix} 2-1 & 0 \\ 0 & 20-1 \end{vmatrix} - \begin{vmatrix} 1^2 & 8.5^2 \\ 0^2 & 10^2 \end{vmatrix} = \begin{vmatrix} 0 & 89.25 \\ 0 & 90 \end{vmatrix},$$

so, for example, the variance of the estimate 8.5 years is 89.25.

Markov and semi-Markov processes

The simple and powerful Markov chain results depend on the transitions being constant. In particular, the probability of dying is assumed to be the same for twenty-year-olds as for sixty-year-olds. Because age must eventually take its toll, it is common in models of continuing disease to have transition probabilities that are not constant. If the transition probabilities depend only on time from the start (and hence on patient age) but not on which states the patient was in prior to the current period, the process is said to satisfy the Markovian assumptions and is called a (time-dependent) Markov process.[13] An alternative formulation of the Markovian assumption is that "history doesn't matter." The mathematical results of Markov chains no longer apply, but the Markovian assumption makes programming the models easy. One simply starts, for example, a cohort of 10,000 identical forty-two-year-old men through a system with transition matrices $P(t)$ that depend only on time and simply applies equations (9.2) and (9.3) with P replaced by $P(t)$ and accumulates statistics. At the end, dividing by 10,000 gives the mean value of statistics for a single patient.[14] Such cohort analysis is a standard option of most decision tree programs.

The identical cohort analysis can be contrasted with sensitivity analyses that repeat the tests of alternatives for patients with characteristics varying over the range commonly seen in the population. Because results are not a linear function of patient characteristics, the average patient will not necessarily have average results, and one may need to model a range of people to get the

Table 9.4. *Mental health spending transition matrix*

	Next period	
This period	Not treated	Under treatment
Not treated	0.936	0.064
Under treatment	0.215	0.785

Box 9.5 Results on Markov chains without death

The long run proportions of those under treatment can be found by either computing P^n for some large n, all of whose rows are approximately the long run proportion, or solving $a = aP$ for the steady state proportion a, which is in fact (23 percent, 77 percent). The transition matrices for those with good and bad insurance similarly lead to the proportion of time (27 percent and 20 percent, respectively) that users will be under treatment. Multiplying by the proportion who ever use the service estimates the total effects of insurance. Statistical tests on these data revealed that there was a considerable difference between patients who had been in treatment for two months in a row and those who had not been treated last month but were in treatment this month. Again by expanding to the four states defined by treatment status in the past two months, the simple Markov chain format could be preserved. In the new model, average length of an episode of treatment was the number of months to go from the state "no treatment last month, treatment this month" to the state "treatment last month, no treatment this month." The matrix algebra calculations show this to be 4.7 months with a standard deviation of 5 months.

---

population average results.[15] Another advantage of repeating the analysis with different types of patients is that the results may indicate for which patients the treatment is best.

Typically, costs and effects occur and are summed in states, such as years × rate of drug treatment × cost of drugs for costs, and years of life for effects. It is also useful to be able to collect costs and effects at transition between states. Consider a model of screening for a silent disease such as hypertension.

When patients with disease are screened, their disease classification changes from undetected to detected. They may have initial workup costs associated with the transition, as well as continuing drug management and purchase costs associated with being in the state of detected disease. Some analysts handle the transition problem by introducing temporary states that fall between the immediate longer continuing (chronic disease) states. An example is the bridge submodel of the Coronary Heart Disease Policy Model (Weinstein et al. 1987).

If the transition probabilities also depend on how long the patient has been in the current state, the process is called a semi-Markov process. For example, in dialysis, the death rate in the initial year may be 15 percent, and death rates for subsequent years may be 10 percent (Table 9.3). This could be considered a semi-Markov process with two states, dialysis and death.

A pattern of falling hazards can also be seen for transplants, whose failure may be high initially but, once the graft takes, may fall to a low level. Drugs may be used to reduce the initial transplant failure rate, and the process will not be well described by assuming a constant failure rate. There are ways for dealing with these processes in standard software, but they have some practical and conceptual problems and will not be discussed much here.[16] Instead, semi-Markov processes will be treated as another reason for doing simulations.

Simulation

Computer power can be used to allow analysts to relax strong assumptions that otherwise would be needed to derive answers. For example, in statistics, bootstrap calculations allow one to compute standard errors of statistical procedures without restrictive assumptions on the distribution of errors or limits on the statistics (Efron and Tibshirani 1991).

In modeling health outcomes, Monte Carlo simulation is used to transform the health of individual patients by applying a random device to generate random "shocks" to see what happens to those at chance nodes, until they reach the end of the tree. Repeating these calculations thousands of times on identical patients, using fresh flips of the coin each time, leads to a distribution of outcomes which should converge to the expected distribution of outcomes for such patients.

With the earlier cohort analysis, the people in a certain state might have had different histories prior to getting there; so the Markov assumption was needed to give a simple determination of what should happen to them next. However, it is not needed in simulations, and indeed, virtually any assumptions about consequences can be simulated. In particular, simulations can handle (1) accumulating history, (2) non-constant hazard functions, (3) unmeasured frailty and effects of Darwinian selection, (4) utilities that are not the sum of annual utilities, and (5) future management decisions. These will be discussed in turn.

Accumulating history: Prognosis may differ strongly for patients with different histories. An AIDS patient who does not tolerate drug A may be switched to drug B but have a different set of results with drug B than a patient who starts with drug B. Or patients with a previous stroke may have quite different probabilities of survival after a heart attack or a stroke. In principle, differences in medical histories can be handled by a Markov process with two sets of states, for example, one for patients without a previous stroke and one for patients with a previous stroke. However, as the number of relevant factors in the histories increases, the number of states becomes unmanageable. It is conceptually and computationally easier to have fewer states with transition probabilities that are a function of history (i.e., at the first stroke, a flag indicating previous stroke is changed from 0 to 1 and transition probabilities are a function of this flag), as well as other patient characteristics (Swain et al. 1992).

Nonconstant hazard functions: Many diseases do not have constant transitions to the next stage. Some might have a high initial probability, but once that stage is survived, the transition probabilities may be low. Others may have a more nearly fixed stage, of say five years, before the next stage is entered. As long as patients are considered one at a time, it is not hard to build models incorporating any distribution of time to transition. It is no longer necessary to pick a particular cycle length. With the transition, accumulated costs and life can be updated as functions of the time to transition. Indeed, these costs can also be stochastic functions of the time to transition, if desired. The trade-off here is more realism in the modeling of transitions and a better idea of the distribution of results in exchange for more computation (the 10,000 or so cloned individuals that might get put through the model to compute the distribution of possible results).

Frailty and heterogeneous populations: Some people may be naturally hardier than others of the same age and apparent disease condition. If so, treatments increasing survival of the less hardy at the early stages of a disease may not have the expected benefit if survivors are more likely to die later than the hardier people who now survive the early stages. This phenomenon is well known in demography. Less advantaged populations such as black Americans have a greater life expectancy at age eighty than eighty-year-old white Americans, who in turn have a greater life expectancy than eighty-year-old Swedes (Shepard and Zeckhauser 1977; Manton, Stallard, and Wing 1991). This process can be depicted in a model by assuming that there is a distribution of unmeasured propensities that affect all transitions, and that each person starts with a draw from that distribution. The distribution may be hypothesized or in some cases estimated from data. Such modeling was important in an analysis of the effects of deductibles and ceilings on health spending (Buchanan et al. 1991).

Utilities for health that are not the sum of annual utilities: In a cohort analysis, utilities are accumulated period by period based on the period utility associated with the health status of survivors. However, utility may depend on health history. For example, people may become anxious if they get horrible headaches on 10 percent of days and actually feel worse than $0.1U$ (headache) $+ 0.9U$ (no headache). Or as another example, individuals may care about trajectories of health, not just the amount of time spent in each state of health, preferring to get the pain over with in an initial treatment rather than experience the same amount of pain spread out over intermittent future painful episodes of illness. In such cases, utilities can only be assigned to entire life histories, and the statistics on the proportion of time in various future states of health which come from cohort analyses do not suffice. Despite these potential problems, analysts almost always compute sums of annual utilities, such as QALYs or discounted QALYs (Chaps. 3 and 7).[17]

Long-term management: For management of chronic disease, the initial choice of drug is only the first decision, and indeed, the effects of that choice depend strongly on how downstream decisions will be made. These later decisions have to be taken into account in evaluating the initial decision. The Bellman principle underlying dynamic programming states that each part of an optimal strategy must be optimal (Bellman 1957). Thus, in deciding present optimal treatment, one should assume future decisions will be made optimally and back up from them to the present. Alternatively, one can pick strategies that decide all future decisions in advance in some reasonable way and "hardwire" those decisions into the model. With discounting, differences in outcomes between future reasonable preset decisions and future optimal decisions may be small.

Choice of models

In cases where there is only one transition of interest following a decision (e.g., from life to death), formulas usually suffice to compute long-term outcomes. When there are transitions between more than two states or back and forth between two nonabsorbing states, Markov models are a simple and powerful tool. Through matrix calculations or easy-to-use software, analysts can get a feel for the outcome implications of data-based or hypothetical transition probabilities. In Markov models, history (e.g., a previous stroke) can be included at the cost of multiplying the number of states. Analysts must use common sense to decide which factors cannot be excluded and, as a result, how many states to allow.

Even though simulations can be performed with arbitrarily complex sets of assumptions, this is not necessarily a good idea. The costs of computing are lower every year, and there are many useful ideas for controlling the number of runs necessary to achieve a certain degree of precision.[18] Still, it may be difficult to conduct a wide range of sensitivity analyses if each analysis requires processing 10,000 individuals through the model. More importantly, the results of a complex simulation may not be transparent, may contain hidden errors, and often are based on assumed details (such as the distribution of unmeasured frailty) that are not verifiable empirically or, at best, require elaborate statistical procedures that were not performed in the underlying research from which the parameters of the models came. A major advantage of formal analyses – clarity about assumptions and about their link to results – may be lost.

Typically, analysts want to abstract to essentials, that is, use "the simplest model that fits." Some of the more complex models currently in use reflect years of effort in building, debugging, and calibrating, and once built and verified have become formidable tools for analysis. Still, in most instances a rough prediction may be all that is useful (or cost–effective) to produce. If one treatment is much better than another, a rough calculation will verify that, and if treatments are close, the costs of the wrong decision may be small or highly dependent on individual circumstances. Even simple models that predict outcomes can substantially aid intuition in judging cost–effectiveness of drugs with long-term effects.

Appendix: Further reading

Readers desiring more details or examples of simple decision trees for treatment, screening, and testing can read textbooks on medical decision making (Weinstein et al. 1980; Sox et al. 1988) or the journal *Medical Decision Making*, in particular its clinical decision making rounds feature, which describes a variety of advanced decision theoretic techniques. Beck and Pauker (1983) provide an excellent introduction to the use of Markov models in clinical decision making. Kemeny and Snell (1960) give the underlying mathematics of Markov chains. Most analyses in *Medical Decision Making* use Decision Maker software developed by Steve Pauker or its spin-off SMLTREE, developed by Jim Hollenberg.

SMLTREE has a tutorial that explains the decision theoretic ideas behind its features as well as how to use them. These programs are DOS based. Other programs not aimed at medicine and typically including decision trees, influence diagrams, and some simulation capabilities include Mac-based DE-MOS (Lumina Decision Systems 415-327-4944), DOS-based Supertree (Strategic Decision Group 415-366-2577, and DPL (Applied Decision Analysis 415-854-7101; Windows Application).

Screening models combined with semi-Markov models of long term results have been widely used in studying cancer. To see the advantage of screening, David Eddy and others have built models of the natural history of disease with and without treatment. These are shown in his prize-winning book (Eddy 1980) and numerous papers (e.g., Eddy 1981, 1983; Eddy et al. 1987; van Oortmarssen et al. 1990).

The May–June 1991 issue of *Interfaces* was devoted to AIDS modeling (Cretin and Larson 1991). Markov and simulation models relating to screening, to needle sharing, to long-term projections of the epidemic, and to the impact of AIDS on the population of intravenous IV drug users were presented.

A large heart disease model that can be used for analyzing prevention or treatment questions has been developed at Harvard (Weinstein et al. 1987).

For an introduction to Monte Carlo simulation in decision-making models, see Swain et al. (1992).

CHAPTER 10

The use of cost–effectiveness/cost–benefit analysis in actual decision making: current status and prospects

Frank A. Sloan and Christopher J. Conover

The whole purpose of cost–effectiveness/cost–benefit analysis is to determine the best way to allocate scarce resources among alternative uses. Because markets for medical care and health insurance have a natural tendency to fail (Enthoven 1993), no country in the world has left these decisions about resource allocation entirely to private markets. Conversely, only a handful of countries have eliminated private markets entirely. Instead, health system policies form a continuum based on the degree to which government intervenes to make health care a social right (Roemer 1991).

Alternative methods of allocating health resources under constraints

There are numerous approaches to allocating health resources. In the current environment, these are often characterized as policies designed to control costs (see CBO 1991). However, it should be kept in mind that health cost containment per se is not an appropriate objective of public policy. Instead, we should be seeking the "right" level of health spending that would bring into balance the benefits and costs of medical care (Pauly 1991). The various approaches to health resource allocation can be categorized into four broad groups based on the locus of resource allocation decisions. That is, decisions about how much to do or how much to spend can be made by patients, payers, providers, or the public (Table 10.1).

The remainder of the chapter describes in more detail various strategies for resource allocation and the potential role of cost–effectiveness/cost–benefit analysis in each.

Table 10.1. *Alternative methods of health resource allocation according to locus of decision making*

Patients	Payers	Providers	Public
Cost sharing	Exclusions from coverage	Capitation	Expenditure controls
Behavioral incentives	Utilization review	Provider education	Supply controls
Competition among plans	Payer education		Price controls
Patient education			Public monopoly

Patient resource allocation strategies

Strategies that encourage greater patient involvement in resource allocation decisions include cost sharing, behavioral incentives, competition among plans, and patient education. These are not mutually exclusive but instead are often combined within different systems of care or types of health plans.

Cost sharing: This approach encourages patients to be more cost conscious when deciding what medical services to buy and how much to pay for them. The best evidence regarding the efficacy of cost sharing comes from the Rand Health Insurance Experiment, which showed that the annual medical expenses for patients with 25 percent cost sharing were nearly 20 percent lower than the expenses of those with free care (Manning et al. 1988). However, these savings cannot be interpreted as pure efficiency gains for two reasons. First, these savings were achieved at the expense of good health: those with free care had slightly better health than those on cost sharing plans, with low income patients being particularly vulnerable to the effects of cost sharing (Brook et al. 1983). Second, it appears that consumers cut back on medical services likely to be highly effective (e.g., treatment of pneumonia) at the same rate as they reduce their use of services where medical care is rarely effective (e.g., treatment of hypoglycemia) (Lohr et al. 1986). Likewise, rates of inappropriate hospital use were comparable under free and cost-sharing plans (Siu et al. 1986). Thus, despite an economic incentive to pick more carefully, patients appear unable to distinguish well between necessary and unnecessary care.

In theory, attention to cost–effectiveness/cost–benefit analysis could improve the decisions of consumers under cost sharing. For example, sophisticated consumers might find Eddy's work on Pap smears to be very illuminating regarding whether to seek such care annually or every three years (Eddy 1990).

In actual practice, however, nearly all cost–effectiveness/cost–benefit analyses are reported in medical journals, where providers, rather than patients, are the intended target audience. In order for this information to be used by consumers, it would have to be translated and made more accessible to them. Moreover, the decision of a patient who pays only 25 percent of the cost will be different from the decision made by a patient without any third-party coverage.

Behavioral incentives: An increasing number of employers are using differential cost sharing as a way to steer employees to particular providers or facilities or are relying on other types of economic incentives to encourage use of preventive services or to alter lifestyles (Ruffenach 1993). Differential cost sharing differs from conventional cost sharing in that the goal is less to reduce use of care than to influence where care is sought. In 1992, more than 58 million workers and 64 million dependents were eligible to use preferred provider organizations (PPOs) (Marion Merrell Dow 1993). Evidence suggests that PPOs are able to attract between 24 and 55 percent of employees and dependents who are enrolled in indemnity plans and that they reduce outpatient but not inpatient utilization (Hosek, Marquis, and Wells 1990).

In theory, cost–effectiveness/cost–benefit analysis could be the basis for selecting certain treatment patterns for comparative provider profiling (i.e., physicians with conservative practice patterns might be less likely to order tests or procedures whose costs are high relative to the benefit obtained).

Competition among plans: This approach encourages patients to make trade-offs at a much higher level of aggregation. Competition among plans allows patients to make an annual plan selection based on price, quality, convenience, and, in some variants, benefits offered instead of simply deciding whether to seek care and where. Although plans or providers themselves actually make many of the resource allocation decisions within this model, the role of the patient is crucial in signaling to plans whether they have the "mix" right. For example, plans can lower their price by eliminating excess capacity, but this may result in occasional bottlenecks where patients must wait for services. Other plans will lower their price by making use of more cost–effective providers, such as nurse practitioners or physician assistants (CBO 1981). Some patients are willing to wait in line or to be seen predominantly by nonphysicians in exchange for lower premiums, whereas others are not.

The limited evidence regarding the cost–reducing potential of choice among plans is mixed. In the Federal Employee Health Benefits Program (FEHBP), for example, the evidence suggests that consumers select plans that minimize cost–sharing requirements but not total out-of-pocket costs (Marquis, Kanouse, and Brodsky 1985) and that large numbers of consumers select plans with net benefits among the lowest offered (Aaron 1983). On the other hand, there is evidence that consumers tend to move from low net benefit plans to high net benefit plans and that patients with particular conditions select plans advantageous to them (Marquis, Kanouse, and Brodsky 1985). However, because the FEHBP allows for some variability in benefits packages, it is not exactly comparable to a managed competition system in which the benefits package is standardized. In contrast, a study of the Minnesota state employees' program, which is more analogous to pure managed competition, found that plan switching produced savings of 5.1–6.9 percent. This is a lower bound on potential savings, since it does not capture the extent to which competition per se resulted in lower premiums for plans that were not the lowest cost plan (Feldman and Dowd 1993).

It is expected that widespread competition among plans (e.g., under managed competition) would result in greater numbers of consumers receiving their care through managed care plans such as health maintenance organizations (HMOs) and PPOs. The U.S. Congressional Budget Office (CBO) (Staines 1993) estimates that various types of managed care plans can deliver services at a cost that is 2–15 percent below that of unmanaged, fee-for-service plans. Therefore, the actual savings that would accrue from widespread competition depends on how consumers would sort themselves into various plans. These uncertainties are so great that the CBO was unable to project whether a full-blown system of universal coverage under managed competition would be less expensive than the current system (CBO 1993). Although decision analysis might be useful to a patient faced with multiple trade-offs, conventional cost–effectiveness/cost–benefit analysis, no matter how well executed or translated to consumers, has virtually no role to play in such decisions. As described in the remainder of the chapter, such methods may have an important role in improving the ability of plans and providers themselves to allocate resources under capitation.

Patient education: Improved information can benefit patient decision making with or without cost sharing. Broadly speaking, the current evidence suggests that consumers are about as well informed about prices for routine physician and dental service as they are for other similarly priced goods or services. However, consumers are less informed about hospital and surgical prices than about prices of other higher-priced goods (Marquis, Kanouse, and Brodsky 1985). There is good evidence that advertising results in lower prices both for eyeglasses (25 percent lower in Benham and Benham 1975; 14 percent lower in Feldman and Begun 1978) and for prescription drugs (4 percent lower in Cady 1976). An emerging trend has been the publication of hospital price lists by coalitions and other groups, but no systematic evidence regarding the impact that such information has on consumer choices or prices has been gathered. However, the Pennsylvania Health Care Cost Containment Council credits its

Hospital Effectiveness Reports (which report on price and quality) with leading to specific hospital price reductions and use of the compiled information in hospital advertising (Sessa 1993).

But better-informed patients may lower their use of medical services even when they face no cost sharing. A video developed to educate prostate patients about the benefits and risks of alternative approaches to treatment reduced the rate of prostate surgery among HMO patients who used the video by 44 percent (Holzman 1992). It is unclear how extensively this strategy might be used to effectively guide patients to an appropriate balancing of risks and benefits. In theory, physicians, acting as perfect agents, already ought to be providing equivalent information to patients. Recently, pharmaceutical companies, in a departure from the earlier practice of advertising only to physicians, have begun marketing prescription drugs directly to consumers by encouraging them to ask their doctor about certain new drugs, such as Minoxidil (Barnet 1991).

Cost–effectiveness/cost–benefit analyses have no role to play in improving price information. The benefits portion of such studies would be highly relevant to the development of materials to educate patients about the benefits and risks of different procedures. However, given patient heterogeneity, there are clear limits on the extent to which mass-produced patient education materials can substitute for or improve on a well-informed physician who assists the patient in reaching an informed decision about whether to undergo a medical procedure.

Payer resource allocation strategies

Payers can include employers, even if not self-funded, as well as third-party payers. Among strategies that entail payer involvement in resource allocation decisions are exclusions from coverage, utilization review, and payer education. The first approach eliminates any provider discretion, and the second attempts to constrain the exercise of that discretion. The third assists payers in getting consumers to make more cost-conscious choices.

Exclusions from coverage: Payers are constantly faced with coverage decisions. Coverage decisions can apply to benefits, procedures, or products. Historically, most coverage decisions have been in the direction of expanding coverage. For example, coverage for drug abuse treatment was included in less than 40 percent of medium- and large-firm benefit plans just ten years ago, whereas today, nearly 100 percent include such coverage (Levit and Cowan 1990). However, employers and the government are under increasing pressure to adjust coverage in the face of budgetary pressures. Adjustment often takes the form of changing the plan structure (e.g., adjusting deductibles and copayments) but at times extends to trimming or limiting benefits as well. Decisions regarding procedures typically revolve around new technology. For example, the Health Care Financing Administration (HCFA) approved Medicare coverage of heart, kidney, liver, and bone marrow transplants and listed detailed criteria regarding what types of patients can receive transplants and where the procedures can be performed (*New York Times* 1991). Also, decisions about products typically are not made by employers, but drug formularies are a common feature in HMOs and state Medicaid plans.

Cost–benefit/cost–effectiveness analyses are rarely used in benefits coverage decisions. Certain benefits are promoted as being cost saving because they either substitute for more expensive services (e.g., home health, hospice care) or lead to reductions in use of medical care generally (see the growing literature on the offset potential of alcohol, drug abuse, and mental health treatment benefits). The reason for the rarity of cost–effectiveness/cost–benefit analysis is that most benefits are far too broad to enable useful assessment of their cost–effectiveness. Is coverage of physician services, for example, cost–effective? Moreover, even when cost calculations are used to justify inclusion of a benefit, they typically focus on demonstrating that a benefit "pays for itself" in terms of reduced medical spending rather than that the benefits from a service are worth their cost. On the other hand, because cost–effectiveness analysis is sufficiently specific for performing reasonable calculations, it has the potential to be very useful in making decisions about covering particular services or products. The actual use of cost–effectiveness/cost–benefit analysis appears to fall far short of its potential, however. A systematic survey by Drummond and Hutton (1987) of economic appraisal of health technology in the United Kingdom found that most such studies were conducted by independent researchers hoping to get published, with the result that relatively few had any influence on coverage decisions. But even if such methods were in greater use, a critical question is whether such analyses performed by private payers should adopt a social or a payer perspective. For example, an employer may get no benefit from a heart transplant performed on a worker who will soon retire, because all the longevity benefits will occur after the worker leaves the firm.

Utilization review: Utilization review includes a wide range of activities designed to influence how medical care is practiced. Among utilization review activities are review of inpatient admissions and length of stay (which can be done prospectively, concurrently, or retrospectively), second opinion surgery programs, and drug utilization review. The CBO (Staines 1993) estimates that in 1990 more than 65 million Americans were in health plans with effective utilization review (defined to include precertification and concurrent review for hospitalization).

The evidence suggests that private utilization review of hospital care reduces costs. One study of a precertification/concurrent review of hospital care showed a reduction in inpatient hospital costs of 8 percent and a reduction in overall health spending of 4–5 percent (Khandker and Manning 1992). Another study, which was not as well controlled as the first, found that a similar hospital review program offered by a large private insurance company reduced hospital expenditures by 11.9 percent and overall health spending by 8.3 percent (Feldstein, Wickizer, and Wheeler 1988), even taking into account the additional outpatient care induced by such review activities (Wickizer, Wheeler, and Feldstein 1991). On the basis of this and other literature, the CBO (Staines 1993) estimates that effective utilization review could reduce health spending by 4 percent compared to unmanaged, fee-for-service coverage.

In theory, cost–effectiveness/cost–benefit analyses could be useful adjuncts to utilization review, establishing thresholds for patients who could receive surgery or be admitted to the hospital and the optimal length of stay for a particular case. In actual practice, utilization review criteria are developed using clinician judgment to set such thresholds, typically using expected efficacy alone as the determinant of whether a patient should be admitted or surgery performed. In this regard, utilization review is quite conservative in the criteria used, since the threshold of what to allow using a cost–effectiveness standard occurs at a more stringent level than that determined only by examining whether there is net medical benefit to doing a procedure.

Payer education: This includes price and quality information developed by public agencies or private coalitions that can be used by payers to steer patients to less expensive providers. The quality of these efforts varies greatly, from simply summarizing hospital charges by procedure or diagnosis-related group (DRG) – with no adjustment for severity – to much more sophisticated efforts to report comparisons that adjust for patient differences (age, race, sex, case mix). The availability of such information is growing. For several years, HCFA has reported on hospital mortality rates for all facilities with Medicare patients, and nearly two-thirds of states have centralized hospital databases from which charge, length of stay, and other information are available on tape or in published reports. In contrast, the state of the art with respect to outpatient care is far behind. However, it is difficult to determine how many payers actually make use of such information in establishing incentives for patients to use particular facilities. Payer educational activity, although theoretically useful in red flagging inefficient facilities, does not require the use of either cost–effectiveness or cost–benefit analysis.

Provider resource allocation strategies

Strategies that entail provider involvement in resource allocation decisions include capitation and provider education. The first approach changes the economic incentives facing providers, and the second reduces uncertainty.

Capitation: Capitation includes all forms of prepaid medical care. Although some countries' national health systems (e.g., Great Britain's) use partial capitation as a way to pay physicians, the most common use of capitation in the United States is by HMOs. However, there are different types of HMOs, ranging from staff- or group-model HMOs, which often pay physicians on salary, to independent practice associations (IPAs), which typically pay their physicians on a fee-for-service basis. As used in HMOs, therefore, capitation provides an incentive for providers to organize and deliver care cost–effectively, but the degree to which that theoretical incentive is manifested in real-world behavior is partly dependent on the incentives facing the physician (Hillman, Pauly, and Kerstein 1989).

The evidence supports this idea. Although a large literature showed that HMOs appeared to deliver care 10–40 percent less expensively than fee-for-service physicians (Luft 1978), the question of whether this was achieved through self-selection of healthier patients was not resolved definitively until a randomized controlled trial (RCT) found that patients who received free medical care through a group model HMO had annual expenses that were 28 percent lower than those given free care through a fee-for-service plan. Most of the savings were attributable to lower inpatient use (Manning et al. 1984). In contrast, little evidence exists showing that IPAs save money (Luft 1978; CBO 1992b). In recent years, hospital utilization in fee-for-service plans has declined considerably. The CBO (Staines 1993) estimates that use of staff- or group-model HMOs would save 15 percent compared to fee-for-service plans today.

Cost–effectiveness/cost–benefit analyses can be effective tools in making capitated arrangements work well. Capitated plans, particularly those that are fully vertically integrated, face a full range of resource allocation decisions, including what services to include in a benefits package, how much resource capacity (staff and facilities) to acquire to serve a given population size, what specific procedures to perform, and what products to select (e.g., pharmaceuticals, durable medical equipment), given multiple possibilities. As noted earlier, the selection of procedures and products is most amenable to cost–effectiveness/cost–benefit analyses in capitated plans.

Provider education: Provider education typically has focused on physicians and includes various methods, such as feedback, medical practice guidelines, and continuing medical education. Of these, various approaches to feedback have been used most often – and have demonstrated most success in reducing costs through influencing physician practice patterns (DHHS 1992).

An early review of physician education efforts concluded that "physician cost containment education can lower costs without reducing the quality of care provided" (GAO/HRD 1982). Since then, there have been a number of studies that confirm this idea. A study by Cummings, Frisof, Long, and Hrynkiewich (1982) showed that feedback of test prices led to a 31.1 percent decline in test costs; Berwick and Coltin's study (1986) showed that feedback of comparative test ordering patterns among peers led to a 14.2 percent decline in test use; a study by Wachtel, Moulton, Pezzullo, and Hamolsky (1986) showed that development of inpatient management protocols led to a 15 percent reduction in total charges. In another case, the decline was 12.9 percent (Tierney, Miller, and McDonald 1990). However, another review showed that many studies of educational programs designed to encourage cost–effective care delivery focused on measuring short-term effects only and that the few studies that examined long-term impacts often found that the effects were, in fact, short lived (Siu, Mayer-Oakes, and Brook 1985).

Public resource allocation strategies

Strategies that entail public involvement in resource allocation decisions include expenditure controls, supply controls, price controls, and public monopoly. The first approach limits spending directly, and the second strategy affects costs indirectly by limiting the availability of capital or staff used to produce health services. The third approach alters incentives by changing unit prices, and the last approach displaces the private market entirely, leaving resource allocation decisions in public hands.

Expenditure controls: Although recent U.S. debate has begun to use the term "global budgets" more broadly, we will restrict the use of that term to operating budgets established for hospitals or other large providers of health services. Within this limit, individual providers are free to allocate the mix of resources and services provided (CBO 1992b). In contrast, expenditure caps or targets establish a ceiling on aggregate spending for all providers of a specified service (e.g., physician care) within a geographic area. Under expenditure targets, spending that exceeds the caps triggers a penalty enforcement mechanism that applies concurrently or prospectively. Under expenditure caps, an absolute spending limit cannot be exceeded during a specified period (CBO 1992b). There are several varieties of expenditure limits, including (1) expenditure limits with all-payer rate setting (e.g., Canada and Germany), (2) expenditure limits with premium regulation, (3) expenditure limits with managed competition (e.g., the Clinton health reform proposal), and (4) a combination of managed competition or premium regulation with all-payer rate setting (Holahan, Blumberg, and Zuckerman 1993).

The limited U.S. experience with such approaches has been mixed. The Rochester hospital experimental payment program established a community-wide cap on hospital revenues for nine hospitals. The consensus is that this has resulted in a slowing of hospital spending per capita relative to New York in general and to the United States (Block, Regenstreif, and Griner 1987; GAO/HRD 1991), but some unique factors may underlie this success (CBO 1992b). The Medicare volume performance standards establish a target annual growth rate in physician payments, with a downward adjustment in fees the following year if spending growth exceeds the target. In the first two years, actual spending exceeded the targets, leading to cutbacks in scheduled fee increases. Thus, the limits "worked" but have raised concerns about whether physicians make up their Medicare losses by changing their practice patterns for non-Medicare patients (CBO 1992b). In contrast, there is extensive experience with expenditure controls if one considers the experiences of countries other than the United States, but most countries combine these with other approaches to cost control. It is difficult, then, to disentangle the independent effects of the expenditure controls per se. A qualitative summary of the experience in the many countries that use expenditure controls suggests that to be effective, ceilings must be implemented in combination with other cost control measures (e.g., all-payer rate setting) and include an enforcement mechanism (GAO/HRD 1991; CBO 1992b). One analysis of changes in the German system concluded that expenditure caps are a more effective mechanism for limiting health (physician) spending growth than are price controls (GAO/HRD 1991).

Cost–effectiveness/cost–benefit analysis plays no role in setting expenditure controls. However, under the constraints of such controls, cost–effectiveness/cost–benefit analysis could be effective, in theory, in showing where expenditures should be trimmed in order to stay within a ceiling. However, this depends very much on how caps are enforced. For example, critics argue that the system of global budgets for each hospital in Canada has led to inefficiencies in resource allocation, since hospital administrators have an incentive to fill beds with less sick or low-cost patients and avoid high-cost patients (Danzon 1992). Likewise, similar inefficiencies can plague the global budget system used for physician services in five Canadian provinces. Under this system, expenditure targets are set which, if exceeded, result in lower fees for all physicians in the next round of fee negotiations. Such a system does not target wasteful expenditures but instead rewards those who bill for excessive visits and penalizes those who do not (Phelps 1992). On the other hand, in theory, a global budget system tied to managed competition would give plans an incentive to trim low-value procedures in a competition to see which plan could offer the most value for the money (Starr and Zelman 1993). In the latter context, there may be extensive use of cost–effectiveness/cost–benefit studies to determine where to trim.

Supply controls: Supply controls include any mechanisms that limit the supply of health providers, pharmaceuticals, or medical equipment. Some Canadian provinces limit the number of medical school graduates, and Britain controls the number of hospital-based physicians by requiring regional approval of all new positions (CBO 1991). Both government approval of new drugs (e.g., the U.S. Food and Drug Administration) and drug formularies such as those used in several European countries have the effect of reducing the availability of pharmaceuticals (Culyer 1989). Most national health care systems control capital acquisition of hospitals through mechanisms such as certificate of need (Germany and most U.S. states), national capital budgets (Great Britain), or government control of prices and/or hospital budgets (Canada and France).

Most U.S. studies of certificate of need consistently have found that it achieved no reduction in per capita hospital spending (Brown 1983), in part because any savings were more than offset by the added costs imposed by the process itself, such as time delays in getting projects started and the cost of the application process. The story may be different in other countries. For example, a recent comparison of the availability of six high-cost technologies (e.g., magnetic resonance imaging [MRI], open heart surgical units) showed that the United States had two to seven times more capacity per million population than did West Germany or Canada (Rublee 1989).

Cost–effectiveness/cost–benefit analysis is largely irrelevant with respect to setting limits on the number of providers but is highly relevant in making decisions about supply controls for pharmaceuticals (see the remainder of this chapter for examples from Australia and Ontario). Such studies may have relevance in determining the optimal scale of high-technology services such as MRI, which would facilitate decisions about regionalization of expensive equipment.

Price controls: Price controls have been used most frequently for hospital services, physician services, and pharmaceuticals. The unit of service can vary widely, from hospital per diem rates (e.g., most state hospital rate-setting programs in the United States) to fixed amounts per case (e.g., Medicare DRGs).

The U.S. experience with all-payer hospital rate setting generally has shown that such programs lower hospital costs by 2–13 percent (CBO 1991), with more-stringent programs achieving the largest results (Thorpe and Phelps 1990). Although the issue of whether such savings come at the expense of patient health is important, the several studies which have addressed this issue have had conflicting results. One early study found that mortality rates were higher in states with rate setting (Shortell and Hughes 1988), but the analysis is plagued with methodological flaws. Another study found a small adverse effect of prospective payment on mortality, but these effects were inconsistent at the state level (Gaumer, Poggio, Coelen, Sennett, and Schmitz 1989). A more recent study found that states with rate regulation had *lower* mortality rates

among elderly patients (Smith, McFall, and Pine 1993). The general experience
with price controls on physician fees is that they are typically offset by volume
adjustments (Gabel and Rice 1985). Thus, countries such as Germany and
Canada have moved away from pure price controls to systems that combine
standardized fee schedules with utilization review designed to detect and pe-
nalize physicians with deviant practice profiles or expenditure targets (CBO
1991). Cost–effectiveness/cost–benefit analysis is not useful in establishing
price controls.

Public monopoly: Under public monopoly, the government provides health
care services using publicly owned facilities and/or publicly salaried physicians
(e.g., British National Health Service, U.S. Veterans' Administration system).
With the demise of the former Soviet Union and economic restructuring of
formerly communist nations in Eastern Europe, only a handful of countries are
left with fully socialist national health systems (e.g., Cuba, North Korea, China,
Vietnam; see Roemer 1991).

   With the exception of the Soviet Union (the only industrialized nation where
life expectancy fell during the 1980s), socialized systems, by providing a
minimum standard of health services accessible to the entire population, appear
to have been successful in achieving life expectancies comparable to those of
much better endowed nations with more weakly organized health systems
(Roemer 1991). Socialist countries tend to spend a lower fraction of gross
domestic product on health, mainly because of the extremely low salaries paid
to health workers (Roemer 1991). Skeptics have argued that public monopolies
are unlikely to be as efficient as privately delivered plans and are likely to be
characterized by lower availability of technology and/or waiting lines to obtain
care (Danzon 1992; Goodman and Musgrave 1992).

   In theory, cost–effectiveness/cost–benefit analysis would be highly relevant
in determining the type and number of services to provide in a public monopoly
system. Nevertheless, there is no indication of substantial use of such methods
in countries using public monopoly systems. But whether that is because of the
socialized system or because these same countries typically have lower per
capita gross national products is unclear (Roemer 1991).

Current applications of cost–effectiveness/cost–benefit analysis in health policymaking

This section reviews three applications of cost–effectiveness/cost–benefit analysis in health policymaking. The Oregon priority-setting system is included as
an illustration of how an effort to rank services according to cost–effectiveness
ratings was supplanted by a much less rational, more subjective ranking process. We then describe the recently implemented Australian guidelines for

coverage of new pharmaceuticals. The section covering the Australian guidelines is followed by a description of Ontario's draft guidelines for coverage of new pharmaceuticals. These systems illustrate a broad range of applications, with the Ontario "checklist" approach representing the most minimalist intervention to encourage use of cost–effectiveness/cost–benefit information in policy decisions. Oregon's system potentially represents the most extensive use of cost–effectiveness/cost–benefit analysis.

Oregon's priority-setting process for Medicaid coverage

Oregon has developed a unique approach to determining the benefits package available to Medicaid eligibles (a "substantially similar" package must be provided to Oregon employees under an employer mandate that becomes effective in July 1997). Rather than deciding which specific types of services to cover (e.g., prescription drugs, chiropractic services) or how to limit them, the Oregon approach eliminates specific treatments for specific conditions based on rankings from a public prioritization process. What is interesting about the Oregon approach is that initial rankings – "the first large-scale public attempt to apply cost–effectiveness analysis to set priorities for medical services" (Eddy 1991a) – were ultimately abandoned in favor of a hybrid process in which cost was not a major factor in determining the final rankings. Moreover, because even this modified process was initially rejected by the federal government, further modifications were required before a federal Medicaid waiver was approved in March 1993.

For all three approaches, the starting point was to develop condition–treatment (CT) pairs. International Classification of Diseases codes (ICD-9) were linked with Current Procedural Terminology codes (CPT-4) for one or more therapies used to treat the disease. Thus, ICD-9 code 201 for Hodgkin's disease would be linked with CPT-4 codes 38100, 49000, 49200, and 49220 for chemotherapy or radiation therapy. An initial list of more than 1,600 CT pairs was finally reduced to 709. Diagnostic services were not included on the prioritized list since all diagnostic services necessary to make a complete diagnosis are part of the benefits package. Likewise, all long-term care services were excluded from the list. In addition, mental health and chemical dependency services were exempted by law from the initial list and were instead ranked separately (they were incorporated into the list in October 1993). Preventive services were lumped into four categories, each of which was ranked on the final list: (1) children's preventive services, (2) adult preventive services of proven effectiveness, (3) preventive dental services, and (4) adult preventive services with little evidence of effectiveness. Under the pure cost–effectiveness approach, priority ratings were obtained based on the following formula (Hadorn 1991):

$$\text{priority rating} = \frac{\text{cost of treatment}}{\text{net expected benefit} \times \text{duration of benefit}}.$$

Cost measurement was based on data from the Oregon Medicaid program and other third-party payers or providers. The cost of treatment was measured using charges for all services pertaining to a diagnosis, including hospitalization, professional fees, drugs, laboratory and imaging services, and ancillary services such as physical or occupational therapy and rehabilitation and social services (Klevit et al. 1991). Subjective judgment was used to fill in gaps in these cost data. Indirect costs were ignored entirely. Since all treatments are assumed to occur in the current year, discounting of costs is unnecessary.

All benefit was measured using the Quality of Well-Being (QWB) Scale, which defines twenty-four functional states ranging from no illness to death – taking into account limitations in physical activity, mobility, and social activity and the presence of physical or mental symptoms (Klevit et al. 1991):

QWB = 1 – (mobility weight) – (physical activity weight)
         – (social activity weight) – (symptom weight)

The net expected benefit equals the expected QWB with treatment minus the expected QWB without treatment. In both cases, expected benefit is calculated as a weighted average for a typical patient, based on the probability of being in a particular state (e.g., death) and the weight attached to that state (0 = death, 1 = perfect health). The duration of benefit depends on the condition. Repetitive or episodic treatments were assumed to last one year, and treatments for self-limiting conditions were assumed to last five years. Specific treatments (e.g., hip replacements) with durations greater than five years but less than a lifetime have benefits that last for the lifetime of the treatment (Klevit et al. 1991). Finally, one-time treatments that are not repeated or replaced are assumed to last a lifetime, based on the life expectancy of a patient who is at the median age that a particular condition occurs. Panels of physician specialists were used to estimate the probabilities of each health state (with and without treatment), the patient age at which conditions occur, and the expected duration of benefits. Where possible, these estimates were based on the literature, with subjective judgment used to fill in missing information. All weights for the various QWB states were based on a random telephone survey of 1,000 Oregon citizens, supplemented by surveys of people in special categories (e.g., bed-ridden, chronically depressed, economically or educationally disadvantaged).

An eleven-member Health Services Commission consisting of three family physicians, an obstetrician, a pediatrician, four consumer representatives, a public health nurse, and a social services worker took eighteen months to develop the priority list. The commission rejected an interim working list that was based purely on cost–effectiveness rankings derived using the aforementioned method because, in the words of the project's first director, the formula did not pass a "gut-level check" (Read 1992, 9). The final list approved by the commission and filed with the state's application for a Medicaid waiver was instead based on an alternative three-step process:

1. Each CT pair was assigned to one of seventeen categories (Table 10.2). The commission ranked these categories using a group consensus method designed to reflect community health values expressed during forty-seven community meetings and twelve public hearings.
2. These categories were stacked (i.e., all items in the highest category were judged to be higher priority than any items, regardless of position, in a lower category). Within each category, CT pairs were ranked according to their net benefit, as previously described.
3. The commission performed a line-by-line review of the preliminary ranked list and used its judgment to move selected CT pairs up or down the list (33–50 percent of the items in the final list were moved in this fashion; see Hadorn 1991). Major factors taken into account during this final review included (a) number of people expected to benefit from treatment, (b) value placed on the treatment by society (prevention, e.g., was valued highly), and (c) cost–effectiveness ratio.

Thus, in the end, costs were taken into account only "to a minor extent" (Hadorn 1991). Once the list was prioritized, an actuarial firm calculated the estimated cost of providing services at various thresholds on the final list of 709 CT pairs, basing estimates on the likely number of Medicaid patients who would be treated during the year and assuming they were treated in managed care plans. The state legislature, which was barred from altering the rankings, appropriated sufficient Medicaid funds to cover all services through number 587 in the initial benefits package. Every two years, the commission will update the list and the legislature must vote on a new threshold for coverage.

The initial Medicaid waiver application was rejected in August 1992 because of concerns that the list "was based in substantial part on the premise that the value of the life of a person with a disability is less than the value of the life of a person without a disability" (Louis W. Sullivan letter to Barbara Roberts, 3 Aug. 1992; cited in Paul and Campion 1993, 10). Specifically, the Americans with Disabilities Act was held to rule out any consideration of the ability of a treatment to eliminate or reduce symptoms or of consumer opinions about quality of life based on residual symptoms. As a result, Oregon again revised its ranking method by (a) consolidating several controversial items

Table 10.2. *Categories of services used in the prioritization process and examples of condition–treatment pairs in Oregon*

Category	Description
Essential services	
1. Acute fatal	Treatment prevents death, with full recovery. *Example: Appendectomy for appendicitis.*
2. Maternity care	Maternity and most newborn care. *Example: Obstetrical care for pregnancy.*
3. Acute fatal	Treatment prevents death, without full recovery. *Example: Medical therapy for acute bacterial meningitis.*
4. Preventive care for children	*Example: Immunizations.*
5. Chronic fatal	Treatment improves life span and quality of life. *Example: Medical therapy for asthma.*
6. Reproductive services	Excludes maternity and infertility services. *Example: Contraceptive management.*
7. Comfort care	Palliative therapy for conditions in which death is imminent. *Example: Hospice care.*
8. Preventive dental care	Adults and children. Example: Cleaning and fluoride applications.
9. Proven effective preventive care for adults	*Example: Mammograms.*
"Very important" services	
10. Acute nonfatal	Treatment causes return to previous health state. *Example: Medical therapy for vaginitis.*
11. Chronic nonfatal	One-time treatment improves quality of life. *Example: Hip replacement.*
12. Acute nonfatal	Treatment, without return to previous health state. *Example: Arthroscopic repair of internal knee derangement.*
13. Chronic nonfatal	Repetitive treatment improves quality of life. *Example: Medical therapy for chronic sinusitis.*
Services that are "valuable to certain individuals"	
14. Acute nonfatal	Treatment expedites recovery from self-limiting conditions. *Example: Medical therapy for diaper rash.*
15. Infertility services	*Example: In vitro fertilization.*
16. Less effective preventive care for adults	*Example: Screening of nonpregnant adults for diabetes.*
17. Fatal or nonfatal	Treatment causes minimal or no improvement in quality of life. *Example: Medical therapy for viral warts.*

(e.g., cirrhosis of the liver caused by alcoholism was combined with cirrhosis of the liver from other causes), (b) eliminating the public survey weights for each QWB state, and (c) eliminating the measures of the treatment effectiveness in diminishing symptoms (Paul and Campion 1993). The revised list included 688 ranked procedures, of which 568 are to be funded in the first year. This revised list was approved by federal Medicaid officials in March 1993 (Fox and Leichter 1993).

Australia's Guidelines for Pharmaceuticals

To date, evaluation of pharmaceuticals by public agencies has been based almost exclusively on criteria of safety and efficacy. Some public agencies, faced with pressures to cut costs, have based selection of pharmaceuticals to be included on the drug formularies exclusively on a comparison of drug charges. The underlying assumption in such cases has been that drugs are about equally efficacious.

Two countries, Australia and Canada (especially the Province of Ontario), have gone a substantial step farther. As of 1993, for a new drug to be included in the Australian Pharmaceutical Benefits Scheme (PBS), manufacturers must submit, among other material, an economic evaluation of the drug (Australian Pharmaceutical Benefits Advisory Committee [PBAC], unpublished data; Drummond 1992; Johannesson 1992a). The guidelines for submissions require that only direct costs, such as the cost of treating the disease or condition, be included. Such nonmedical costs as home help, day care, meals on wheels, and nursing and physiotherapy cost may be included, but inclusion should be justified and sufficient detail should be provided to permit an independent assessment of such costs.

Indirect costs, such as lost earnings, are to excluded from the calculations. The arguments used to support the decision to exclude such costs are that (a) workers make up lost production after returning from short-term absences, (b) there is usually excess capacity in the labor force to cover absenteeism, and (c) for long-term absences, ill workers are replaced by otherwise unemployed workers. The text of the guidelines implies that the marginal product of labor in Australia is zero (PBAC). To standardize the prices used to compute cost, it was recommended that PBS develop a set of medical care shadow prices to be used in the economic analysis.

Unless drugs have clinically identical effects, in which case the cheaper drug is selected, costs and effects of the new drug are compared with the most commonly utilized drug for the indication – incremental cost–effectiveness analysis (see this volume's Chaps. 1, 2, and 5). If appropriate, the new drug is compared with nonpharmaceutical clinical strategies. If there is no drug for the indication, costs and effects of the new drug are compared with costs and effects without the drug.

The guidelines call for use of life years gained for drugs that mainly affect life expectancy and for intermediate-outcome indicators, such as change in blood pressure caused by antihypertensive drugs and change in cholesterol level caused by lipid-lowering drugs. Since there is little experience with using utility concepts to measure outcome in Australia (see Chap. 3 for a discussion of these utility-based approaches), the guidelines discourage use of such measures as change in quality-adjusted life years (QALYs) as measures of drug outcome. If quality-of-life measures are used, the authors of the evaluations are asked to provide supportive methodological detail and references. The guidelines encourage authors to report actual underlying changes in daily activities when summary measures of quality-of-life change are used. Cost–benefit analysis is not performed.

Authors are encouraged to base their evaluations on results of RCTs to the extent possible. However, the guidelines recognize that economic analysis requires information generally not available from RCTs. The evaluations use a discount rate of 5 percent, and future costs are measured in current prices. Sensitivity analysis on key parameters is performed. Authors consider the possibility in their sensitivity analysis that the cost–effectiveness of a drug may diminish if the drug is used by persons with less severe disease. Further, some consideration is given to the possibility that users of the comparable drug in the community may experience better outcomes than did the patients in the trial. The guidelines admit, however, that such alternative calculations may be difficult, given the lack of concrete empirical evidence. The PBS is to develop "yardsticks" to compare the cost–effectiveness ratios associated with alternative clinical strategies.

Ontario's draft guidelines for pharmaceuticals

In Canada, provincial formulary review committees consider effectiveness, safety, and cost of pharmaceutical products. At present, each province reviews drugs independently (Detsky 1993). An interprovincial economic working group has proposed that a single review committee be established countrywide to review economic evaluations of drugs. Ontario will begin using cost–effectiveness information routinely in formulary decision making and has established quidelines for manufacturers.

As in Australia, in making recommendations about listing pharmaceutical products, on provincial formularies, consideration is already given to effectiveness, safety, and cost. The draft guidelines do not introduce the concept of cost measurement, because provincial formularies already require this. Rather, they provide guidance about the information manufacturers should provide to decision-making bodies to enable them to more fully understand the economic implications of reimbursement for new products (Ontario Ministry of Health 1992).

The draft guidelines provide a worksheet for preparation of pharmacoeconomic analysis (Detsky 1993). To the extent possible, submissions to DQTC are responsive to the worksheet queries. The draft guidelines express a preference for information from RCTs or meta-analyses of RCTs (Chap. 2). It is recognized that there may not be data on long-term effects of clinical strategies from either RCTs or nonexperimental studies. When such data are unavailable, authors use modeling techniques to project lifetime costs and benefits (Chap. 9).

As a first pass, comparisons between costs and effects of the new drug are made with the least expensive currently available strategy, such as a generic product, although comparisons with the most commonly used alternative product may also be included (this contrasts with Australia, which uses the latter as the benchmark). Also in contrast to Australia, the evaluations may include indirect costs. Ontario's draft guidelines do not prescribe a particular method for outcome measurement. Willingness-to-pay measures of benefit are permitted. Ontario's argument for permitting diversity of approaches to outcome/benefit assessment is that the science of measuring outcomes is insufficiently developed to justify requiring a specific methodology. Overall, use of QALYs for computing incremental cost–effectiveness ratios receives greater encouragement in Ontario than in Australia.

The study authors must indicate who performed the analysis (Detsky 1993, 358). This requirement reflects concern over the level of competence of the individuals who prepare the report and about bias resulting from conflict of interest.

Evaluation

Oregon's, Australia's, and Ontario's programs represent the best attempts to incorporate the approaches described in this book into the policy making process. They span the gamut from a global approach that undertakes to prioritize a wide range of health services along the lines described by Weinstein (Chap. 5) to a set of open-ended instructions on how to structure presentation of economic analysis when submitting a new drug for consideration for coverage. The Australian approach is between the two extremes. Although the guidelines are more specific than those proposed by Ontario, the approach is still much closer to Ontario's than to Oregon's. Several specific aspects of these programs merit discussion, particularly as they relate to key points covered in this book.

Choice of effectiveness parameters: Evidence on effectiveness derived from RCTs is generally preferred to evidence from other sources, such as observational data and expert judgment based on clinicians' experiences (Chaps. 2 and 8). The scope of Oregon's undertaking precludes exclusive reliance on RCT-based evidence. Such information simply is not available for many of the treatment–procedure/diagnosis–condition combinations. Also, the combinations are broad, often encompassing several distinct therapies. If RCTs or observational studies were used to gauge effectiveness, it would often be difficult to know which studies to use. Since the two approaches for valuing new drugs are much less ambitious in scope than Oregon's, using RCT-based information is more realistic, even given the limitations of such evidence. Many of the mistakes made in Oregon, such as in gauging the duration of benefit (Eddy 1991a), may reflect the sheer enormity of the task of comparing so many benefits.

Heterogeneity of effect among patients is always an issue. Measures of average effect may be less useful than understanding variability of effect and the circumstances under which such variability occurs. Such heterogeneity is particularly important when the unit of analysis is a broad patient category, as in the Oregon plan.

Because some assumptions about effectiveness must inevitably be made, it is important to perform sensitivity analysis. Rankings of the type proposed in Oregon are likely to be quite sensitive to values of effectiveness and other parameters assumed (Petrou, Malek, and Davey 1993). Moreover, a large component of subjectivity was involved in the final rankings: the Office of Technology Assessment (OTA 1992a) found that one-fourth of all CT pairs moved up or down at least 100 lines on the list. So even if an identical process were replicated in another state, there might be substantial differences in the resultant lists.

Outcome measures: Before its waiver application was rejected, the Oregon plan was based on a quality-of-life measure of outcome. Although the QWB Scale is a well-regarded method of measuring quality of life, its twenty-four health states do not discriminate very well in terms of severity of symptoms (Eddy 1991a). For example, state number 6 is "abdominal pain," which can include a wide range of discomforts running from mild indigestion to an excruciatingly painful hernia. Moreover, even if this measure could capture substantially more fine-grained differences in health states, another serious flaw in the modified Oregon approach is that it is based on *average* outcomes for *average* patients, with no recognition of the heterogeneity of both clinical outcomes (health states) and patient preferences for those states (Eddy 1991b; Hadorn 1991; Ferrara 1993). Eddy notes that "ideally, in a priority-setting exercise, services should be defined narrowly enough so that every person who receives a particular service will have the same expected benefits and costs" (Eddy 1991b, 2136). But this requires that services be defined in detail by (*a*) patient indications (e.g., age, race, sex, severity of symptoms, comorbid conditions) and (*b*) procedural variations considering differing benefits and risks (e.g., there are numerous ways, ranging from surgery to drugs, to unclog arteries). The Oregon procedure would have been entirely unmanageable if performed at that level of detail. Such limitations may explain why the Australian guidelines are skeptical about using such measures, especially in their current state of development. Critics of using quality-of-life measures in practical applications have argued that different estimation procedures of health utilities yield different results, that the estimates are not reliable, and that obtaining a global measure of life quality is inadvisable (Drummond 1992).

Part of the skepticism about quality-of-life measures comes from groups who believe they are likely to lose if health services allocations are based on such measures – the disabled, the elderly, and some patients facing life threatening situations. In Chapter 3, Kaplan argued that opposition to the Oregon plan, based on the view that it discriminates against disabled persons, is misplaced. Yet, aside from the issue of whether or not the Oregon plan violated a federal law, the Americans with Disabilities Act of 1990, the fact is that the plan was opposed by groups representing the disabled, not just the Bush administration (Fox and Leichter 1993). When the losers are the vulnerable members of society, it is especially incumbent on the research community to be sure that the measures proposed for use by policymakers are both valid and reliable. If preferences do indeed differ by health state, a decision must be made about how much weight to give the preferences of individuals in particular states. Current policy is to give the views of the unhealthy considerable weight in certain situations, such as when to terminate life support. Oregon originally tried to use general public opinion supplemented by surveys of those in special categories, but this was judged to violate the recently passed Americans with Disabilities Act. Hence the final rankings were made without regard to any preference weights for different health states.

Measuring cost: Neither Oregon's nor Australia's method counts indirect costs like work loss. This implies that there is no value to a drug that allows a depressed person to return to work and no distinction between the benefit of returning to some household activity such as shaving or watching television and returning to work in the marketplace. Certainly, it is doubtful that employers would be indifferent between the two outcomes. Further, because of hiring cost and specific investments (on-the-job training), hiring a new worker to replace an existing one and treating the existing one so that he or she can return to work is unlikely to be a matter of indifference, especially for skilled jobs. More fundamental are objections that such costs are not sufficiently inclusive and that they discriminate against persons not likely to be employed. As Pauly states in Chapter 6, wage loss is likely to be a lower bound on the conceptually correct willingness-to-pay measure. In computing the benefit from a drug such as Clozeril, which allows schizophrenics to return to work (often in a sheltered setting), it is not so much the output gain that matters as much as the feeling of newly found independence and the relief provided other family members. This, however, is not to imply that the value of such output, if positive once one has subtracted out supervision cost, is worthless.

Even if, as argued here, the value of time lost because of illness of individual patients and their families is a legitimate social cost, government agencies in the health sphere may have difficulty giving full credit to such costs in practice. In cost–effectiveness analysis, such costs appear as cost offsets in the numerator of the ratio. When such offsets are subtracted from the sum of various medical costs, it is conceivable that the resulting numerator will sometimes be nearly zero or even negative, thus placing the clinical strategy in question at the top of the priority list for funding. If the medical costs place an appreciable burden on the agency's budget, at least some agencies may be reluctant to fund it, even though in principle the agency should maintain a social perspective of the costs and benefits of the programs it funds. The reason for this reluctance is that an agency, such as the Ministry of Health, may get little credit for a benefit like reducing work loss days, which is the purview of the Ministry of Labor. This consideration may lurk behind some of the reasoning for excluding indirect cost from cost–effectiveness calculations. Indirect costs were ignored entirely in the original Oregon cost–effectiveness rankings, probably in part because health officials in that state wanted to take a narrower perspective of social costs and benefits.

If indirect cost is to be considered, practitioners would do well to follow some of the suggestions made by Dranove in Chapter 4. Particularly tricky is measurement of the unit value of time. In some cases, use of a wage rate may greatly overstate the opportunity cost at the margin. The Australian guidelines diagnose the situation correctly, but their cure is too extreme. Ontario's draft guidelines ask how capital costs and overhead costs are treated in the economic analysis (Detsky 1993); however, they provide no guidance about how these cost items should be treated. Although various accounting procedures for attributing capital and overhead cost to particular preventive, diagnostic, and therapeutic procedures exist, there is no really accurate way to do this, even though regression analysis may sometimes be helpful, as Dranove suggests. Thus, at a minimum, it is important to know the allocation methodology employed and how sensitive the final calculations are to choice of methodology. Even Ontario does not mention the cost of drug research and development. For discussion of the issue of sunk versus incremental costs, we refer readers to Chapter 4.

Use of cost–benefit analysis: In the health area, cost–effectiveness studies far outnumber cost–benefit studies. The final version of the Oregon plan did not use cost–benefit or cost–effectiveness analysis. Nevertheless, since the allocations were performed subject to a budget constraint and a specific cut point, in effect the value of the least desirable funded program is being compared with the value of resources applied to uses other than personal health services. Benefit–cost analysis is expressly forbidden by the Australian guidelines. More specifically, the guidelines state that "such analyses are not likely to be helpful to PBAC in its deliberations and are not encouraged" (PBAC, 12). Ontario's draft guidelines do not appear to exclude cost–benefit analysis (Detsky 1993), but they do not encourage its use either.

In Chapter 6, Pauly argues rather persuasively that cost–benefit analysis is the conceptually correct approach. In fact, benefits are negative costs. In cost–effectiveness analysis, a reduction in wage loss appears as a negative cost offset in the numerator of the ratio. In cost–benefit analysis, costs (such as those associated with diagnosis and treatment) are subtracted from benefits, which are positive numbers. A comprehensive accounting of costs in cost–effectiveness analysis comes close to cost–benefit analysis. The only difference is that in cost–benefit analysis, life extension and quality-of-life extension are valued in dollar terms, and in cost–effectiveness analysis, they are not.

Lack of popularity (perhaps an understatement) among researchers and practitioners seems to stem from both distributional concerns and a judgment that willingness-to-pay measures are neither valid nor reliable. As Pauly states, it should be possible, at least in principle, for policymakers to reweigh benefits to reflect their distributional concerns. In practice, it is by no means easy to develop and implement explicit weights.

The measurement issues represent serious deficiencies. The wide range of estimates obtained in value-of-life studies (Fisher, Chestnut, and Violette 1989) is reason for real concern about the measures' validity and reliability. Yet it is reasonable to expect that this problem could be overcome by serious in-depth research. To the extent that the techniques discussed in this book will be used for making health policy decisions, undertaking such research should merit a high priority.

Discounting: The discounting of costs and returns and the choice of the discount rate remain controversial topics. Petrou, Malek, and Davey (1993) present a table of alternative discount rates used in economic evaluations of health care programs. The rates vary from zero to 20 percent. Discounting health is conceptually different from discounting financial values, in that health cannot be traded between time periods and among individuals (Chap. 7). The case for discounting in a health context is strong. However, the extreme variation in implicit health discounts obtained from empirical research, as with valuation of life measures, is unsettling (see Chap. 7 for a discussion of evidence on such discount rates).

Oregon, Australia, and Ontario have different policies on discounting, from no discounting of either costs or benefits in Oregon, to uncertainty about the discount rate to be used in Ontario, to specification of a 5 percent rate be used in Australia. A 5 percent rate is considerable for a social discount rate, considering that monetary values are to reflect prices prevailing in the year the evaluation is done. Real rates in financial markets (i.e., private, rather than social, rates) have tended to be far less than 5 percent. If anything, one would expect social rates to be less than private rates (e.g., the historical rate of return on U.S. Treasury bills has been roughly 3 percent). If practitioners in the health field are to use anything but real rates prevalent in financial markets (2 or 3 percent), further empirical research is needed to determine what the rate should be.

One's choice of a real rate critically depends on how one handles future inflation of medical care prices. Historically, medical care prices have risen far faster than the rate of general inflation. Perhaps this is a justification for using a higher than "normal" discount rate, such as 5 percent. But it is not at all clear that the authors of the Australian guidelines had this consideration in mind when they arrived at the 5 percent rate. Although consistency across economic evaluations is desirable, some justification for selecting a particular rate would be useful.

Gauging long-term effects of clinical strategies: Relatively little thought has been given in the Oregon, Australian, and Ontario approaches to modeling long-term costs and effects. The Australian guidelines provide little concrete help. They ask that the economic evaluator's time horizon be specified. For example, the guidelines state that "in the case of urinary tract infection 5–7 days might be appropriate. In the case of hypertension or peptic ulcer, maintenance treatment over several years might need to be considered" (PBAC, 12). At a minimum, best-practice techniques for accounting for long-term costs and outcomes should be disseminated, unless it is known that analysts are already familiar with these techniques.

A problem with Oregon's initial approach for establishing a rank ordering of health programs was estimating duration of benefit (Eddy 1991a). Given the huge number of procedures to be ranked, the four-category heuristic used to determine duration of benefits was an understandable simplification. Nevertheless, use of the more sophisticated approaches described in Chapter 9 probably would have produced considerably different results (particularly if long-term health benefits had been discounted properly). The guidelines from Australia and Canada certainly do not rule out the use of sophisticated methodologies for gauging long-run phenomena, but they do not provide guidance about choice of methodology either. How long-term costs and effects are calculated often has an important effect on program ranking. Here, additional practical experience with best practice techniques are needed, coupled with more longitudinal data on costs and outcomes of various clinical strategies. Recognizing that having longitudinal data is no panacea, particularly since technologies evolve as they are used (see, e.g., Chap. 4), in the final analysis, the sophisticated methods are only imperfect substitutes for the "real McCoy," that is, data on costs and outcomes.

Who should prepare economic evaluations? Various sources of bias may result from industry evaluations. The evaluations in Oregon were prepared by a public process that entailed a great deal of subjective judgment on the part of a highly visible eleven-member commission. Ontario's draft guidelines suggest that different weight be given to evaluations depending on how much freedom the authors have in preparing their report and in reporting their results. Australia's guidelines are silent on this point.

Bias is only one risk when decision makers rely entirely on estimates prepared by others. Another risk is lack of comparability across studies, though some lack of comparability is inevitable. Also, private analysts may not have complete access to information that is available to competitors. The bottom line is that total reliance on the work of others by public or private decision makers who use cost–effectiveness or cost–benefit analysis is not a good idea. Some direct access to personnel with technical knowledge of the relevant methodologies and time to apply this knowledge in scrutinizing economic evaluations is a must.

A brief research agenda

It is often customary to conclude articles and books with suggestions for further research. This book has presented the state of the art in cost–effectiveness/cost–benefit analysis of pharmaceuticals and other health care technologies. We have not presented the results of heretofore unpublished research but rather have discussed currently used methodologies, their advantages, and their deficiencies. Judging from this review, research topics that merit a high priority include the following.

Quantification of quality of life

On the whole, having an index of quality of life is very useful. Unfortunately, there is currently a lack of consensus about which measures to use. Further work on the measures, preferably by interdisciplinary teams sensitive to the alternative disciplinary perspectives, is likely to be very fruitful. Not to be neglected is input from persons with practical experience in policymaking. If such measures are to be used, not only must their basic underpinnings must not only be understood, but the measures must also be seen as essentially fair to the various constituent groups to whom policymakers are ultimately responsible.

Quantifying benefits in monetary terms

For cost–benefit analysis to be used, policymakers need to be able to trust willingness-to-pay measures. Therefore, further work on measurement of willingness to pay merits a high priority. To the extent that different approaches lead to different values of outcomes, researchers should address the reasons for these differences.

Determining appropriate discount rates for evaluation of health care programs

Again, more work on appropriate discount rates is needed. Here too, reasons for differences need to be identified. Lacking more solid empirical evidence, real financial rates should probably be used as long as forecasts of the likely relative rate of medical care inflation are taken into account.

Methods for securing cost information

The pluses and minuses of obtaining cost information from RCTs are not well understood. To the extent that accurate information cannot be obtained from trials, such as on rare adverse effects and their cost, attention should be devoted to how to incorporate information from observational data sets.

Final comment

During the past decade, there has been a growing realization that new approaches must be found for managing the allocation of resources devoted to personal health care services. At the same time, we have learned that no one disciplinary perspective provides all the answers. The dual problem of rising health care expenditures and pressures on public budgets is not unique to any country. Ways must be found to fund collaborative research on these issues, both across disciplines and across countries.

Notes

Chapter 2

1. A more detailed discussion of the choice of input prices will be covered by Dranove in Chapter 4.
2. Chapters 3 and 6 explore these measurement issues more fully.

Chapter 4

1. Benefits to individual providers usually take the form of extracting rents from the consumers in the form of higher prices. Such rents fall out in the calculation of total benefits since they do not accrue to society as a whole.
2. Freedberg et al. (1991) state: "The analysis was from a societal perspective, so total costs were considered without regard to the source of payment" (523). It is difficult to tell what the authors had in mind by this statement.
3. Note that "not affected by" refers to the practical importance of the intervention rather than its statistical significance. Differences in outcomes, treatment costs, etc., that are large in magnitude should usually be considered even when they are not significant. (Such differences often turn out to be significant when sample sizes are increased.) Although this introduces noise into the analysis, failure to include these differences introduces bias, which is usually worse.
4. Luft, Hunt, and Maerki 1987 documented a statistically significant relationship between volume and quality for a number of surgical procedures and argued that this is due to a learning curve.
5. The coefficient of variation equals the standard error of a distribution divided by the mean.
6. See Destache et al. 1990, Dranove 1989b, and Saywell et al. 1989, for studies that used this method.
7. See Les, Smith-Erichsen, and Lind 1987 and Ewald 1991 for discussions of variations in nursing time across patients within departments.

8. The distribution of costs within a cost center is likely to be highly skewed. Thus, the mean estimated cost will overstate the true cost for over 50 percent of the illness types treated in that center.
9. This estimate, however, does not take into account other characteristics of the job, such as risk, which may differ from characteristics of the home environment.

Chapter 5

1. This solution presumes that programs with both positive cost ($C_i > 0$) and negative effectiveness ($E_i < 0$) have been ruled out, and that programs with both negative cost ($C_i < 0$) and positive effectiveness ($E_i > 0$) have already been accepted. See Kaplan and Bush 1981.
2. See Box 5.4 for an example of this point concerning cholesterol reduction in different age groups.
3. The reciprocal of the C/E ratio for this marginal program may be interpreted as the shadow price of the budget constraint. That is, it represents the number of QALYs that would be sacrificed per dollar removed from the budget or diverted to other uses.
4. It can be argued that a portion of this economic benefit also accrues to the health care sector, the portion being the marginal contribution of earnings to health care resources via taxes, insurance premiums, and out-of-pocket expenditures. Analyses from the perspective of the health care sector should ideally include at least this portion of indirect benefits in the numerators of C/E ratios. More commonly, sensitivity analyses test the implications of either fully including or excluding the indirect benefits of morbidity reduction.
5. This is the principle known as extended dominance. See Weinstein et al. 1980b.
6. See Doubilet, Weinstein and McNeil 1986 for discussion of this caveat in interpreting C/E ratios.
7. If more than one program would have to be cut, or cut back, then the relevant cost-effectiveness criterion would be the weighted average of the C/E ratios of the reduced programs. Strictly speaking, the averaging would optimally be a harmonic average (i.e., weighting of the reciprocals), and the weights would be the costs diverted from each program.
8. The calculation is as follows. Each dollar diverted reduces funds for programs D and E each by $0.50. This results in the loss of $(0.5)(1/8,000)$ QALYs from D and $(0.5)(1/12,000)$ QALYs from E. The sum is $1/9,600$ QALY. Hence the new program, to be worth funding, must yield $1/9,600$ QALY per dollar, or $9,600/QALY.
9. If indirect mortality benefits are already subtracted from the numerator of the C/E ratio, which is *not* recommended, the human capital approach would lead to a threshold value of zero for the C/E ratio. This formulation strongly suggests that human capital provides a lower bound at best.

Chapter 6

1. One of the controversial issues in analyses that use a constitutional (or "veil of ignorance") perspective is whether the expected utility criterion is the right one to

use, and if so, what is the relevant utility function to use. In the interest of simplicity, this chapter assumes that a single utility function prevails in all states of the world. Kamlet (DHHS 1992b) also adopts an expected utility model but does not use it to evaluate the desirability of alternative decision rules. The use of this constitutional perspective, defined in terms of political economy, not of the law, was pioneered by Rawls (1971) and Buchanan and Tullock (1962).

2. The ratio approach is used in this exposition even though it can sometimes be misleading, especially if projects are large relative to the budget or are mutually exclusive. Chapter 5 discusses these problems in detail.

3. This argument does not contradict Kaplan's conclusion (Chap. 3) that populations appear to weight different health states in a similar fashion, for two reasons: (1) Kaplan has not investigated trade-offs between health and other goods (which is what the "monetary value" represents); and (2) Kaplan does not argue that all persons within a population have the same trade-offs—he only argues that the average trade-offs differ little.

4. Studies of willingness to pay under different survival probabilities do show that people at the same income levels report different willingnesses to pay (Acton 1973). People at equal wealth levels do take different chances on life-threatening behavior (e.g., driving without a seat belt). We cannot, of course, easily distinguish differences in true preferences from possible misconceptions of probability.

5. The analogous marketing technique of conjoint analysis is sometimes used for drugs.

6. If others in the community place positive value on benefits to lower-income persons, those values should be added.

Chapter 7

1. For a review of the debate over the choice of the appropriate discount rate for health effects, see Fuchs and Zeckhauser 1987, Keeler and Cretin 1983, and Lipscomb 1989.

2. This estimate of a 9 percent real rate of interest is based on the estimates provided in the recent analysis by Grabowski and Vernon 1990, which is based on the rates of return that pharmaceutical companies earn on their research and development investments.

3. The inflation adjustment to the discount rate ideally should take into account the particular commodity mix being valued, such as the medical care component of the Consumer Price Index (CPI). The overall medical component of the CPI is certainly not ideal, however, in that it abstracts from quality changes and encompasses a broad mix of goods and services with quite different rates of inflation.

4. For a review of the discounting controversies and the underlying economics, see Stokey and Zeckhauser 1978.

5. The income elasticity for health insurance is documented in Phelps 1973, Newhouse and Phelps 1976, and Phelps 1980.

6. Complex payoff streams with a large number of sign reversals or complex un-

certainties may make it difficult to compare different payoff streams and make judgments about present or future orientation.

7. See Viscusi 1992 for a comprehensive survey of the value-of-life literature.

8. See Viscusi and Evans 1990. Estimates of the implicit value of job injuries, for example, indicate that the income elasticity of job injuries is approximately 1.0.

9. Health is not the only outcome for which one could claim that the impacts are special. Advocates of increased national spending on housing, defense, and education likewise would argue that these allocations have special appeal. National defense ensures our very survival and education is fundamental to individual welfare and society. However, the government does not generally have a menu of different discount rates applicable to environmental programs, transportation programs, civil rights efforts, and similar policies. In all cases, one can make the argument that these programs merit special treatment. However, these arguments really are not a rationale for distinctive discounting so much as an indication of the importance of properly assessing these benefits.

10. Examples abound of analyses in which no discounting of long-term effects was undertaken. See, for example, Eddy 1980.

11. Keeler and Cretin 1983 discuss a variety of analytical ramifications of inadequate discounting.

12. I do, however, assume that there is additive separability across periods and that the within-year value of life (set equal to 1) is the same in each period.

13. These are the results of a poll undertaken by Lawrence Summers, reported in the *Washington Post,* national weekly edition, 16 July 1986, p. A22.

Chapter 8

1. This discussion is cast in terms of "effectiveness." Whether "effectiveness" or "efficacy" is more appropriate in a given context is discussed elsewhere.

2. See Gehan 1984 for a summary of the relative merits of randomized and observational studies.

3. In practice, it is often difficult to obtain an estimate of the cost of real-world implementation of the treatment from data collected during the trial. The costs of the trial include the costs of design, monitoring, and evaluation, in addition to the costs of treatment provided. Further, the providers used may be atypical of the community to be served or may already have the cost structure that will prevail only when all providers have gained experience with the new regimen.

4. We will provide some indication of where the results are sensitive to modeling assumptions. Because ANOVA formulations can also be expressed in a regression mode, much of what follows applies to that method or ANOCOVA.

5. For example, a study may not have a sample size adequate to detect a 10 percent increase in costs or mortality. Such an effect size is very important, but an estimate of 10 percent effect may not be statistically significant. Similarly, very large studies may have sufficient power to detect effects too small to merit much economic or clinical concern.

6. See Goldberger 1972 for an overview of structural models in social science research.

7. Cook and Campbell (1979, Chap. 1) and Holland 1986 provide excellent summaries of the views on this issue.

8. Holland 1986 provides an overview of Rubin's framework and how it fits into the overall context of studying causality with empirical data. Although Rubin has been credited with developing the model in its present form, the core idea of the model, understanding causation from the counterfactual, is long-standing and has, for example, been at the core of agricultural experimental work for decades (see Fisher 1926).

9. "Unit" here could be an agricultural plot, a laboratory animal, a human subject, or any unit of interest. The discussion will be conducted as if human subjects are of interest. The reason the individual index j is used will become immediately apparent; the reasons a time subscript is also used will be made clear later on.

10. By assuming that R is invariant over j and t, the r index can be left unsubscripted to reduce notational clutter.

11. For the moment assume that a sample of individuals to be studied has already been defined and is being observed. There is no harm is viewing this "sample" as an entire population if the discussion is kept at an abstract level.

12. The analysis is easily extended to the case of arbitrary $S \geq 2$ but is not done so here to keep things as simple as possible.

13. To this point nothing has been said about the way the $y_r(j, t)$ are measured. In practice, $y_r(j, t)$ may be measured as binary (e.g., dead/alive, success/failure), continuous (e.g., weight, survival time, progression time), counts (e.g., symptom counts, cell counts), etc. Some issues are specific to the kind of response, but it is sufficient for present purposes to assume only that the expected values of these responses exist (i.e., are finite).

14. That is, one might specify

$$Y_C(j, t) = f[d(j, t), X_C(j, t), \eta_C(j, t); \rho_C(j)], \quad \text{for} \quad d(j, t) = 0$$

and

$$Y_T(j, t) = g[d(j, t), X_T(j, t), \eta_T(j, t); \rho_T(j)], \quad \text{for} \quad d(j, t) = 1.$$

Because the $\rho_r(j)$ are free parameters, it involves no loss of generality to let $X_C(j, t) = X_T(j, t)$ and to call this common covariate vector $x = x(j, t)$. Where it leads to no confusion, the j and t indexes will be suppressed in the following to keep notational clutter to a minimum.

15. The presentation here suggests that binary comparisons between a treatment regime and the control are of primary interest. However, when a range of treatments is considered, for example, varying dose strengths (d), the treatment effect can be viewed as one point on some dose–response function $\delta(d)$. In the context of the linear model developed below, δ would represent the slope of the dose–response surface when d is allowed to vary continuously.

16. In moving from the general model to a linear treatment effect regression model with fixed parameters, several key assumptions made in any particular application may

or may not be reasonable. For a one-period model, a brief listing of such assumptions includes the following:

1. $f(\cdot) = g(\cdot)$; that is, the treatment does not affect the functional relationship between outcomes, causes, and controls and $\rho_T = \rho_C$ (i.e., parameters are the same in both models).

2. $\eta_T = \eta_C$; that is, treatment does not affect unobservables.

3. $\rho_r(j) = \rho_r(k)$; that is, the parameters are fixed, not varying (see Heckman and Robb 1985 for a discussion of the varying parameters case). This is a particularly strong assumption that suggests a form of homogeneity that may not characterize the population. Actually, in the linear model context, varying parameters can often be easily admitted with the recognition that only their mean is estimated using standard regression methods.

4. Separability: η is additively separable; for example, $f(\cdot) = f_1(d, x; \rho) + f_2(d, x, \eta; \rho) = f_1(d, x; \rho) + \varepsilon$ such that $E(\varepsilon | d,x) = 0$ or $E(\varepsilon | Z) = 0$, where Z are instrumental variables. Note that this allows for heteroscedastic errors; that is, $f_2(\cdot)$ depends on d, x; for example, $f_2(d, x, \eta; \rho) = h(d, x; \rho)\eta$.

5. Linearity in parameters: $f_1(d, x; \rho) = d\delta + x\beta + dx\gamma$ is essentially the model considered by Hausman and Wise (1985) and others. Note that allowing for interaction effects may be important; see the comments by Conlisk and McFadden on the Hausman–Wise paper.

When multiple time periods are involved, additional assumptions may be needed. For instance, what Holland (1986) calls temporal stability essentially implies that the functional relationships do not vary over time. In addition, in a temporal context, the covariance structure of unobservables, $\mathrm{cov}\{\varepsilon(j, t), \varepsilon(j, \tau)\} = \sigma(j)_{t\tau}$, may be important to consider.

Nonlinear-in-parameters models are quite common in applied research. Insofar as the analysis we present below is concerned, whether nonlinearity has different implications than linearity will depend on the particular application. In many instances, the important distinction is not between linearity in parameters versus nonlinearity in parameters but rather between models that are separable in unobservables versus models that are nonseparable in unobservables (see Manski 1988 and Angrist 1991 for discussion of separability and its implications). In many formulations, nonlinear-in-parameters models are nonseparable in unobservables and, as such, are problematic. Most probit and logit models are formulated so unobservables are nonseparable. Moreover, nonlinear models that have otherwise separable unobservable components will generally be plagued by nonseparable unobservables if covariate measurement error is present. See Carroll 1989 for a discussion of these issues.

17. An analogous result applies if d and/or x are matrices. To keep the algebra simple, we focus on the scalar case. In addition, the variables are taken as deviations from their grand means to simplify the algebra.

18. An important issue in any such analysis is the definition of the population for which the results of the study are presumed to be applicable. Moses (1985) discussed such inferential issues under the rubric of the internal versus the external validity of the study. Even if an RCT provides statistically sound results for some subpopulation (i.e., is internally valid), it may fail to be externally valid if its conclusions do not

extend to other subpopulations. Important examples of the possibility of internally valid studies failing to be externally valid are when the results of animal studies are used to infer something about human populations or, even more subtly, when the results of studies based on samples of males (females) are used to infer something about the female (male) subpopulation. As will be seen below, these issues become even more complex when the population/sample definition is based on endogenous variables (e.g., health status, amount of smoking/drinking) rather than on exogenous variables (e.g., sex, race, age).

19. See Brook et al. 1983 and Newhouse and The Health Insurance Experiment Group 1993 for discussions of refusal and attrition biases in the Rand Health Insurance Experiment.

20. Treatments assigned on the basis of endogenous characteristics are neither exogenous nor orthogonal to other characteristics. Hausman and Wise (1985) discuss these issues for income maintenance and electricity rate studies.

21. In some instances, controlling for confounders (e.g., severity) and/or allowing for interaction effects (e.g., severity with treatment) could circumvent channeling bias.

22. See Rubin's commentary on the Efron and Feldman 1991 article.

23. See Judge, Griffiths, Hill, and Lee 1980, Chap. 13, for details on alternative methods for errors in x-variables.

24. See Little and Rubin 1986 for a good general discussion of missing data.

25. The reader should consult Jorgenson 1983 for a general survey of these econometric issues.

26. The use of a random effects model will also be inconsistent unless μ_i is independent and identically distributed across individuals i (clusters).

27. This is mathematically equivalent to including a dummy variable for each individual (or cluster).

28. Conditioning works in recent logit and Poisson regression models but not, for instance, in probit models (Chamberlain 1980; Greene 1990).

29. See Rosenzweig and Schultz 1983 and Mullahy and Portney 1990 for examples in health economics.

30. Although this example provides an excellent illustration of how IV estimation can work in practice, it is a rather simple example in which no other covariates appear. More generally, the model includes a vector of covariates x, a subset of which may be problematic in the sense described. In this case, the IV vector z must contain at least as many elements as does x (typically including the nonproblematic elements of x). With Z and X representing the matrices of z and x stacked across observations, and with W some projection of X onto Z (e.g., $W = Z(Z'Z)^{-1}Z'X$), the general IV estimator of $\hat{\beta}$ is given by $\beta_{IV} = (W'X)^{-1})W'y$. Defining the $N \times 2$ matrices $S = [1, s]$ and $D = [1, d]$ and the $N \times 1$ vector $B = [b]$, the IV estimator of the intercept and slope parameters (a_2, b_2) in the birth weight model presented here can be written simply as $\hat{\beta}_{IV} = (D'S)^{-1}D'B$.

31. For example, in economic studies, economic theory itself can provide guidance in the choice of appropriate exclusion restrictions because profit maximization, competitive markets, and other economic paradigms often imply certain model structures that provide the identifying restrictions on which the choice of IVs can be based.

32. Heckman's (1979) original labor market formulation used reasonable assumptions about labor market behavior to provide such identifying information. Restrictions on how reservation wages and wage offers depend on family structure and labor market experience were the source of such identifying information.

33. Indeed, the probability limit of the estimate of δ can be signed opposite that of the subsample δ_i. Blyth (1972) presented a numerical example which, translated for the linear regression context, gives point estimates $\hat{\delta}_A = .05$, $\hat{\delta}_B = .45$, but $\hat{\delta}_{pooled} = -.35$.

34. See Koenker and Bassett 1982 for a conceptual overview and Manning et al. 1992 for a recent application.

35. Our reading of the literature suggests that, until recently, quantile estimation has not been utilized much in social science and other evaluation research. Estimation constraints may have been part of the reason, but now that some popular microcomputer software packages have added quantile regression procedures to their cache of estimation programs, we predict that published applications of quantile regression methods will grow substantially in the near future.

36. Some HMOs use tertiary facilities for rarer treatments or severe cases.

37. For example, Manning et al. (1989, 1991) found that the optimal Pigouvian tax on cigarettes was quite sensitive to modest changes in discount rates. See Chapter 7 of this volume for a discussion of discounting.

38. As noted in Chapter 6 of this volume, the relevant concern is not the average cost per unit effect size but the incremental cost of achieving that gain.

39. However, if the numerator and denominator were independent unit normals with mean zero, the ratio would be a standard Cauchy or a t with one degree of freedom. That distribution has moments <1 but no higher-order moments.

40. The differences in mean incremental efficacy and costs have been captured in the ratio of means, which captures the possibility that more-effective treatments are more likely to be more costly *on average*.

41. A similar situation occurs in the case of the log normal. If $\ln(y)$ is distributed as $N(\mu, \sigma^2)$, and if the estimates of μ and σ are m and s, respectively, then the true 95 percent confidence interval for the median is $[\exp(m - 1.96s/n^{0.5}), \exp(m + 1.96s/n^{0.5})]$. By the delta method, the confidence interval is $\exp(m) \pm \exp(m) \cdot s/n^{0.5}$. The true confidence interval is symmetric on the logarithmic scale but not on the raw scale, because the exponential is nonlinear. The delta method generates an approximation that is symmetric on the raw scale. Note: If we were concerned about the mean, then we must also include the term for the multiplicative retransformation factor $\exp(\sigma^2)$. If $\ln(y) \sim$ iid $N(\mu, \sigma^2)$, then a consistent estimate of the mean on the raw or untransformed scale is $E(y) = \exp(m + s^2/2)$.

42. See the note to Table 8.1 for an example.

Chapter 9

1. Making policy for classes of patients involves more than just deciding what is best for each patient. For individual patients, physicians may choose to tailor treatments to suit the particular wishes and circumstances of each patient within the constraints

of cost and availability of treatments. For classes of patients, society may have to set universal constraints to promote effectiveness, administrative simplicity, or fairness even if those constraints harm patients with unusual clinical circumstances or tastes. Surveyed physicians place more weight on effectiveness when considering policy decisions than when making decisions about individual patients (Redelmeier and Tversky 1990). Typically, cost–effectiveness studies aim at policy, rather than individual, choices and try to estimate average costs and effects for typical patients with average preferences. Decisions tailored to unusual patients are left to sensitivity analyses or are not considered.

2. An example of an analysis that used a decision tree to evaluate management of fever for infants (Lieu et al. 1991).

3. Throughout the chapter, "toy" models that ignore some of the complications of real clinical decisions are presented. This is done to make the key concepts clearer; in any real analysis, important complications in the models would have to be included.

4. Because the decision analysis method involves taking averages weighted by the probability of occurrence, the outcomes must be represented in a form that can sensibly be averaged. Decision analysts call such quantities "utilities." In decision trees for business or personal financial decisions, the dollar outcomes on each branch might be estimated. But if the decision maker places decreasing value on each extra dollar when wealth is high than when it is low, so that, for example, he or she would be indifferent between $350,000 with certainty and a lottery with a 50 percent chance of a $1,000,000 gain and a 50 percent chance of no gain (decreasing marginal utility of wealth), the outcomes should be measured in utility terms that reflect these "risk-averse" preferences rather than in raw dollars. See Raiffa 1968 or Keeney and Raiffa 1976 for more discussion of how utilities might be assessed, for example, how to efficiently define a function $U(\$)$ so that $U(\$1,000,000)$ is twice as big as $U(\$350,000)$. Psychologists have criticized these methods on the grounds that people do not act to maximize expected utility and in fact fail to do so in predictable ways (Tversky and Kahneman 1981). Decision analysts reply that their methods are supposed to be normative, not predictive. In health cost–effectiveness analyses, it is reasonable to use average dollar costs as an appropriate criterion, ignoring risk aversion for financial losses. The dollar consequences of a particular clinical situation are small relative to overall health costs paid by insurers or society, so that it would be inefficient to weight extremely large losses at more than their expected costs. Indeed, a major goal of insurance and government financing is to shift risks from individuals to bigger entities that are in a better position to bear such risks.

5. The double vertical lines on the branches following "test for strep" signify that the action on their right always follows next. In this case, with a perfect test, treatment always follows a positive test result.

6. The initial probability for a protocol is usually the prevalence of strep in the population of interest.

7. The methods and controversies concerning measurement of costs and benefits that are appropriate are discussed in Chapters 3 through 6. Rationale and techniques for discounting are discussed in Chapter 7.

8. There are numerous difficulties in going from percentage reduction in risk factor to

changes in life expectancy. See Weinstein and Stason 1976, 21–39 and Berwick, Cretin, and Keeler 1980, 95–126 for previous attempts to do this.

9. Because decisions are based on the differences between outcomes of treatments, this statement is true, but it is unlikely that formulas would be wrong in this way. Indeed, errors in estimates of disease hazards might have a small impact on short horizons but larger impacts if natural remaining life expectancy was long. Analysts might well check the sensitivity of results to such errors.

10. Recursive trees are another way of handling recurrent events. When modeling treatment of headaches, for example, the outcome of treatment might be temporary relief followed by some probability of a recurrence of the headache. The assumption that the clinical situation is essentially the same in a recurrence as in the initial headache (the Markovian assumption) permits a recursive tree. In the decision tree software, the branch "headache" is "pasted" in as a possible consequence of treatment. The program knows the set of branches following the initial state of headache and assumes they reapply. Programmers have to be careful to avoid infinite looping through the tree, and several other potential bugs, but in principal recursive trees can be useful.

11. In this example, the cycle length is 1 year. In general, one must decide whether to make the cycle long, which keeps down the number of cycles one needs to compute and hence the expense of a computation, or use a short cycle (one month, one day?), which avoids problems such as when in the cycle people die. Analysts must make sure that the transition probabilities are appropriate for the chosen cycle length. For example, if the instantaneous hazard of going from dialysis to death is h, and the cycle has length t, then the probability of a transition to death is $1 - \exp(-ht)$ in each cycle, which would be much smaller for a month than for a year. The given model is a discrete version of the DEALE, so the result that life expectancy $= 1/d$ is not surprising.

12. A regular Markov chain is one in which every state can be eventually reached from any other state. In other words, there exists an N so that P^N has all positive entries. For any regular Markov chain P, as $n \to \infty$, $P^n \to A$, which is a matrix all of whose rows are a positive vector a that gives the long-run proportion of time in the states from any starting point. The fundamental matrix Z is defined by $Z = [I - P - A]^{-1}$. For a patient in state i, the first passage time to state j is the number of steps before entering state j for the first time after the initial position. The mean first passage time matrix $M = (I - Z + EZ_{dg})D$, where E is the matrix of all 1s, Z_{dg} is the matrix whose diagonal elements equal those of Z and whose off-diagonal elements are 0, and D is the diagonal matrix with diagonal elements $d_{ii} = 1/a_i$. See Kemeny and Snell 1960, Chap. 4, for proofs and related results.

13. Hazard models involve the transition from one state to another but allow for the transition probabilities to change over time. Thus they can be considered two-state Markov processes (because everyone starts out alive, there is no history of previous transitions to worry about), and the DEALE is actually a two-state Markov chain.

14. Demographers have developed an extensive theory for constructing and using life tables. Life tables are simple two-state models (life, death) with values of $p(t)$, the probability of dying calculated for each group of interest (normally people categorized by age, gender, race, and possibly location). Annual vital statistics data are

commonly used by decision analysts to fill in their models for "normal" deaths. "Life expectancy at birth" is not a prediction of the mean length of life of babies born in 1993, which would depend on death rates for forty-year-olds in 2033, but rather the hypothetical construct of how long people would live on average if they had the death rates at age forty of today's (1993) forty-year-olds, and at fifty of today's fifty-year-olds, and so on. This convention is almost always used in cost–effectiveness studies, because the alternative (guessing what death rates far in the future will be) is thought to be too difficult and conjectural.

15. To see why we need to look at average results rather than results of the average patient, suppose a cholesterol-lowering drug reduces cholesterol values by 20 mg/dl, and a program gives the drug to a proportion p of the population. Mean patient cholesterol values will fall by $20p$ mg/dl, no matter which people make up the proportion p. Many diagnostic activities (screening, testing) are designed precisely to find out who will benefit the most from taking the drug. But if one bases analysis on "the average patient," one may not see any added benefit of diagnostic activities.

16. SMLTREE automatically allows for "tunnel" of states for which the time spent in a state matters by incorporating the trick we used for dialysis of defining each time in the state as a separate state. The tunnel is a vector of numbered states and allows clear models but can use up enormous quantities of memory and computing time if the necessary number of states is large. The decision maker allows tunnels to be created explicitly but also uses "limited" memory approximation to deal with survival functions of form $S(t) = K - bt$. The method has some conceptual problems and is not totally successful but may be good enough in practice.

17. The assumptions that lead to utility of life and health being expressible as S (discount factor), U (health), with U independent of time, are quite stringent (Pliskin, Shepard and Weinstein 1980). Utility representations that are more complex than discounted QALYs are rarely used in cost–effectiveness studies because (1) cost–effectiveness studies are generally done for typical patients, and little survey work has been done to estimate complex utilities in various populations; and (2) incorporating them would restrict the models that can be used to one-at-a-time simulations, making results less interpretable.

18. There is much of art and of science in performing Monte Carlo simulations in an efficient manner (Fishman 1978). The issues are very similar to those in efficient sample design in flesh and blood experiments and observational studies. Clever design can minimize the variance between two treatments that is due to different luck. Ideas to do this include matching on "luck," that is, using the same random number strings to compute outcomes on each branch; importance sampling, that is, oversampling the events that make the most difference and then using inverse sampling weights to calculate averages; antithetic variates, which pair streams of experience so that good luck in one stream is balanced by bad luck in another. These approaches were used in Buchanan et al. (1991) to calculate the effects of insurance on spending (where bad luck typically was large hospital bills), but they can be applied just as well to rare long-term health outcomes. On the other hand, it may be more efficient not to waste time figuring out how to have smart simulations but to just let the computer plug away longer.

References

Aaron, Henry. 1983. Orange Light for the Competitive Model. *Journal of Health Economics* 2(3): 281–4.

Abrams, Howard B., Allan S. Detsky, Leslie L. Roos, and Andre Wajda. 1988. Is There a Role for Surgery in the Acute Management of Infective Endocarditis? A Decision Analysis and Medical Claims Database Approach. *Medical Decision Making* 8(3): 165–74.

Acton, P. 1973. *Evaluating Public Programs to Save Lives: The Case of Heart Attacks*. R-950-RC, Jan. Santa Monica, Calif.: Rand Corp.

Amemiya, Takeshi. 1985. *Advanced Econometrics*. Cambridge: Harvard Univ. Press.

Anderson, Norman H., ed. 1990. *Contributions to Information Integration Theory*. 3 vols. Hillsdale, N.J.: Erlbaum Associates.

Angrist, Joshua D. 1991. Instrumental Variables Estimation of Average Treatment Effects in Econometrics and Epidemiology. NBER Technical Working Paper No. 115.

Antiplatelet Trialists' Collaboration Group. 1988. Secondary Prevention of Vascular Disease by Prolonged Antiplatelet Treatment. *British Medical Journal* 296(6618): 320–1.

Appel, Lawrence J., Earl P. Steinberg, Neil R. Powe, Gerard F. Anderson, Sharon A. Dwyer, and Ruth R. Faden. 1990. Risk Reduction from Low Osmolality Contrast Media – What Do Patients Think It Is Worth? *Medical Care* 28, pt. 1(4): 324–37.

Arrow, Kenneth J. 1951. *Social Choice and Individual Values*. New York: John Wiley & Sons.

Ashton, T. 1991. Cost-Effectiveness of Alternative Medications in the Treatment of Duodenal Ulcer. *Scandinavian Journal of Gastroenterology* 26, pt. 1(1): 82–8.

Atkinson, Scott E., and Robert Halvorsen. 1990. The Valuation of Risks to Life: Evidence from the Market for Automobiles. *Review of Economics and Statistics* 72(1): 133–6.

Balaban, Donald J., Philip C. Fagi, Neil I. Goldfarb, and Steven Nettler. 1986. Weights for Scoring the Quality of Well-Being Instrument among Rheumatoid Arthritics: A Comparison of General Population Weights. *Medical Care* 24, pt. 2(11): 973–80.

Ball, Stuart F., and Ellen Schneider. 1992. Cost of β-Adrenergic Receptor Blocking Agents for Ocular Hypertension. *Archives of Ophthalmology* 110, pt. 1(15): 654–7.

Barnet, Jim. 1991. Tagamet Radically Changed Drug Marketing. *News and Observer* (Raleigh, N.C.) 14 Apr., sec 8A.

Barrett, Brendan J., Patric S. Parfrey, Hilary M. Vavasour, Frank O'Dea, Gloria Kent, and Eric Stone. 1992. A Comparison of Nonionic, Low-Osmolality Radiocontrast Agents with Ionic, High-Osmolality Agents during Cardiac Catheterization. *New England Journal of Medicine* 326(7): 431–6.

Bator, Francis M. 1957. The Simple Analytics of Welfare Maximization. *American Economic Review* 47(1): 22–59.

Bauer, Paul W. 1990. Recent Developments in the Econometric Estimation of Frontiers. *Journal of Econometrics* 46(1/2): 39–56.

Beck, J. Robert, Jerome P. Kassirer, and Stephen G. Pauker. 1982. A Convenient Approximation of Life Expectancy (The "DEALE"). I. Validation of the Method. *The American Journal of Medicine* 73(6): 883–8.

Beck, J. Robert, Stephen G. Pauker, Jonathan E. Gottlieb, Karen Klein, and Jerome P. Kassirer. 1982. A Convenient Approximation of Life Expectancy (The "DEALE"). II. Use in Medical Decision-Making. *American Journal of Medicine* 73(6): 889–97.

Beck, J. Robert, and Stephen G. Pauker. 1983. The Markov Process in Medical Prognosis. *Medical Decision Making* 3(4): 419–58.

Bell, E. David, and Peter H. Farquhar. 1986. Perspectives on Utility Theory. *Operations Research* 34(1): 179–83.

Bellman, Richard E. 1957. *Dynamic Programming.* Princeton: Princeton Univ. Press.

Benham, Lee, and Alexandra Benham. 1975. Regulating through the Professions: A Perspective on Information Control. *Journal of Law and Economics* 18(2): 421–47.

Berger, Mark C., Glenn C. Blomquist, Don Kenkel, and George S. Tolley. 1989. Valuing Changes in Health Risks: A Comparison of Alternative Measures. *Southern Economic Journal* 53(4): 967–84.

Berwick, Donald M., and Kathryn L. Coltin. 1986. Feedback Reduces Test Use in a Health Maintenance Organization. *Journal of the American Medical Association* 255(11): 1450–54.

Berwick, Donald M., Shan Cretin, and Emmett B. Keeler. 1980. *Cholesterol, Children and Heart Disease: An Analysis of Alternatives.* New York: Oxford Univ. Press.

Birch, Stephen, and Amiram Gafni. 1992. Cost Effectiveness/Utility Analyses: Do Current Decision Rules Lead Us to Where We Want to Be? *Journal of Health Economics* 11(3): 279–96.

Block, James A., Donna I. Regenstreif, and Paul F. Griner. 1987. A Community Hospital Payment Experiment Outperforms National Experience: The Hospital Experimental Payment Program in Rochester, New York. *Journal of the American Medical Association* 257(2): 193–7.

Blyth, Colin R. 1972. On Simpson's Paradox and the Sure-Thing Principle. *Journal of the American Statistical Association* 67(338): 364–6.

Bombadier, C., P. Tugwell, A. Sinclair, C. Dok, G. Anderson, W. W. Buchanan. 1982. Preference for Endpoint Measures in Clinical Trials: Results of Structural Workshops. *Journal of Rheumatology* 9(5): 798–801.

Boyle, Michael H., George W. Torrance, John C. Sinclair, and Sargent P. Horwood. 1983. Economic Evaluation of Neonatal Intensive Care of Very-Low-Birth-Weight Infants. *New England Journal of Medicine* 308(22): 1330–7.

Breyer, Friedric. 1987. The Specification of a Hospital Cost Function: A Comment on the Recent Literature. *Journal of Health Economics* 6(2): 147–57.

Briggs, Gerald S., Brian R. Moore, Ray Bahado-Singh, Suk Lange, Pat Bogh, and Thomas J. Garite. 1987. Cost–Effectiveness of Cefonicid Sodium versus Cefoxitin Sodium for the Prevention of Postoperative Infections after Nonelective Caesarian Section. *Clinical Pharmacy* 6(9): 718–21.

Brook, Robert H., John E. Ware Jr., William H. Rogers, Emmett B. Keeler, Allyson R. Davies, Cathy A. Donald, George A. Goldberg, Kathleen N. Lohr, Patricia C. Masthay, and Joseph P. Newhouse. 1983. Does Free Care Improve Adults' Health? *New England Journal of Medicine* 309(23): 1426–34.

Brown, Lawrence D. 1983. Common Sense Meets Implementation: Certificate-of-Need Regulation in the States. *Journal of Health Politics, Policy and Law* 8(3): 80–94.

Buchanan, James, and Gordon Tullock. 1962. *Calculus of Consent.* Ann Arbor: Univ. of Michigan Press.

Buchanan, Joan, Emmett Keeler, John Rolph, and Martin Holmer. 1991. Simulating Health Expenditures under Alternative Insurance Plans. *Management Science* 37(9): 1067–90.

Burner, Sally T., Daniel R. McKusick, and David R. Waldo. 1992. National Health Expenditures Projections through 2030. *Health Care Financing Review* 14(1): 1–29.

Buxton, M., J. Ashby, and M. O'Hanlon. 1987. Alternative Methods of Valuing Health States. Health Economics Research Group, Brunel University. Mimeo.

Cady, John F. 1976. An Estimate of the Price Effects of Restrictions on Drug Price Advertising. *Economic Inquiry* 14(4): 493–510.

Calvert, A. Hilary, and Jane Urie. 1991. The Costs of Carboplatin Treatment. *Seminars in Oncology* 18, supp. 2(1): 28–31.

Campbell, Donald T., and Julian C. Stanley. 1963. *Experimental and Quasi-Experimental Designs for Research.* Boston: Houghton Mifflin.

Carroll, Raymond J. 1989. Covariance Analysis in Generalized Linear Measurement Error Models. *Statistics in Medicine* 8(9): 1075–93.

Carson, Jeffrey L., Brian L. Strom, Keith A. Soper, Suzanne L. West, and K. Lee Morse. 1987a. The Association of Nonsteroidal Anti-inflammatory Drugs with Upper Gastrointestinal Tract Bleeding. *Archives of Internal Medicine* 147(1): 85–8.

Carson, Jeffrey L., Brian L. Strom, M. Lee Morse, Suzanne L. West, Keith A. Soper, Paul D. Stolley, and Judith K. Jones. 1987b. The Relative Gastrointestinal Toxicity of the Nonsteroidal Anti-inflammatory Drugs. *Archives of Internal Medicine* 147(6): 1054–9.

CBO (U.S. Congressional Budget Office). 1981. *The Impact of PSROs on Health-Care Costs: Update of CBO's 1979 Evaluation* by Daniel M. Koretz. Jan. Washington, D.C.: Government Printing Office.

———. 1991. *Rising Health Care Costs: Causes, Implications, and Strategies.* Apr. Washington, D.C.: Government Printing Office.

———. 1992a. *The Potential of Direct Expenditure Limits to Control Health Care Spending.* CBO Staff Memorandum. Aug. Washington, D.C.: Government Printing Office.

———. 1992b. *Projections of National Health Expenditures.* Oct. Washington, D.C.: Government Printing Office.

———. 1993. *Managed Competition and Its Potential to Reduce Health Spending.* May. Washington, D.C.: Government Printing Office.

Chalmers, Thomas C., Harry Smith Jr., Bradley Blackburn, Bernard Silverman, Biruta

Schroeder, Dinah Reitman, and Alexander Ambroz. 1981. A Method for Assessing the Quality of a Randomized Control Trial. *Controlled Clinical Trials* 2(1): 31–49.

Chamberlain, Gary. 1980. Analysis of Covariance with Qualitative Data. *Review of Economic Studies* 47(1): 225–38.

Chapekis, Anthony T., Karen Burek, and Eric J. Topol. 1989. The Cost:Benefit Ratio of Acute Intervention for Myocardial Infarction: Results of a Prospective, Matched Pair Analysis. *American Heart Journal* 118, pt. 1(5): 878–82.

Chen, Xinhua, Henry Glick, and John Eisenberg. 1989. Comparison of Two Methods of Utility Assessment in Metabolic Control of Diabetes. *Society for Medical Decision Making and Abstracts, Scientific Session,* 324.

Christianson, Jon B., and Steven G. Bender. 1982. Benefit–Cost Analysis and Medical Care Delivery System Change. *Evaluation Review* 6(4): 481–504.

Clancy, Carol, R. Cebul, and S. Williams. 1988. Guiding Individual Decisions: A Randomized, Control Trial of Decision Analysis. *American Journal of Medicine* 84(2): 283–8.

Conley, Bryan C. 1976. The Value of Human Life in the Demand for Safety. *American Economic Review* 66(1): 45–55.

Cook, Deborah J., Gordon H. Guyatt, Andreas Laupacis, and David L. Sackett. 1992. Rules of Evidence and Clinical Recommendations on the Use of Antithrombotic Agents. *Chest* 102(4): 305S–11S.

Cook, Thomas D., and Donald T. Campbell. 1979. *Quasi-Experimentation: Design and Analysis Issues for Field Settings.* Boston: Houghton Mifflin.

Crawford, Jeffrey, Howard Ozer, Ronald Stoller, David Johnson, Gary Lyman, Imad Tabbara, Mark Kris, John Grous, Vincent Picozzi, Gregory Rausch, Roy Smith, William Gradishar, Anne Yahanda, Martha Vincent, Morgan Stewart, and John Glaspy. 1991. Reduction by Granulocyte Colony-Stimulating Factor of Fever and Neutropenia Induced by Chemotherapy in Patients with Small-Cell Lung Cancer. *New England Journal of Medicine* 315(3): 164–70.

Cretin, Shan, and Richard C. Larson. 1991. Introduction to the Special Issue on AIDS Modeling. *Interfaces* 21(3): 1–4.

Culyer, A. J. 1989. Cost Containment in Europe. *Health Care Financing Review* 11(annual supp.): 21–32.

Cummings, K. Michael, Kenneth B. Frisof, Michael J. Long, and George Hrynkiewich. 1982. The Effects of Price Information on Physicians' Test-Ordering Behavior. *Medical Care* 20(3): 293–301.

Dajani, Adnan S., Alan L. Bisno, Kyung J. Chung, David T. Durack, Michael Freed, Michael A. Gerber, Adolf W. Karchmer, H. Dean Millard, Shahbudin Rahimtoola, Stanford T. Shulman, Chatrchai Watanakunakorn, and Kathryn A. Tauber. 1990. Prevention of Bacterial Endocarditis: Recommendations by the American Heart Association. *Journal of the American Medical Association* 264(22): 2919–22.

Dalen, James E., and Jack Hirsh, eds. 1992. Antithrombotic Therapy. Introduction. *Chest* 102, supp.(4): 303S–4S.

Daniels, Norman. 1991. Is the Oregon Rationing Plan Fair? *Journal of the American Medical Association* 265(17): 2232.

Danzon, Patricia. 1992. Hidden Overhead Costs: Is Canada's System Really Less Expensive? *Health Affairs* 11(1): 21–43.

Department of Clinical Epidemiology and Biostatistics, McMaster University Health Sciences Centre. 1981. How to Read Clinical Journals: V. To Distinguish Useful from Useless or Even Harmful Therapy. *Canadian Medical Association Journal* 124(9): 1156–62.

Destache, Christopher J., Sharon K. Meyer, Marvin J. Bittner, and Kenneth G. Hermann. 1990. Impact of a Clinical Pharmacokinetic Service on Patients Treated with Aminoglycosides: A Cost–Benefit Analysis. *Therapeutic Drug Monitoring* 12(5): 419–26.

Detsky, Allan S. 1993. Guidelines for Economic Analysis of Pharmaceutical Products: A Draft Document for Ontario and Canada. *PharmacoEconomics* 3(5): 354–61.

Detsky, Allan S., and I. Gary Naglie. 1990. A Clinician's Guide to Cost–Effectiveness Analysis. *Annals of Internal Medicine* 113(2): 147–54.

Detsky, Allan S., Jeffrey P. Baker, Keith O'Rourke, and Vivek Goel. 1987. Perioperative Parenteral Nutrition: A Meta-analysis. *Annals of Internal Medicine* 107(2): 195–203.

DHHS (U.S. Department of Health and Human Services). National Center for Health Statistics. 1989. *Vital Statistics of the United States 1989.* 2 vols. Washington, D.C.: Government Printing Office.

————. Agency for Health Care Policy and Research. 1992. *Information Dissemination to Health Care Practitioners and Policymakers: Annotated Bibliography.* Apr. Rockville, Md.: Government Printing Office.

————. Office of Disease Prevention and Promotion. 1992b. *A Framework for Cost–Utility Analysis of Government Health Care Program,* by Mark S. Kamlet. Washington, D.C.: Government Printing Office.

Dittus, Robert S., Stephen D. Roberts, and James R. Wilson. 1989. Quantifying Uncertainty in Medical Decisions. *Journal of the American College of Cardiology* 14, pt. 1(3): 23A–8A.

Doll, Richard, and A. Bradford Hill. 1950. Smoking and Carcinoma of the Lung: Preliminary Report. *British Medical Journal* 2(4682): 739–48.

Doll, Richard, and Richard Peto. 1976. Mortality in Relation to Smoking: 20 Years' Observations on Male British Doctors. *British Medical Journal* 2(6051): 1525–36.

Donaldson, Cam. 1990. Willingness to Pay for Publicly Provided Goods: A Possible Measure of Benefit? *Journal of Health Economics* 9(1): 103–18.

Doubilet, Peter, Milton C. Weinstein, and Barbara J. McNeil. 1986. Use and Misuse of the Term "Cost–Effective" in Medicine. *New England Journal of Medicine* 314(4): 253–6.

Dranove, David. 1989a. Medicaid Drug Formulary Restrictions. *Journal of Law and Economics* 32, pt. 1(2): 143–62.

————. 1989b. What Impact Did the Programs Have on the Costs of Caring for Ventilator Assisted Children? In *Pediatric Home Care: Results of a National Evaluation of Programs for Ventilator Assisted Children,* ed. Lu Ann Aday, Marlene J. Aitken, and Donna Hope Wegener, 295–321. Chicago: Pluribus Press.

Dranove, David, Mark Shanley, and William White. 1991. How Fast Are Hospital Prices Really Rising? *Medical Care* 29(8): 690–6.

Drummond, Michael. 1992. Cost–Effectiveness Guidelines for Reimbursement of Pharmaceuticals: Is Economic Evaluation Ready for Its Enhanced Status? *Health Economics* 1:85–92.

Drummond, Michael F., and J. Hutton. 1987. Economic Appraisal of Health Technology in the United Kingdom. In *Economic Appraisal of Health Technology in the European Community,* ed. M. F. Drummond, 239–62. New York: Oxford Univ. Press.

Duan, Naihua, Willard G. Manning Jr., Carl N. Norris, and Joseph P. Newhouse. 1983. A Comparison of Alternative Models for the Demand for Medical Care. *Journal of Business and Economics Statistics* 1(2): 115–26.

EC/IC Bypass Study Group. 1985. Failure of Extracranial–Intracranial Arterial Bypass to Reduce the Risk of Ischemic Stroke. *New England Journal of Medicine* 313(19): 1191–200.

Eddy, David M. 1980. *Screening for Cancer: Theory, Analysis, and Design.* Englewood Cliffs, N.J.: Prentice-Hall.

———. 1981. The Economics of Cancer Prevention and Detection: Getting More for Less. *Cancer* 47, supp.(5): 1200–9.

———. 1983. A Mathematical Model for Timing Repeated Medical Tests. *Medical Decision Making* 3(1): 45–62.

———. 1984. Variations in Physician Practice: The Role of Uncertainty. *Health Affairs* 3(2): 74–89.

———. 1990. Screening for Cervical Cancer. *Annals of Internal Medicine* 113(3): 214–26.

———. 1991a. Oregon's Methods: Did Cost-Effectiveness Analysis Fail? *Journal of the American Medical Association* 266(15): 2135–41.

———. 1991b. What's Going on in Oregon? *Journal of the American Medical Association* 266(3): 417–20.

Eddy, David M., F. Warren Nugent, Judy F. Eddy, John Coller, Victor Gilbertsen, Leonard Gottlieb, Reed Rice, Paul Sherlock, and Sidney Winawer. 1987. Screening for Colorectal Cancer in a High-Risk Population. *Gastroenterology* 92, pt. 1(3): 682–92.

Edelson, Jonathan T., Anna N. A. Tosteson, and Paul Sax. 1990. Cost Effectiveness of Misoprostol for Prophylaxis against Nonsteroidal Anti-inflammatory Drug-Induced Gastrointestinal Tract Bleeding. *Journal of the American Medical Association* 264(1): 41–7.

Efron, Bradley, and D. Feldman. 1991. Compliance as an Explanatory Variable in Clinical Trials (with Comments and Rejoinder). *Journal of the American Statistical Association* 86(413): 9–26.

Efron, Bradley, and Robert Tibshirani. 1991. Statistical Data Analysis in the Computer Age. *Science* 253:390–5.

Eisenberg, John M. 1989. Clinical Economics: A Guide to the Economic Analysis of Clinical Practices. *Journal of the American Medical Association* 262(20): 2879–86.

Ellenberg, Susan S., Dianne M. Finkelstein, and David A. Schoenfeld. 1992. Statistical Issues Arising in AIDS Clinical Trials (with Comments and Rejoinder). *Journal of the American Statistical Association* 87(418): 562–83.

Enthoven, Alain C. 1993. The History and Principles of Managed Competition. *Health Affairs* 12, supp.: 24–48.

Enthoven, Alain C., and Richard Kronick. 1989. A Consumer-Choice Health Plan for the 1990s: Universal Health Insurance in a System Designed to Promote Quality and Economy (First of Two Parts). *New England Journal of Medicine* 320(1): 29–37.

European Carotid Surgery Trialists' Collaborative Group. 1991. MRC European Carotid Surgery Trial: Interim Results for Symptomatic Patients with Severe (70-99%) or with Mild (0-29%) Carotid Stenosis. *Lancet* 337(8752): 1235–43.

Ewald, Uwe. 1991. What Is the Actual Cost of Neonatal Intensive Care? *International Journal of Technology Assessment in Health Care* 7, supp. 1: 155–61.

Fanshel, Sol, and James W. Bush. 1970. A Health-Status Index and Its Applications to Health-Services Outcomes. *Operations Research* 18(6): 1021–66.

Farrell, Phillip, and Victor R. Fuchs. 1982. Schooling and Health: The Cigarette Connection. *Journal of Health Economics* 1(3): 217–30.

Feinstein, Alvan R. 1985. *Clinical Epidemiology: The Architecture of Clinical Research.* Philadelphia: W. B. Saunders.

Feldman, Roger, and James W. Begun. 1978. The Effect of Advertising: Lessons from Optometry. *Journal of Human Resources* 13, supp.: 253–62.

Feldman, Roger, and Bryan Dowd. 1993. The Effectiveness of Managed Competition: Results from a Natural Experiment. *Health Care Expenditure Controls: Political and Economic Issues.* Washington, D.C.: American Enterprise Institute for Public Policy Research.

Feldstein, Paul J., Thomas M. Wickizer, and John R. C. Wheeler. 1988. The Effects of Utilization Review Programs on Health Care Use and Expenditures. *New England Journal of Medicine* 318(20): 1310–14.

Ferrara, Peter J. 1993. *The Oregon Health Plan – Good Intentions Aren't Enough: What's Wrong, What's Better.* Portland, Oreg.: Cascade Policy Institute.

Fingarette, Herbert. 1988. *Heavy Drinking.* Berkeley and Los Angeles: Univ. of California Press.

Fischl, Margaret A., Douglas D. Richman, Michael H. Grieco, Michael S. Gottlieb, Paul A. Volberding, Oscar L. Laskin, John M. Leedom, Jerome E. Groopman, Donna Mildvan, Robert T. Schooley, George G. Jackson, David T. Durack, Dannie King, and the AZT Collaborative Working Group. 1987. The Efficacy of Azidothymidine (AZT) in the Treatment of Patients with AIDS and AIDS-Related Complex: A Double-Blind, Placebo-Controlled Trial. *New England Journal of Medicine* 317(4): 185–91.

Fisher, Anne, Lauraine G. Chestnut, and Daniel M. Violette. 1989. The Value of Reducing Risks of Death: A Note on New Evidence. *Journal of Policy Analysis and Management* 8(1): 88–100.

Fisher, Ronald A. 1926. The Arrangement of Field Experiments. *Journal of Ministry of Agriculture* 33:503–13.

Fishman, George S. 1978. *Principles of Discrete Event Simulation.* New York: John Wiley & Sons.

Fletcher, Robert H., Suzanne W. Fletcher, and Edward H. Wagner. 1982. *Clinical Epidemiology – The Essentials.* Baltimore: Williams & Wilkins.

Ford, Larry C., Hunter A. Hammil, and Thomas B. Lebherz. 1987. Cost–Effective Use of Antibiotic Prophylaxis for Cesarean Section. *American Journal of Obstetrics and Gynecology* 157(2): 506–10.

Fox, Daniel M., and Howard M. Leichter. 1993. The Ups and Downs of Oregon's Rationing Plan. *Health Affairs* 12(2): 66–70.

Frech, H. E., ed. 1991. *Regulating Doctors' Fees: Competition, Benefits, and Controls under Medicare.* Washington, D.C.: American Enterprise Institute Press.

Freedberg, Kenneth A., Anna N. A. Tosteson, Calvin J. Cohen, and Deborah J. Cotton. 1991. Primary Prophylaxis for Pneumocystis Crinii Pneumonia in HIV-Infected People with CD4 Counts below 200/mm^3: A Cost–Effectiveness Analysis. *Journal of Acquired Immune Deficiency Syndromes* 4, pt. 1(5): 521–31.

Freedman, David, Robert Pisani, and Roger Purves. 1991. *Statistics.* 2d ed. New York: W. W. Norton.

Freund, Deborah A., and Robert S. Dittus. 1992. Principles of Pharmacoeconomic Analysis of Drug Therapy. *PharmacoEconomics* 1(1): 20–9.

Froberg, Debra G., and Robert L. Kane. 1989a. Methodology for Measuring Health

State Preferences I: Measurement Strategies. *Journal of Clinical Epidemiology* 42(4): 345–54.

———. 1989b. Methodology for Measuring Health State Preferences II: Scaling Methods. *Journal of Clinical Epidemiology* 42(5): 459–71.

———. 1989c. Methodology for Measuring Health State Preferences III: Population and Context Effects. *Journal of Clinical Epidemiology* 42(7): 585–92.

———. 1989d. Methodology for Measuring Health State Preferences IV: Progress and a Research Agenda. *Journal of Clinical Epidemiology* 42(7): 675–85.

Fuchs, Victor. 1986. *The Health Economy.* Cambridge: Harvard Univ. Press.

Fuchs, Victor, and Richard Zeckhauser. 1987. Valuing Health – A Priceless Commodity. *American Economic Review Papers and Proceedings* 77(2): 263–88.

Gabel, Jon R., and Thomas Rice. 1985. Reducing Public Expenditures for Physician Services: The Price of Paying Less. *Journal of Health Politics, Policy, and Law* 9(4): 595–609.

Gafni, Amiram. 1991. Willingness-to-Pay as a Measure of Benefits: Relevant Questions in the Context of Public Decisionmaking Health Care Programs. *Medical Care* 29(12): 1246–52.

GAO/HRD (U.S. General Accounting Office, Human Resources Division). 1982. *Physician Cost-Containment Training Can Reduce Medical Costs: Report to the Secretary of Health and Human Services.* Feb. Washington, D.C.: Government Printing Office.

———. 1991. *Health Care Spending Control: The Experience of France, Germany, and Japan: Report to Congressional Requesters/U.S. General Accounting Office.* Nov. Washington, D.C.: Government Printing Office.

Gately, Dermot. 1980. Individual Discount Rates and the Purchase and Utilization of Energy-Using Durables: Comment. *Bell Journal of Economics* 11(1): 373–6.

Gaumer, G. L., E. L. Poggio, C. G. Coelen, C. S. Sennett, and R. J. Schmitz. 1989. Effects of State Prospective Reimbursement Programs on Hospital Mortality. *Medical Care* 27(7): 724–36.

Gehan, Edmund A., 1984. The Evaluation of the Therapies: Historical Control Studies. *Statistics in Medicine* 3(4): 315–24.

Gerking, Shelby, and Linda R. Stanley. 1986. An Economic Analysis of Air Pollution and Health: The Case of St. Louis. *Review of Economics and Statistics* 68(1): 115–21.

Geweke, John, and Burton A. Weisbrod. 1981. Some Economic Consequences of Technological Advance in Medical Care: The Case of a New Drug. In *Drugs and Health Economic Issues and Policy Objectives,* ed. Robert B. Helms, 235–71. Washington, D.C.: American Enterprise Institute for Public Policy Research.

Goel, Vivek, Raisa B. Deber, and Allan S. Detsky. 1989. Nonionic Contrast Media: Economic Analysis and Health Policy Development. *Canadian Medical Association Journal* 140(4): 389–95.

Goldberger, Arthur S. 1972. Structural Equation Methods in the Social Sciences. *Econometrica* 40(6): 979–1001.

Goldman, Lee, S. T. Benjamin Sia, E. Francis Cook, John D. Rutherford, and Milton C. Weinstein. 1988. Costs and Effectiveness of Routine Therapy with Long-Term Beta-Adrenergic Antagonists after Acute Myocardial Infarction. *New England Journal of Medicine* 319(3): 152–7.

Goldman, Lee, Milton C. Weinstein, Paula A. Goldman, and Lawrence W. Williams. 1991. Cost–Effectiveness of HMG-CoA Reductase Inhibition for Primary and

Secondary Prevention of Coronary Heart Disease. *Journal of the American Medical Association* 265(9): 1145–51.

Gompertz, Benjamin. 1825. On the Nature of the Function Expressive of the Law of Human Mortality. *Philosophical Transactions of the Royal Society of London* 115:513–85.

Goodman, John C., and Gerald L. Musgrave. 1992. *Patient Power: Solving America's Health Care Crisis.* Washington, D.C.: Cato Institute.

Goughnour, Barry R., and William W. Arkinstall. 1991. Potential Cost-Avoidance with Oral Extended-Release Morphine Sulphate Tablets versus Morphine Sulfate Solution. *American Journal of Hospital Pharmacy* 48, pt. 1(1):101–4.

Grabowski, Henry, and John Vernon. 1990. A New Look at the Returns and Risks to Pharmaceutical R&D. *Management Science* 36(7): 804–21.

Grannemann, Thomas W., Randall S. Brown, and Mark V. Pauly. 1986. Estimating Hospital Costs: A Multiple-Output Analysis. *Journal of Health Economics* 5(2): 107–27.

Green, Sylvan B., and David P. Byar. 1984. Using Observational Data from Registries to Compare Treatments: The Fallacy of Omnimetrics. *Statistics in Medicine* 3(4): 361–70.

Greene, William H. 1990. *Econometric Analysis.* New York: Macmillan.

Grobbee, Diederick E., Eric B. Rimm, Edward Giovannucci, Graham Colditz, Meir Stampfer, and Walter Willett. 1990. Coffee, Caffeine, and Cardiovascular Disease in Men. *New England Journal of Medicine* 323(15): 1026–32.

Hadorn, David C. 1991. Setting Health Care Priorities in Oregon: Cost–Effectiveness Meets the Rule of Rescue. *Journal of the American Medical Association* 265(17): 2218–25.

Hall, J. C., J. Mander, K. Christiansen, C. Reid, M. Cooney, and S. M. Gibb. 1988. Cost–Efficiency of a Long-Acting Cephalosporin Agent. *Australian and New Zealand Journal of Surgery* 58, pt. 2(9): 733–5.

Hansen, Lars P. 1982. Large Sample Properties of Generalized Method of Moments Estimators. *Econometrica* 50(4): 1029–54.

Hass, William K., J. Donald Easton, Harold P. Adams, William Pryse-Phillips, Basil A. Molony, Sharon Anderson, and Barbara Kamm. 1989. A Randomized Trial Comparing Ticlopidine Hydrochloride with Aspirin for the Prevention of Stroke in High-Risk Patients. *New England Journal of Medicine* 321(8): 501–7.

Hatziandreu, Evridiki I., Jeffrey P. Koplan, Milton C. Weinstein, Carl J. Caspersen, and Kenneth E. Warner. 1988. A Cost–Effectiveness Analysis of Exercise as a Health Promotion Activity. *American Journal of Public Health* 78(11): 1417–21.

Hausman, Jerry A. 1979. Individual Discount Rates in the Purchase and Utilization of Energy-Using Durables. *Bell Journal of Economics* 10(1): 33–54.

Hausman, Jerry A., Bronwyn H. Hall, and Zvi Griliches. 1984. Econometric Methods for Count Data with an Application to the Patents–R&D Relationship. *Econometrica* 52(4): 909–38.

Hausman, Jerry A., and David A. Wise. 1985. Technical Problems in Social Experimentation: Cost versus Ease of Analysis (with Comments by J. Conlisk and D. L. McFadden). In *Social Experimentation,* ed. Jerry A. Hausman and David A. Wise, 187–219. Chicago: Univ. of Chicago Press for National Bureau of Economic Research.

Hay, Joel W. 1988. Cost–Effectivenss of Three Transdermal Nitroglycerin Controlled-Release Systems. *Clinical Therapeutics* 10(4): 450–5.

Hay, Joel W., and Eugene D. Robin. 1991. Cost–Effectiveness of Alpha-1 Antitrypsin

Replacement Therapy in Treatment of Congenital Chronic Obstructive Pulmonary Disease. *American Journal of Public Health* 8(41): 427–33.

Heather, Nick, and Ian Robertson. 1989. *Problem Drinking.* 2d ed. New York: Oxford Univ. Press.

Heckman, James J. 1979. Sample Selection Bias as a Specification Error. *Econometrica* 47(1): 153–61.

Heckman, James J., and V. Joseph Hotz. 1989. Choosing among Alternative Non-experimental Methods for Estimating the Impact of Social Programs: The Case of Manpower Training (with Comments and Rejoinder). *Journal of the American Statistical Association* 84(408): 862–80.

Heckman, James J., and Richard Robb. 1985. Alternative Methods for Evaluating the Impact of Interventions: An Overview. *Journal of Econometrics* 30(1/2): 239–67.

Henry, David. 1992. Economic Analysis as an Aid to Subsidization: The Development of Australian Guidelines for Pharmaceuticals. *PharmacoEconomics* 1(1): 54–67.

Herve, C., D. Castiel, M. Gaillard, R. Boisvert, and V. Leroux. 1990. Cost–Benefit Analysis of Thrombolytic Therapy. *European Heart Journal* 11, pt. 3(11): 1006–10.

Hillman, Alan L., Mark V. Pauly, and Joseph J. Kerstein. 1989. How Do Financial Incentives Affect Physicians' Clinical Decisions and the Financial Performance of Health Maintenance Organizations? *New England Journal of Medicine* 321(2): 86–92.

Himmelberg, Cheryl J., Roy A. Pleasants, David J. Weber, John M. Kessler, Gregory P. Samsa, J. Michael Spivey, and Theresa L. Morris. 1991. Use of Antimicrobial Drugs in Adults before and after Removal of a Restriction Policy. *American Journal of Hospital Pharmacy* 48, pt. 1(6): 1220–7.

Holahan, John, Linda Blumberg, and Stephen Zuckerman. 1993. *Strategies for Implementing Global Budgets.* July. Washington, D.C.: Urban Institute, No. 18524.

Holland, Paul W. 1986. Statistics and Causal Inference (with Comments and Rejoinder). *Journal of the American Statistical Association* 81(396): 945–70.

Hollenberg, James P., Leslee L. Subak, John J. Ferry Jr., and James B. Bussel. 1988. Cost–Effectiveness of Splenectomy versus Intravenous Gamma Globulin in Treatment of Chronic Immune Thrombocytopenic Purpura in Childhood. *Journal of Pediatrics* 112(4): 530–39.

Holzman, David. 1992. Interactive Video Promotes Patient/Doctor Partnership. *Business and Health* 10:42–9.

Horwitz, Ralph I., Catherine M. Viscoli, Lisa Berkman, Robert M. Donaldson, Sarah M. Horwitz, Carolyn J. Murray, David F. Ransohoff, and Jody Sindelar. 1990. Treatment Adherence and Risk of Death after a Myocardial Infarction. *Lancet* 336(8714): 542–5.

Hosek, Susan D., M. Susan Marquis, and Kenneth B. Wells. 1990. *Health Care Utilization in Employer Plans with Preferred Provider Organization Options.* R-3800-HS/NIMH, Feb. Santa Monica, Calif.: Rand Corp.

Howard, Ronald A. 1988. Decision Analysis: Practice and Promise. *Management Science* 34(6): 679–95.

Hsiao, William C., Peter Braun, Daniel Dunn, Edmund R. Becker, Margaret DeNicola, and Thomas R. Ketchum. 1988. Results and Policy Implications of the Resource-Based Relative Value Scale. *New England Journal of Medicine* 319(13): 881–88.

Iams, J. D., and Ashok Chawla. 1984. Patient Costs in the Prevention and Treatment of Post-Cesarean Section Infection. *American Journal of Obstetrics and Gynecology* 149(4): 363–6.

Iezzoni, Lisa I., Susan M. Foley, Jennifer Daley, John Hughes, Elliott S. Fisher, Timothy Heeren. 1992. Comorbidities, Complications, and Coding Bias: Does the Number of Diagnoses Codes Matter in Predicting In-Hospital Mortality? *Journal of the American Medical Association* 267(16): 2197–203.

Institute of Medicine. 1991a. *Adverse Effects of Pertussis and Rubella Vaccines.* Washington, D.C.: National Academy Press.

———. 1991b. *The Artificial Heart: Prototypes, Policies, and Patients. Appendix E.* Washington, D.C.: National Academy Press.

Jacobson, J. J., D. E. LaTurno, F. K. Johnston, and C. Shipman, Jr. 1987. Cost Effectiveness of Prevaccination Screening for Hepatitis β Antibody. *Journal of Dental Education* 51(2): 94–7.

Jencks, Stephen F. 1992. Accuracy in Recorded Diagnoses. *Journal of the American Medical Association* 267(16): 2238–9.

Jencks, Stephen F., Deborah K. Williams, and Terrence L. Kay. 1988. Assessing Hospital-Associated Deaths from Discharge Data: The Role of Length of Stay and Comorbidities. *Journal of the American Medical Association* 260, pt. 2(15): 2240–6.

Johannesson, Magnus. 1992a. The Australian Guidelines for Subsidisation of Pharmaceuticals: The Road to Cost–Effective Drug Prescribing? *PharmacoEconomics* 2(5): 355–62.

———. 1992b. Economic Evaluation of Lipid Lowering – A Feasibility Test of the Contingent Valuation Approach. *Health Policy* 20(3): 309–20.

Johannesson Magnus, and Björn Fagerberg. 1992. A Health-Economic Comparison of Diet and Drug Treatment in Obese Men with Mild Hypertension. *Journal of Hypertension* 10, pt. 2(9): 1063–70.

Johannesson, Magnus, Bengt Jönsson, and L. Borgquist. 1991. Willingness to Pay for Antihypertensive Therapy – Results of a Swedish Pilot Study. *Journal of Health Economics* 10(4): 461–73.

Jönsson, Bengt, and Per Carlsson. 1991. The Effects of Cimetidine on the Cost of Ulcer Disease in Sweden. *Social Science and Medicine* 33, pt. 1(3): 275–82.

Jönsson, Bengt, et al. 1988. Quality of Life in Angina Pectoris: A Swedish Randomized Cross-Over Comparison between Transderm-Nitro and Long-Acting Oral Nitrates. In *Socioeconomic Evaluation of Drug Therapy*, ed. W. van Eimeren and B. Horisberger. Berlin: Springer-Verlag.

Jorgenson, Dale W. 1983. Econometric Methods for Modeling Producer Behavior. In *Handbook of Econometrics*, ed. Zvi Griliches and Michael D. Intriligator, 1841–1915. 3 vols. Amsterdam: North-Holland.

Judge, G. G., W. E. Griffiths, C. Hill, and T.-C. Lee. 1980. *The Theory and Practice of Econometrics.* New York: John Wiley and Sons.

Kahneman, Daniel, and Amos Tversky. 1979. Prospect Theory: An Analysis of Decision under Risk. *Econometrica* 47(2): 263–91.

———. 1984. Choices, Values, and Frames. *American Psychologist* 39(4): 341–50.

Kaplan, Norman M. 1991. Cost–Effectiveness of Antihypertensive Drugs. Fact or Fancy? *American Journal of Hypertension* 4, pt. 1(5): 478–80.

Kaplan, Robert M. 1982. Human Preference Measurement for Health Decisions and the Evaluation of Long-term Care. In *Values and Long-Term Care*, ed. Robert L. Kane and Rosalie A. Kane, 157–88. Lexington, Mass.: Lexington Books.

———. 1990. Behavior as a Central Outcome in Health Care. *American Psychologist* 45(11): 1211–20.

———. 1993a. Application of a General Health Policy Model in the American Health Care Crisis. *Journal of the Royal Society of Medicine* 86(5): 277–81.

————. 1993b. *The Hippocratic Predicament: Affordability, Access, and Accountability in Health Care.* San Diego: Academic Press.

Kaplan, Robert M., and John P. Anderson. 1988. A General Health Policy Model: Update and Applications. *Health Services Research* 23(2): 203–35.

————. 1990. The General Health Policy Model: An Integrated Approach. In *Quality of Life Assessments in Clinical Trials,* ed. Bert Spilker, 131–49. New Haven: Raven Press.

Kaplan, Robert M., and Charles C. Berry. 1990. Adjusting for Confounding Variables. In *AHCPR Conference Proceedings, Research Methodology: Strengthening Causal Interpretations of Nonexperimental Data,* ed. Lee Sechrest, Edward Perrin, and John Bunker, 105–114. U.S. Department of Health and Human Resources. Rockville, Md.: U.S. Government Printing Office.

Kaplan, Robert M., and James W. Bush. 1981. Health-Related Quality of Life Measurement for Evaluation Research and Policy Analysis. *Health Psychology* 1(1): 61–80.

Kaplan, Robert M., James W. Bush, and Charles C. Berry. 1976. Health Status: Types of Validity and the Index of Well-Being. *Health Services Research* 11(4): 478–507.

————. 1978. The Reliability, Stability, and Generalizability of a Health Status Index. *American Statistical Association, Proceedings of the Social Status Section,* 704–9.

————. 1979. Health Status Index: Category Rating versus Magnitude Estimation for Measuring Levels of Well-Being. *Medical Care* 17(5): 501–25.

Kaplan, Robert M., and S. J. Coons. 1992. Relative Importance of Dimensions in the Assessment of Health-Related Quality of Life for Patients with Hypertension. *Progress in Cardiovascular Nursing* 7(2): 29–36.

Kaplan, Robert M., Marget DeBon, and Barry F. Anderson. 1991. Effects of Number of Rating Scale Points upon Utilities in a Quality of Well-Being Scale. *Medical Care* 29(10): 1061–4.

Kaplan Robert M., and John A. Ernst. 1983. Do Category Rating Scales Produce Biased Preference Weights for a Health Index? *Medical Care* 21(2): 193–207.

Kawachi, Ichiro, and Lawrence A. Malcolm. 1991. The Cost–Effectiveness of Treating Mild-to-Moderate Hypertension: A Reappraisal. *Journal of Hypertension* 9(3): 199-208.

Keeler, Emmett B., and Robert Bell. 1992. New DEALEs: Other Approximations of Life Expectancy. *Medical Decision Making* 12(4): 307–11.

Keeler, Emmett B., and Shan Cretin. 1983. Discounting of Life-Saving and Other Non-monetary Effects. *Management Science* 29(3): 300–6.

Keeler, Emmett B., Kenneth B. Wells, and Willard G. Manning. 1987. Markov and Other Models of Mental Health Treatment. *Advances in Health Economics and Health Services Research* 8:279–98.

Keeney, Ralph L. 1976. A Group Preference Axiomatization with Cardinal Utility. *Management Sciences* 23(2): 140–5.

Keeney, Ralph L., and Howard Raiffa. 1976. *Decisions with Multiple Objectives: Preferences and Value Tradeoffs.* New York: John Wiley & Sons.

Kemeny, John G., and J. Laurie Snell. 1960. *Finite Markov Chains.* New York: Springer-Verlag.

Khandker, Rezaul K., and Willard G. Manning. 1992. The Impact of Utilization Review on Costs and Utilization. In *Health Economics Worldwide,* ed. Peter Zweifel and H. E. Frech III. Norwell, Mass.: Kluwer Academic Publishers.

Killip, Thomas, and Thomas J. Ryan. 1985. Randomized Trials in Coronary Bypass Surgery (Editorial). *Circulation* 71(3): 418–21.

Kitzhaber, John A. 1993. Prioritising Health Services in an Era of Limits: The Oregon Experience. *British Medical Journal* 307(6900): 373–7.

Klepper, Steven I., Mark S. Kamlet, and Richard G. Frank. 1993. Regressor Diagnostics for the Errors-in-Variables Model – An Application to the Health Effects of Pollution. *Journal of Environmental Economics and Management* 24(3): 190–212.

Klevit, Harvey D., Alan C. Bates, Tina Castanares, E. Paul Kirk, Paige R. Sipes-Metzler, and Richard Wopat. 1991. Prioritization of Health Care Services: A Progress Report by the Oregon Health Services Commission. *Archives of Internal Medicine* 151(5): 912–16.

Koenker, Roger, and Gilbert Bassett. 1982. Robust Tests for Heteroskedasticity Based on Regression Quantiles. *Econometrica* 50(1): 43–61.

Krumholz, Harlan M., Richard C. Paternak, Milton C. Weinstein, Gottlieb C. Friesinger, Paul M. Ridker, Anna N. A. Tosteson, and Lee Goldman. 1992. Cost Effectiveness of Thrombolytic Therapy with Streptokinase in Elderly Patients with Suspected Acute Myocardial Infarction. *New England Journal of Medicine* 327(1): 7–13.

LaPuma, John, and Edward F. Lawlor. 1990. Quality-Adjusted Life-Years: Ethical Implications for Physicians and Policymakers. *Journal of the American Medical Association* 263(21): 2917–21.

Lau, Joseph, Elliott M. Antman, Jeanette Jimenez-Silva, Bruce Kupelnick, Frederick Mosteller, and Thomas C. Chalmers. 1992. Cumulative Meta-analysis of Therapeutic Trials for Myocardial Infarction. *New England Journal of Medicine* 327(4): 248–54.

Laupacis, Andreas, Gregory W. Albers, Marvin I. Dunn, and William M. Feinberg. 1992a. Antithrombotic Therapy in Atrial Fibrillation. *Chest* 102(4): 426S–33S.

Laupacis, Andreas, David Feeny, Allan S. Detsky, and Peter X. Tugwell. 1992b. How Attractive Does a New Technology Have to Be to Warrant Adoption and Utilization? Tentative Guidelines for Using Clinical and Economic Evaluations. *Canadian Medical Association Journal* 146(4): 473–81.

Lave, Lester B. 1981. *The Strategy of Social Regulation*. Washington, D.C.: Brookings.

Lee, Jeff T., and Lisa A. Sanchez. 1991. Interpretation of "Cost–Effective" and Soundness of Economic Evaluations in the Pharmacy Literature. *American Journal of Hospital Pharmacy* 48, pt. 2(12): 2622–7.

Levit, Katherine R., and Cathy A. Cowan. 1990. The Burden of Health Care Costs: Business, Households, and Governments. *Health Care Financing Review* 12(2): 127–37.

Leviton, Alan, Jane Schulman, Lisa Kammerman, Douglas Porter, Warner Slack, and John R. Graham. 1980. A Probability Model of Headache Recurrence. *Journal of Chronic Diseases* 33(7): 407–12.

Lieu, Tracy A., J. Sanford Schwartz, David M. Jeffe, and Gary R. Fleisher. 1991. Strategies for Diagnosis and Treatment of Children at Risk for Occult Bacteremia: Clinical Effectiveness and Cost–Effectiveness. *Journal of Pediatrics* 118(1): 21–9.

Linnerooth, Joanne. 1979. The Value of Human Life: A Review of the Models. *Economic Inquiry* 17(1): 52–74.

Lipscomb, Joseph. 1989. Time Preference for Health in Cost–Effectiveness Analysis. *Medical Care* 27(3): S233–53.

Littenberg, Benjamin. 1988. Aminophylline Treatment in Severe, Acute Asthma: A Meta-analysis. *Journal of the American Medical Association* 259(11): 1678–84.

Little, Roderick J. A., and Donald B. Rubin. 1987. *Statistical Analysis with Missing Data*. New York: John Wiley & Sons.

Llewellyn-Thomas, H., H. J. Sutherland, R. Tibshirani, A. Ciampi, J. E. Till, and N. F. Boyd. 1984. Describing Health States: Methodologic Issues in Obtaining Values for Health States. *Medical Care*, 22(6): 543–2.

Lobo, Patricia J., Ray L. Powles, Angela Hanrahan, and Derek K. Reynolds. 1991. Acute Myeloblastic Leukaemia – A Model for Assessing Value for Money for New Treatment Programmes. *British Medical Journal* 302(6771): 323–6.

Løes, Øyuind, Nils Smith-Erichsen, and Bjørn Lind. 1987. Intensive Care: Cost and Benefit. *Acta Anaesthesiologica Scandanavica* 31, supp.(84): 3–19.

Lohr, Kathleen N., Robert H. Brook, Caren J. Kamberg, George A. Goldberg, Arleen Leibowitz, Joan Keesey, David Reboussin, and Joseph P. Newhouse. 1986. *Use of Medical Care in the Rand Health Insurance Experiment: Diagnosis- and Service-Specific Analyses in a Randomized Controlled Trial*. R-3469-HS, Dec. Santa Monica, Calif.: Rand Corp.

Lord, Frederic M. 1960. Large Sample Covariance Analysis When the Control Variable Is Fallible. *Journal of the American Statistical Association* 55(290): 307–21.

———. 1967. A Paradox in the Interpretation of Group Comparisons. *Psychological Bulletin* 68(5): 304–5.

———. 1969. Statistical Adjustments When Comparing Pre-existing Groups. *Psychological Bulletin* 72(5): 336–7.

Luce, R. Duncan. 1981. Axioms for the Averaging and Addition Representations of Functional Measurement. *Mathematical Social Sciences* 1:139–44.

Luft, Harold S. 1978. How Do Health Maintenance Organizations Achieve Their Savings? *New England Journal of Medicine* 298(24): 1336–43.

Luft, Harold S., Sandra S. Hunt, and Susan C. Maerki. 1987. The Volume–Outcome Relationship: Practice Makes Perfect or Selective Referral Patterns? *Health Services Research* 22(2): 159–82.

MacKeigan, Lynn D. 1990. Context Effects in Health State Utility Assessment: Etiology, Framing and Delay of Health Outcomes. Ph.D. diss., Univ. of Arizona, Tucson.

Maddala, G. S. 1971. *Econometrics*. New York: McGraw-Hill.

———. 1983. *Limited-Dependent and Qualitative Variables in Econometrics*. New York: Cambridge Univ. Press.

———. 1987. Limited Dependent Variable Models Using Panel Data. *Journal of Human Resources* 22(3): 305–38.

Maddala, G. S., and J. Jeong. 1992. On the Exact Small Sample Distribution of the Instrumental Variable Estimator. *Econometrica* 60(1): 181–3.

Mamtani, Ravinder, Joseph A. Cimino, Jack M. Cooperman, and Robert Kugel. 1990. Comparison of Total Costs of Administering Calcium Polycarbophil and Psyllium Mucilloid in an Institutional Setting. *Clinical Therapeutics* 12(1): 22–5.

Manning, Willard G., Emmett B. Keeler, Joseph P. Newhouse, Elizabeth M. Sloss, and Jeffrey Wasserman. 1989. The Taxes of Sin: Do Smokers and Drinkers Pay Their Way? *Journal of the American Medical Association* 261(11): 1604–9.

———. 1991. *The Costs of Poor Health Habits*. Cambridge: Harvard Univ. Press.

Manning, Willard G., A. Leibowitz, George A. Goldberg, William H. Rogers, and Joseph P. Newhouse. 1984. A Controlled Trial of the Effect of a Prepaid Group Practice on Use of Services. *New England Journal of Medicine* 310(23): 1505–10.

Manning, Willard G., Joseph P. Newhouse, Naihua Duan, Emmett B. Keeler, Bernadette

Benjamin, Arleen Leibowitz, and M. Susan Marquis. 1987. Health Insurance and the Demand for Medical Care. *American Economic Review* 77(3): 251–77.

Manning, Willard G., Joseph P. Newhouse, Naihua Duan, Emmett B. Keeler, Bernadette Benjamin, Arleen Leibowitz, M. Susan Marquis, and Jack Zwanziger. 1988. *Health Insurance and the Demand for Medical Care: Evidence from a Randomized Experiment.* R-3476-HHS, Feb. Santa Monica, Calif.: Rand Corp.

Manning, Willard G., et al. 1992. The Demand for Alcohol: The Differential Response to Price. Paper presented at the Third Annual Health Economics Workshop. Baltimore, Md.: Johns Hopkins Univ., May.

Manski, Charles F. 1988. *Analog Estimation Methods in Econometrics.* New York: Chapman & Hall.

———. 1990. Nonparametric Bounds on Treatment Effects. *American Economic Review (Papers and Proceedings)* 80(2): 319–23.

Manton, Kenneth G., Eric Stallard, and Steve Wing. 1991. Analysis of Black and White Differentials in the Age Trajectory of Mortality in Two Closed Cohort Studies. *Statistics in Medicine* 10(7): 1043–59.

Marglin, Stephen. 1967. *Public Investment Criteria.* Cambridge: MIT Press.

Marion Merrell Dow. 1993. *Managed Care Digest: PPO Edition.* Kansas City, Mo.: Marion Merrell Dow.

Marquis, M. Susan, David E. Kanouse, and Laurel Brodsky. 1985. *Informing Consumers about Health Care Costs: A Review and Research Agenda.* R-3262-HCFA, Sept. Santa Monica, Calif.: Rand Corp.

McCullagh, Peter, and J. A. Nelder. 1989. *Generalized Linear Models.* 2d ed. London: Chapman & Hall.

McGeer, Allison J., Allan S. Detsky, and Keith O'Rourke. 1990. Parenteral Nutrition in Cancer Patients Undergoing Chemotherapy: A Meta-analysis. *Nutrition* 6(3): 233–40.

McNeil, Barbara J., Ralph Weichselbaum, and Stephen G. Pauker. 1981. Speech and Survival: Tradeoffs between Quantity and Quality of Life in Laryngeal Cancer. *New England Journal of Medicine* 305, pt. 2(17): 982–7.

Mehrez, Abraham, and Amiram Gafni. 1989. Quality-Adjusted Life Years, Utility Theory, and Health Year Equivalents. *Medical Decision Making* 9(2): 142–9.

———. 1990. The Healthy-Years Equivalents: How to Measure Them Using the Standard Gamble Approach. *Medical Decision Making* 10(2): 148–9.

Milkovich, G., and C. J. Piazza. 1991. Considerations in Comparing Intravenous and Intramuscular Antibiotics. *Chemotherapy* 37, supp.(2): 1–13.

Miller, Anthony B., Cornelia J. Baines, Teresa To, and Claus Wall. 1992. Canadian National Breast Screening Study: 1. Breast Cancer Detection and Death Rates among Women Aged 40 to 49 Years. *Canadian Medical Association Journal* 147(10): 1459–76.

Mishan, Edward J. 1976. *Cost–Benefit Analysis.* New York: Praeger.

Moffitt, Robert. 1991. Program Evaluation with Nonexperimental Data. *Evaluation Review* 15(3): 291–314.

Moore, Michael J., and W. Kip Viscusi. 1988. The Quantity-Adjusted Value of Life. *Economic Inquiry* 26(3): 369–88.

———. 1990a. Discounting Environmental Health Risks: New Evidence of Policy Implications. *Journal of Environmental Economics and Management* 18, pt. 2(2): S51–S62.

———. 1990b. Models for Estimating Discount Rates for Long-Term Health Risks Using Labor Market Data. *Journal of Risk and Uncertainty* 3(4): 381–401.

Moses, Lincoln E. 1985. Statistical Concepts Fundamental to Investigations. *New England Journal of Medicine* 312(14): 890–7.

Mullahy, J., and P. R. Portney. 1990. Air Pollution, Cigarette Smoking, and the Production of Respiratory Health. *Journal of Health Economics* 9(2): 193–205.

Mulley, Albert J. 1989. Assessing Patient's Utilities: Can the Ends Justify the Means? *Medical Care* 27, supp.(3): S269–81.

Nelson, Charles R., and Richard Startz. 1990. The Distribution of the Instrumental Variables Estimator and Its *t*-Ratio When the Instrument Is a Poor One. *Journal of Business* 63, pt. 1:S125–40.

Nerenz, David R., K. Golob, and Donald L. Trump. 1990. Preference Weights for the Quality of Well-Being Scale as Obtained from Oncology Patients. Detroit: Henry Ford Hospital. Photocopy

Newhouse, Joseph P., and Charles E. Phelps. 1976. New Estimates of Price and Income Elasticities of Medical Care Services. In *The Role of Health Insurance in the Health Services Sector*, ed. Richard N. Rosett, 261–313. New York: National Bureau of Economic Research.

Newhouse, Joseph P., and The Health Insurance Experiment Group. 1993. *Free for All? Lessons from the Rand Health Insurance Experiment.* Cambridge: Harvard Univ. Press.

New York Times. 1991. Medicare Coverage Is Approved for Liver Transplant Operations. 14 Apr.

Nord, Erik. 1991. The Validity of a Visual Analogue Scale in Determining Social Utility Weights for Health States. *International Journal of Health Planning and Management* 6(3): 234–42.

———. 1992. Methods for Quality Adjustment of Life Years. *Social Science and Medicine* 34(5): 559–69.

North American Symptomatic Carotid Endarterectomy Trial Collaborators. 1991. Beneficial Effect of Endarterectomy in Symptomatic Patients with High-Grade Carotid Stenosis. *New England Journal of Medicine* 325(7): 445–53.

O'Connor, Gerald T., and Robert F. Nease Jr. 1993. The Descriptive Epidemiology of Health-State Values and Utilities. *Medical Decision Making* 13(2): 87–8.

Olson, Craig A. 1981. An Analysis of Wage Differentials Received by Workers on Dangerous Jobs. *Journal of Human Resources* 16(2): 167–85.

Ontario Ministry of Health. 1992. Cost Effectiveness of Drugs. Report submitted to the Federal/Provincial Territorial Subcommittee on Pharmaceutical Policy Issues. May.

Oster, Gerry, and Arnold M. Epstein. 1987. Cost–Effectiveness of Antihyperlipemic Therapy in the Prevention of Coronary Heart Disease: The Case of Cholestyramine. *Journal of the American Medical Association* 258(17): 2381–7.

OTA (U.S. Office of Technology Assessment). 1992a. *Evaluation of Oregon Medicaid Proposal.* May. Washington, D.C.: Government Printing Office.

———. 1992b. *Evaluation of the Oregon Medicaid Proposal: Summary.* May. Washington, D.C.: Government Printing Office.

Parducci, Allen. 1968. The Relativism of Absolute Judgements. *Scientific American* 219(6): 84–90.

Parr, Michael D., Lea Ann Hansen, and Robert P. Rapp. 1988. Cost Comparison of Ceftazidime versus Tobramycin/Ticarcillin Therapy in Three Hospitals. *Drug Intelligence and Clinical Pharmacy* 22(7/8): 628–31.

Parsonage, Michael, and Henry Neuberger. 1992. Discounting and Health Benefits. *Health Economist* 1:71–9.

Patrick, Donald L., James W. Bush, and Milton M. Chen. 1973. Methods for Measuring Levels of Well-Being for a Health Status Index. *Health Services Research* 8(3): 228–45.

Patrick Donald L., Yoga Sittanpalam, Sheena M. Somerville, William B. Carter, and Marilyn Bergner. 1985. A Cross-Cultural Comparison of Health Status Values. *American Journal of Public Health* 75, pt. 2(12): 1402–7.

Paul, Rebecca R., and Daniel M. Campion. 1993. *Lessons from State Efforts to Develop Standard Benefits Packages.* Washington, D.C.: Alpha Center.

Pauly, Mark V. 1991. The Economics of Growing Health Care Expenditures. *LDI Health Policy & Research Quarterly* 1(3): 1–2.

Permutt, Thomas, and J. Richard Hebel. 1989. Simultaneous-Equation Estimation in a Clinical Trial of the Effect of Smoking on Birth Weight. *Biometrics* 45(2): 619–22.

Petri, H., and J. Urquhart. 1991. Channeling Bias in the Interpretation of Drug Effects. *Statistics in Medicine* 10(4): 577–81.

Petrou, Stavros, Mo Malek, and Peter G. Davey. 1993. The Reliability of Cost-Utility Estimates in Cost-per-QALY League Tables. *PharmacoEconomics* 3(5): 345–53.

Pharmaceutical Benefits Advisory Committee (Australia). N.d. Guidelines for the Pharmaceutical Industry on Preparation of Submissions to the Pharmaceutical Benefits Advisory Committee. Unpublished.

Phelps, Charles E. 1973. Demand for Health Insurance: A Theoretical and Empirical Investigation. R-1054-OEO, July. Santa Monica, Calif.: Rand Corp.

———. 1980. National Health Insurance: Mandated Employee Benefits. In *National Health Insurance*, ed. M. Pauly, 52–73. Washington, D.C.: American Enterprise Institute.

———. 1992. *Health Economics.* New York: HarperCollins.

Phelps, Charles E., and Alvin I. Mushlin. 1988. Focusing Technology Assessment Using Medical Decision Theory. *Medical Decision Making* 8(3): 279–89.

———. 1991. On the Near Equivalence of Cost–Effectiveness and Cost–Benefit Analysis. *International Journal of Technology Assessment in Health Care* 7(1): 12–21.

Pliskin, Joseph S., Donald S. Shepard, and Milton C. Weinstein. 1980. Utility Functions for Life Years and Health Status. *Operations Research* 28(1): 206–24.

Podrid, Philip J., Peter R. Kowey, William H. Frishman, Renée J. Goldberg Arnold, Diana J. Kaniecki, J. Robert Beck, and Joni R. Beshansky. 1991. Comparative Cost–Effectiveness Analysis of Quinidine, Procainamide and Mexiletine. *American Journal of Cardiology* 68, pt. 2(17): 1662–7.

Raiffa, Howard. 1968. *Decision Analysis: Introductory Lectures on Choices under Uncertainty.* Reading, Mass.: Addison-Wesley.

Rao, C. Radhakrishna. 1973. *Linear Statistical Inference and Its Applications.* 2d ed. New York: John Wiley & Sons.

Rawls, John. 1971. *A Theory of Justice.* Cambridge: Belknap Press of Harvard Univ. Press.

Read, J. L., R. J. Quinn, D. M. Berwick, H. V. Fineberg, and M. C. Weinstein. 1984. Preferences for Health Outcomes: Comparison of Assessment Methods. *Medical Decision Making* 4(3): 315–29.

Read, Lynn. 1992. Health Care Reform: Can States Lead the Way? Paper presented to Health Policy Forum, 15–16 June, Washington, D.C.

Redelmeier, Donald A., and Amos Tversky. 1990. Discrepancy between Medical Decisions for Individual Patients and for Groups. *New England Journal of Medicine* 322(16): 1162–4.

Revicki, David A., and Robert M. Kaplan. (1993). Relationship between Psychometric and Utility-Based Approaches to the Measurement of Health-Related Quality of Life. *Quality of Life Research.* 2, 477–487.

Rice, Teresa Duryea, Anne K. Duggan, and Catherine DeAngelis. 1992. Cost–Effectiveness of Erythromycin versus Mupirocin for the Treatment of Impetigo in Children. *Pediatrics* 89(2): 210–14.

Richardson, James. 1991. Economic Assessment of Health Care: Theory and Practice. *Australian Economic Review* 81(93): 4–21.

RISC Group. 1990. Risk of Myocardial Infarction and Death during Treatment with Low-Dose Aspirin and Intravenous Heparin in Men with Unstable Coronary Artery Disease. *Lancet* 336(8719): 827–30.

Roemer, Milton I. 1991. *National Health Systems of the World.* Vol. 1, *The Countries.* New York: Oxford Univ. Press.

Rokeach, Milton. 1973. *The Nature of Human Values.* New York: Free Press.

Rose, Geoffrey, P. J. S. Hamilton, L. Colwell, and M. J. Shipley. 1982. A Randomised Controlled Trial of Anti-smoking Advice: 10-Year Results. *Journal of Epidemiology and Community Health* 36(2): 102–8.

Rosenzweig, Mark R., and T. Paul Schultz. 1983. Estimating a Household Production Function: Heterogeneity, the Demand for Health Inputs, and their Effects on Birth Weight. *Journal of Political Economy* 91(5): 723–46.

Rosser, R., and P. Kind. 1978. A Scale of Valuations of States of Illness: Is There a Social Consensus? *International Journal of Epidemiology* 7: 347–58.

Rubin, Donald B. 1974. Estimating Causal Effects of Treatments in Randomized and Nonrandomized Studies. *Journal of Educational Psychology* 66(5): 688–701.

Rublee, Dale A. 1989. Medical Technology in Canada, Germany and the United States. *Health Affairs* 8(3): 178–81.

Ruffenach, Glenn. 1993. Firms Use Financial Incentives to Make Employees Seek Lower Health-Care Fees. *Wall Street Journal,* 9 Feb., B1, B6.

Russell, Louise B. 1986. *Is Prevention Better than Cure?* Washington, D.C.: Brookings Institution.

Sackett, David L., R. Brian Hayes, and Peter Tugwell. 1985. *Clinical Epidemiology: A Basic Science for Clinical Medicine.* 2d ed. Boston: Little, Brown.

Safran, Charles. 1991. Using Routinely Collected Data for Clinical Research. *Statistics in Medicine* 10(4): 559–64.

Saxena, Sunita, Gerald L. Endahl, and Ira A. Shulman. 1988. Use of a Table-Top Analyzer for Predonation Screening for Alanine Aminotransferase – A Cost–Effective Approach? *American Journal of Clinical Pathology* 90(3): 296–9.

Saywell, Robert M., Jr., John R. Woods, Harold G. Halbrook, Stephen J. Jay, Allen W. Nyhuis, and Rosemary G. Lohrman. 1989. Cost Analysis of Heart Transplantation from the Day of Operation to the Day of Discharge. *Journal of Heart Transplantation* 8(3): 244–52.

Schieber, George J., Jean-Pierre Poullier, and Leslie M. Greenwald. 1993. Health Spending, Delivery and Outcomes in OECD Countries. *Health Affairs* 12(2): 120–9.

Schulman, Kevin A., Bruce Kinosian, Terry A. Jacobson, Henry Glick, Mary Kaye William, Harris Koffer, and John M. Eisenberg. 1990. Reducing High Blood Cholesterol Level with Drugs: Cost–Effectiveness of Pharmacologic Management. *Journal of the American Medical Association* 264(23): 3025–33.

Scitovsky, Anne A., Mary W. Cline, and Donald I. Abrams. 1990. Effects of the Use of AZT on the Medical Care Costs of Persons with AIDS in the First 12 Months. *Journal of Acquired Immune Deficiency Syndromes* 3, pt. 2(9): 904–12.

Sessa, Ernest J. 1993. A Message from the Executive Director. The PHC⁴ Bulletin. (Pennsylvania Health Care Cost Containment Council), Aug.

Shepard, Donald S., and Richard J. Zeckhauser. 1977. Heterogeneity among Patients as a Factor in Surgical Decision Making. In *Costs, Risks and Benefits of Surgery*, ed. John P. Bunker, Benjamin A. Barnes, and Frederick Mosteller, 56–69. New York: Oxford Univ. Press.

———. 1982. The Choice of Health Policies with Heterogeneous Populations. In *Economic Aspects of Health*, ed. Victor R. Fuchs, 255–98. Chicago: Univ. of Chicago Press.

Shibley, Louise, Martin Brown, James Schuttinga, Mace Rothenberg, and Judith Whalen. 1990. Cisplatin-Based Combination Chemotherapy in the Treatment of Advanced-Stage Testicular Cancer: Cost–Benefit Analysis. *Journal of the National Cancer Institute* 82(3): 186–92.

Shortell, Stephen, and Edward F. X. Hughes. 1988. The Effects of Regulation, Competition, and Ownership on Mortality Rates among Hospital Inpatients. *New England Journal of Medicine* 318(17): 1100–7.

Sintonen, H. 1981. An Approach to Measuring and Valuing Health States. *Social Science and Medicine* 15C: 55–65.

Siu, Albert L., S. Allison Mayer-Oakes, and Robert H. Brook. 1985. Innovations in Medical Curricula: Templates for Change? *Health Affairs* 4(2): 60–71.

Siu, Albert L., Frank A. Sonnenberg, Willard G. Manning, George A. Goldberg, Ellyn S. Bloomfield, Joseph P. Newhouse, and Robert H. Brook. 1986. Inappropriate Use of Hospitals in a Randomized Trial of Health Insurance Plans. *New England Journal of Medicine* 315(20): 1259–66.

Smith, D., and P. McKercher. 1984. The Elimination of Selected Drug Products from the Michigan Medicaid Formulary: A Case Study. *Hospital Formulary* 19:366–72.

Smith, David W., Stephanie L. McFall, and Michael B. Pine. 1993. State Rate Regulation and Inpatient Mortality Rates. *Inquiry* 30(1): 23–33.

Smith, M., and D. MacClayton. 1977. The Effect of Closing a Medicaid Formulary on the Prescription of Analgesic Drugs. *Hospital Formulary* 12:36–41.

Sommer, Alfred, and Scott L. Zeger. 1991. On Estimating Efficacy from Clinical Trials. *Statistics in Medicine* 10(4): 45–52.

Sovie, Margaret D. 1988. Variable Costs of Nursing Care in Hospitals. *Annual Review of Nursing Research* 6:131–50.

Sox, Harold C., Jr., Marshal A. Blatt, Michael C. Higgins, and Keith I. Marton. 1988. *Medical Decision Making*. Boston: Butterworths.

Staines, Verdon S. 1993. Potential Impact of Managed Care on National Health Spending. *Health Affairs* 12, supp.: 248–57.

Stark, Paul, and C. David Hardison. 1985. A Review of Multicenter Controlled Studies of Fluoxetine vs. Imipramine and Placebo in Outpatients with Major Depressive Disorder. *Journal of Clinical Psychiatry* 46(3, sec. 2): 53–8.

Starr, Paul, and Walter A. Zelman. 1993. A Bridge to Compromise: Competition under a Budget. *Health Affairs* 12, supp.: 7–23.

Steinberg, Earl P., Richard D. Moore, Neil R. Powe, Ramana Gopalan, Amy J. Davidoff, Marc Litt, Sandra Graziano, and Jeffrey A. Brinker. 1992. Safety and Cost Effectiveness of High-Osmolality as Compared with Low-Osmolality Contrast Material in Patients Undergoing Cardiac Angiography. *New England Journal of Medicine* 326(7): 425–30.

Stevens, S. S. 1966. A Metric for the Social Consensus: Methods of Sensory Psychophysics Have Been Used to Gauge the Intensity of Opinions and Attitudes. *Science* 151(710): 530–41.

Stewart, Anita L., and John E. Ware, eds. 1993. *Measuring Functioning and Well-Being: The Medical Outcomes Study Approach.* Durham, N.C.: Duke Univ. Press.

Stiglitz, Joseph E. 1988. *Economics of the Public Sector.* New York: W. W. Norton.

Stokey, Edith, and Richard Zeckhauser. 1978. *A Primer for Policy Analysis.* New York: W. W. Norton.

Strom, Brian L., and Jeffrey L. Carson. 1989. Automated Data Bases Used for Pharmacoepidemiology Research. *Clinical Pharmacology and Therapeutics* 46(4): 390–8.

Strom, Brian L., Jeffrey L. Carson, M. Lee Morse, Suzanne L. West, and Keith A. Soper. 1987. The Effect of Indication on Hypersensitivity Reactions Associated with Zomepirac Sodium and Other Non-steroidal Anti-inflammatory Drugs. *Arthritis and Rheumatism* 30(10): 1142–8.

Subcutaneous Sumatriptan International Study Group. 1991. Treatment of Migraine Attacks with Sumatriptan. *New England Journal of Medicine* 325(5): 316–21.

Swain, James J., D. Goldman, Robert C. Crane, and James R. Wilson, eds. 1992. Markov Process Based Monte Carlo Simulation: A Tool for Modeling Complex Disease and Its Application to the Timing of Liver Transplantation. *Proceedings of the 1992 Winter Simulation Conference.* Arlington, Va.: Winter Simulation Conference Board.

Tanouye, Elyse. 1993. Drug Prices Get Dose of Market Pressure. *Wall Street Journal,* 3 Nov., B1, B3.

Theil, Henri. 1971. *Principles of Econometrics.* New York: John Wiley & Sons.

Theroux, Pierre, Helene Ouimet, John L. McCans, Jean-Gilles Latour, Patrick Joly, Gilles Levy, Edouard Pelletier, Martin Juneau, Jerome Stasiak, Pierre DeGuise, Guy Pelletier, David Rinzler, and David D. Waters. 1988. Aspirin, Heparin, or Both to Treat Acute Unstable Angina. *New England Journal of Medicine* 319(17): 1105–11.

Third International Study of Infarct Survival Collaborative Group. 1992. ISIS-3: A Randomised Comparison of Streptokinase vs. Tissue Plasminogen Activator vs. Anistreplase and of Aspirin plus Heparin vs. Aspirin Alone among 41,299 Cases of Suspected Acute Myocardial Infarction. *Lancet* 339(8796): 753–70.

Thompson, Mark S. 1986. Willingness-to-Pay and Accept Risks to Cure Chronic Disease. *American Journal of Public Health* 76(4): 392–6.

Thompson Mark S., J. Leighton Read, and Matthew Liang. 1984. Feasibility of Willingness-to-Pay Measurement in Chronic Arthritis. *Medical Decision Making* 4(2):199–215.

Thorpe, Kenneth E., and Charles E. Phelps. 1990. Regulatory Intensity and Hospital Cost Growth. *Journal of Health Economics* 9(2): 143–66.

Tierney, William M., Michael E. Miller, and Clement J. McDonald. 1990. The Effect on Test Ordering of Informing Physicians of the Charges for Outpatient Diagnostic Tests. *New England Journal of Medicine* 322(21): 1449–1504.

Tompkins, Richard A., Daniel C. Burnes, and William E. Cable. 1977. An Analysis of the Cost–Effectiveness of Pharyngitis Management and Acute Rheumatic Fever Prevention. *Annals of Internal Medicine* 86(4): 481–92.

Tønnesen, Philip, Jesper Nørregaard, Kåre Simonsen, and Urbain Säwe. 1991. A Double-Blind Trial of 16-Hour Transdermal Nicotine Patch in Smoking Cessation. *New England Journal of Medicine* 325, pt. 1(5): 311–15

Toronto Leukemia Study Group. 1986. Results of Chemotherapy for Unselected Patients with Acute Myeloblastic Leukaemia: Effect of Exclusions on Interpretation of Results. *Lancet* 1, pt. 1(8484): 786–8.

Torrance, George W. 1976. Social Preferences for Health States. An Empirical Evaluation of Three Measurement Techniques. *Socio-economic Planning Sciences* 10:129–36.

———. 1986. Measurement of Health State Utilities for Economic Appraisal: A Review. *Journal of Health Economics* 5(1): 1–30.

Torrance, George W., and David Feeny. 1989. Utilities in Quality-Adjusted Life Years. *International Journal of Technology Assessment in Health Care* 5(4): 559–75.

Tosteson, A. N., D. I. Rosenthal, L. J. Melton, and M. C. Weinstein. 1990. Cost Effectiveness of Screening Perimenopausal White Women for Osteoporosis: Bone Densitometry and Hormone Replacement Therapy. *Annals of Internal Medicine* 113(8): 594–603.

Transdermal Nicotine Study Group. 1991. Transdermal Nicotine for Smoking Cessation. *Journal of the American Medical Association* 266(22): 3133–8.

Tversky, Amos, and Daniel Kahneman. 1981. The Framing of Decisions and the Psychology of Choice. *Science* 211(4481): 453–8.

Tversky, Amos, Paul Slovic, and David Kahneman. 1990. The Causes of Preference Reversals. *American Economic Review* 80(1): 205–17.

Udvarhelyi, Steven, Graham A. Colditz, Arti Rai, and Arnold M. Epstein. 1992. Cost–Effectiveness and Cost–Benefit Analyses in the Medical Literature: Are the Methods Being Used Correctly? *Annals of Internal Medicine* 116(3): 238–44.

van Oortmarssen, Gerrit J., J. Dik F. Habbema, Paul van der Maas, Harry J. de Koning, Hubertine J. A. Collette, AndrÀ)À L. M. Verbeek, Ada T. Geerts, and Koos T. N. Lubbe. 1990. A Model for Breast Cancer Screening. *Cancer* 66, pt. 2(7): 1601–12.

Viscusi, W. Kip. 1979. *Employment Hazards: An Investigation of Market Performance.* Cambridge: Harvard Univ. Press.

———. 1989. Prospective Reference Theory: Toward an Explanation of the Paradoxes. *Journal of Risk and Uncertainty* 2(3): 235–64.

———. 1992. *Fatal Tradeoffs: Public and Private Responsibilities for Risk.* New York: Oxford Univ. Press.

Viscusi, W. Kip, and William Evans. 1990. Utility Functions That Depend on Health Status: Estimates and Economic Implications. *American Economic Review* 80(3): 353–74.

Viscusi, W. Kip, and Michael J. Moore. 1989. Rates of Time Preference and Valuations of the Duration of Life. *Journal of Public Economics* 8(3): 397–417.

Vogel, Ronald J., and Jon B. Christianson. 1986. The Evaluation of Economic Development Projects Where Military Conflict Is Present: Investing in Health Care in El Salvador. *Journal of Policy Analysis and Management* 5(2): 292–310.

von Neumann, John, and Oscar Morgenstern. 1944. *Theory of Games and Economic Behavior.* Princeton: Princeston Univ. Press.

Wachtel, Tom, Anne W. Moulton, John Pezzullo, and Milton Hamolsky. 1986. Inpatient Management Protocols to Reduce Health Care Costs. *Medical Decision Making* 6(2): 101–9.

Wagner, Judith L., and Roger C. Herdman. 1990. Well-Child Care: The Authors Respond. *Health Affairs* 9(1): 202–3.

Wagner, Judith L., Roger C. Herdman, and David W. Alberts. 1989. Well-Child Care: How Much Is Enough? *Health Affairs* 8(3): 147–57.

Walsh, Diane C., Ralph W. Hingson, Daniel M. Merrigan, Suzette Morelock Levenson, L. Adrienne Cupples, Timothy Heeren, Gerald A. Coffman, Charles A. Becker,

Thomas A. Barker, Susan K. Hamilton, Thomas G. McGuire, and Cecil A. Kelly. 1991. A Randomized Trial of Treatment Options for Alcohol-Abusing Workers. *New England Journal of Medicine* 325(11): 775–82.

Warner, K., and B. Luce. 1982. *Cost–Benefit and Cost–Effectiveness Analysis in Health Care.* Ann Arbor, Mich.: Health Administration Press.

Weeks, Jane C., Maureen R. Tierney, and Milton C. Weinstein. 1991. Cost Effectiveness of Prophylactic Intravenous Immune Globulin in Chronic Lymphocytic Leukemia. *New England Journal of Medicine* 325(2): 81–6.

Weinstein, Milton C. 1990. Principles of Cost–Effective Resource Allocation in Health Care Organizations. *International Journal of Technology Assessment in Health Care* 6(1): 93–103.

———. 1991. The Cost–Effectiveness of Orphan Drugs. *American Journal of Public Health* 81(4): 414–15.

Weinstein, Milton C., Pamela G. Coxson, Lawrence W. Williams, Theodore M. Pass, William B. Stason, and Lee Goldman. 1987. Forecasting Coronary Heart Disease Incidence, Mortality, and Cost. *American Journal of Public Health* 7(11): 1417–26.

Weinstein, Milton C., Harvey V. Fineberg, Arthur S. Elstein, Howard S. Frazier, Duncan Neuhauser, Raymond R. Neutra, and Barbara J. McNeil. 1980. *Clinical Decision Analysis.* Philadelphia: W. B. Saunders.

Weinstein, Milton C., Donald S. Shepard, and Joseph S. Pliskin. 1980. The Economic Value of Changing Mortality Probabilities: A Decision-Theoretic Approach. *Quarterly Journal of Economics* 95(2): 373–96.

Weinstein, Milton C., and William B. Stason. 1976. *Hypertension: A Policy Perspective.* Cambridge: Harvard Univ. Press.

———. 1977. Foundations of Cost–Effectiveness Analysis for Health and Medical Practices. *The New England Journal of Medicine* 296(13): 716–21.

———. 1983. *Cost–Effectiveness of Coronary Artery Bypass Surgery.* Cambridge: Harvard Univ. Center for Analysis of Health Practice.

Weinstein, Milton C., and Richard J. Zeckhauser. 1972. Critical Ratios and Efficient Allocation. *Journal of Public Economics* 2(2): 147–57.

Weisbrod, Burton A. 1961. *The Economics of Public Health.* Philadelphia: Univ. of Pennsylvania Press.

———. 1983. *Economics and Medical Research.* Washington, D.C.: American Enterprise Institute for Public Policy Research.

Wickizer, Thomas M., John R. C. Wheeler, and Paul J. Feldstein. 1991. Have Hospital Inpatient Cost Containment Programs Contributed to the Growth in Outpatient Expenditures? Analysis of the Substitution Effect Associated with Hospital Utilization Review. *Medical Care* 29(5): 442–50.

Wiklund, I., L. Gorkin, Y. Pawitan, E. Schron, J. Schoenberger, L. L. Jared, and S. Shumaker. 1992. Methods for Assessing Quality of Life in the Cardiac Arrhythmia Suppression Trial (CAST). *Quality of Life Research* 1(3): 187–201.

Willems, Jane Sisk, Claudia R. Sanders, Michael A. Riddiough, and John C. Bell. 1980. Cost Effectiveness of Vaccination against Pneumococcal Pneumonia. *New England Journal of Medicine* 303(10): 553–59.

Williams, Alan. 1981. Welfare Economics and Health Status Measurement. In *Health, Economics, and Health Economics,* ed. J. van der Gaag and M. Perlman, 271–81. Amsterdam: North-Holland.

Winslow, Constance M., David H. Solomon, Mark R. Chassin, Jaqueline Kosecoft, Nancy J. Merrick, and Robert H. Brook. 1988. The Appropriateness of Carotid Endarterectomy. *New England Journal of Medicine* 318(12): 721–7.

Winslow, Ron. 1992. Prescribing Decisions Increasingly Are Made by the Cost-Conscious: Doctors Are Pressured to Bow to Votes of Committees and Their Formularies. Effect on Drug Firms' Profits. *Wall Street Journal*, 25 Sept., A1, A4.

Wong, John B., Frank A. Sonnenberg, N. Salem Deeb, and Stephen G. Pauker. 1990. Myocardial Revascularization for Chronic Stable Angina: Analysis of the Role of Percutaneous Transluminal Coronary Angioplasty Based on Data Available in 1989. *Annals of Internal Medicine* 113(11): 852–71.

Zhu, Shu Hong, and Norman H. Anderson. 1991. Self-Estimation of Weight Parameter in Multiattribute Analysis. *Organizational Behavior and Human Decision Processes* 48(1): 36–54.

Ziegler, Elizabeth J., Charles J. Fisher, Charles L. Sprung, Richard C. Straube, Jerald C. Sadoff, Garrett E. Foulke, Cornelius H. Wortel, Mitchell P. Fink, R. Phillip Dellinger, Nelson N. H. Teng, I. Elaine Allen, Harvey J. Berger, Gennell L. Knattrud, Albert E. LoBuglio, Craig R. Smith, and the HA-1A Sepsis Study Group. 1991. Treatment of Gram-Negative Bacteremia and Septic Shock with Human Monoclonal Antibody against Endotoxin – A Randomized, Double-Blind, Placebo-Controlled Trial. *New England Journal of Medicine* 324(7): 429–36.

Index

Printed in the United States
27621LVS00004B/173